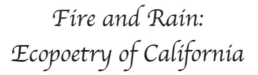

*Fire and Rain:*
*Ecopoetry of California*

# Fire and Rain: Ecopoetry of California

Edited by

Lucille Lang Day
and Ruth Nolan

*Foreword by Dana Gioia*
*Introduction by Jack Foley*

BOOKS
Oakland, California

Cover photograph: Sunset and creosote bush, by Ruth Nolan. Taken with
an iPhone 6 in February 2018 on the Hopalong Cassidy Trail, Cahuilla
Hills/Palm Desert, California.

Cover and interior design: Melanie Gendron
melaniegendron999@gmail.com

Scarlet Tanager Books
P.O. Box 20906
Oakland, CA 94620
www.scarlettanager.com

ISBN 978-0-9768676-9-2
Library of Congress Control Number: 2018905704

*For our grandchildren,*
*Brandon, Sabine, Autumn, Devlin,*
*Simon, Luke, and Eve*

*and in memory of*
*Ursula K. Le Guin (1929-2018)*

# Contents

## II. Coastal Redwoods

## IV. Fields and Meadows

## V. Desert

## VI. Rivers, Lakes, and Lagoons

## VII. Sierra Nevada and Cascades

## VIII. Cities, Towns, and Roads

We are married to plants. We are only one half of what we really are. We, in all of our fullness, are only one side of the wheel of Earth life.
　　—Paul R. Fleischman, *Wonder: When and Why the World Appears Radiant*

We are not in an environmental crisis, [we] *are* the environmental crisis.
　　—Neil Evernden, *The Natural Alien: Humankind and Environment*

Had the funeral been ours, the pigeons would hardly have mourned us.
　　—Aldo Leopold, *A Sand County Almanac*

# *Foreword*

Dana Gioia
California Poet Laureate

California poetry has a double identity. It is both part of American literature and its own distinctive enterprise. The history of our state, its enormous size, its singular culture, its particular natural and geographical position make it different from the rest of the country, especially the Northeast. To a critic in Boston or New York, California poets often seem like foreigners who happen to speak English—indeed speak it with an accent different from Cambridge or Manhattan. Even the perspective seems odd. Why do Californians talk more about Asia and Latin America than Europe? Why all the fuss about nature and the environment?

The Californian literary imagination has—from the beginning—been populist, visionary, multicultural, apocalyptic, and anti-establishmentarian. Our culture is rooted in the natural landscape and driven by the idea that its new society could escape and transform history. California writers immediately departed from the literary conventions of New England and New York, though they never stopped longing for approval from those elder siblings. Not surprisingly our writers have been dismissed, marginalized, or ignored by Eastern tastemakers, despite the immense influence they have had on the broader culture. Our masters have almost always been outsiders to the official curriculum of American literature—Jack London, John Muir, Charlotte Perkins Gilman, Robinson Jeffers, Dashiell Hammett, Raymond Chandler, John Steinbeck, Ray Bradbury, Philip K. Dick, Amy Tan, Kenneth Rexroth, Richard Rodriguez, William Everson, Charles Bukowski, Octavia Butler, and Kay Ryan. The California literary canon has always been problematic to Ivy League mandarins. Readers, however, have never shared those impediments.

Lucille Lang Day and Ruth Nolan's *Fire and Rain: Ecopoetry of California*, therefore, stands in the center of a California literary tradition—not only of poetry but anthologies. The editors cite recent books as precedent for their timely anthology, but another great model was the influential *Continent's End: An Anthology of Contemporary California Poets* (1925), edited by George Sterling, Genevieve Taggard, and James Rorty. Published by John Henry Nash for the Book Club of California, this book not only launched Robinson Jeffers to national attention, it fully articulated the natural landscape as the central theme of the state's poetry. Many of the writers in the book are now forgotten, but the concerns remain urgently present.

The editors of *Fire and Rain* have made the clarifying decision to organize the book not around poets but around places and habitats. The emphasis is on the world we share and the dangers and despoliations it faces, the irreplaceable beauty it offers. Day and Nolan have done a considerable service to select and gather these poems. Their ample anthology provides a generous record of California poets' love and concern for their common world. What more important theme can we in this golden land share?

W. H. Auden famously declared that "poetry makes nothing happen." I concur. Poetry is a way of articulating reality, not an expression of power. But reading this book, I wondered if California poetry might aspire to something simultaneously practical and noble. Perhaps if we write well enough about our endangered coasts and forests, deserts and streams, marshes and mountain lakes, we might see the world clearly enough to *stop* something from happening. We might protect our beautiful, wounded world and help it heal.

# Introduction

## "O Paradise, O Child's World"[1]: Ecology and Poetry

### Jack Foley

Every plant that stands in the light of the sun is a saint and
an outlaw. Every tree that brings forth blossoms without
the command of man is powerful in the sight of God. Every
star that man has not counted is a world of sanity and
perfection. Every blade of grass is an angel singing in a
shower of glory.
    —Thomas Merton, "Atlas and the Fatman"

Ecology is...learning anew *to-be-at-home* in the region
of our concern. This means that human homecoming is a
matter of learning how to dwell intimately with that which
resists our attempts to control, shape, manipulate and
exploit it.
    —Joseph Grange, "On the Way towards Foundational
    Ecology," *Soundings* 60 (1977)

    the poem,
the ground we stand on
constantly shifts.
    —David Meltzer, "Notes for Asaph"

*I*n his brilliant book *The Natural Alien* (1985), environmental
historian Neil Evernden elucidates philosopher Martin
Heidegger's term *Dasein* (German for "being there" or "presence"),
a word Heidegger uses to designate specifically human being.

---

1. The title of this essay quotes Thomas Merton's poem "Grace's House":

> O paradise, O child's world!
> Where all the grass lives
> And all the animals are aware!

Quoting Heidegger, Evernden writes, "'The being of *Dasein* itself is to be made visible as care.' We know a territory by the actions of its occupant; we know *Dasein* by the evidence of care." Evernden goes on to quote Heidegger's interpreter William Barrett, who in his book *Irrational Man* (1958) offers "an especially useful description of how it is to be such a field of care":

> *Now, there is nothing at all remote or abstract about this idea of man, or Dasein, as a field. It checks with our everyday observation in the case of the child who has just learned to respond to his own name. He comes promptly enough at being called by name; but if asked to point out the person to whom the name belongs, he is just as likely to point to Mommy or Daddy as to himself—to the frustration of both eager parents. Some months later, asked the same question the child will point to himself. But before he has reached that stage, he has heard his name as naming a field or region of Being with which he is concerned, and to which he responds, whether the call is to come to food, to mother, or whatever. And the child is right. His name is not the name of an existence that takes place within the envelope of his skin: that is merely the awfully abstract social convention that has imposed itself not only on his parents but on the history of philosophy. The basic meaning the child's name has for him does not disappear as he grows older; it only becomes covered over by the more abstract social convention. He secretly hears his own name called whenever he hears any region of Being named with which he is vitally involved.*

Earlier, Evernden has quoted historian Donald Worster, who concludes that "the best that might be hoped for from the science of ecology, at present, is the more careful management of... resources, to preserve the biotic capital while maximizing the income." "In other words," continues Evernden, "ecology can help us pursue the goals we have already set for ourselves: the maximum utilization of the earth as raw material in the support of one species. Yet environmentalism has typically been a revolt against the presumption that this is indeed a suitable goal....Ecology [in Worster's sense] can help one to criticize inefficient exploitation or destructive utilization of nature, *but it cannot help illuminate the experience that inspires one to be an environmentalist* [my italics]….In combatting exploitation, environmentalists have tutored the developer in the art of careful exploitation."

How does one turn away from "the art of careful exploitation"? How does one regain the child-sense of care (the German term is *Sorge*)?

When William Wordsworth says he wanders "lonely as a cloud" and sees daffodils "dancing," he is deliberately merging the natural world and the human world. Clouds aren't lonely; people are. Daffodils don't dance; people do. Yet seeing a cloud can make a person think of his separateness and loneliness, and the poem is about the continual interaction of nature, mind, feeling, and language. I suggest this as well in these lines from my poem "Viriditas":

> (describe a scene—
> scene vanishes—
> mind appears—)

Similarly, Brenda Hillman's phrase "green ideas leap furiously" (from her "Hydrology of California") is a version (or inversion) of Noam Chomsky's famous sentence "Colorless green ideas sleep furiously." Appearing in Chomsky's book, *Syntactic Structures* (1957), the sentence was originally meant to demonstrate the separation of meaning from syntax: the sentence was grammatically correct but, for Chomsky, meaningless, nonsensical. Hillman takes Chomsky's abstract sentence and resolutely turns it back into the natural world—the green world—and to the notion of ecological thinking: "Green ideas leap furiously." Again, interaction, and a movement from "sleep" to "leap." In Wordsworth's poem, the daffodils "flash upon that inward eye / Which is the bliss of solitude": they have moved from the outward eye, which "saw a crowd, / A host, of golden daffodils" to the inward eye, which is not "lonely" but in a state of blissful solitude; though physically distant, the daffodils are not absent but *there* (*Dasein*, being there), in a transfigured state.

"We need to remember," writes Evernden, "that *Dasein* is not just a different way of saying 'man,' but represents a different concept of being human, a 'field of care.' And being such a field means more than being a body; it means being-in-the-world, and it also implies a different sense of environment."

It is in the often despised, neglected, grossly manipulated, vastly misunderstood, ancient, outlaw art of poetry that such a "different concept of being human" begins to be enunciated. Here is Wordsworth's poem in its entirety. Isn't it, precisely, an expression of *Sorge*, of care?

> I wandered lonely as a cloud
> That floats on high o'er vales and hills,
> When all at once I saw a crowd,
> A host, of golden daffodils;
> Beside the lake, beneath the trees,
> Fluttering and dancing in the breeze.
>
> Continuous as the stars that shine
> And twinkle on the milky way,
> They stretched in never-ending line
> Along the margin of a bay:
> Ten thousand saw I at a glance,
> Tossing their heads in sprightly dance.
>
> The waves beside them danced; but they
> Out-did the sparkling waves in glee:
> A poet could not but be gay,
> In such a jocund company:
> I gazed—and gazed—but little thought
> What wealth the show to me had brought:
>
> For oft, when on my couch I lie
> In vacant or in pensive mood,
> They flash upon that inward eye
> Which is the bliss of solitude;
> And then my heart with pleasure fills,
> And dances with the daffodils.

~

*Fire and Rain: Ecopoetry of California*, expertly edited by Lucille Lang Day and Ruth Nolan, is a majestic hymn to living in localities. Its sections are not themes but landscapes: Coast and Ocean; Coastal Redwoods; Hills and Canyons; Fields and Meadows; Desert; Rivers, Lakes, and Lagoons; Sierra Nevada and Cascades; and, finally, Cities, Towns, and Roads. The book opens, properly, with an evocation of California's fabulous, famous light—a gift of the sea. Mary B. Moore's wonderful poem, "Abundance," begins,

> The light differs here, half wild and whiter
> than the tamer light that gilds the inland
>
> cities gold. It ricochets
> off silicates—mica flakes, sand grains,
>
> quartz bits. Stasis can't stay.
> Even southward off Highway One
>
> where flower herders grow mum,
> larkspur, zinnia all the way
>
> to the cliff-edge, the rocks
> beyond shimmer, jut and glint;
>
> the chicken-wire fences catch fire,
> banter, undulate, wink. Nothing
>
> holds still.

Nothing holds still in this exercise in geography as spirit either. It is as specific, prickly, and ecstatic as the landscape it deliberately mirrors. Moore's poem ends with a reference to "this place that mints / new light each minute, its gift, the unstinting."

And that's just the opening poem. It's immediately followed by David St. John's not "Big" but "Little Sur." St. John's poem, a love poem for landscape and for woman, includes these lines:

> These last wisps of morning fog & rags of sunlight
>    lift into the redwoods rising up along

The canyon walls & in the inlet below us elephant seals
    announce their daily dawn arguments

With those lessons of pre-history & your hair floats across
    the bed as easily as strands of the ruby kelp

That just yesterday rose silently beside the kayak as you
    carved a singular quiet along the waking bay


The founding father of all this activity is no doubt Kenneth Rexroth (1905–1982), whose own poems of the California landscape are masterful and often erotic meditations. Rexroth notoriously remarked, "I write poetry to seduce women and to overthrow the capitalist system. In that order." On the subject of ecology he told David Meltzer, "And don't forget [Berkeley radio station] KPFA's connection with all of this. KPFA has given hundreds of programs, thousands of programs, in the past twenty years on the ecological crisis. And I, on my own program [the half-hour review show "Book"], have never let up on it. There has never been a book, even a bad book, on ecology and on the environmental problem that I haven't reviewed and used…as a peg to hang a long ecology speech on."

Rexroth in turn had a profound influence on poets Gary Snyder and Michael McClure, both of whom became prominent in the Bay Area ecological movement. McClure's "For the Death of 100 Whales," first recited at the famous Six Gallery reading in 1955, became a signature poem both for McClure and for the emerging ecological consciousness. It also marked the first time that McClure center-justified his verse—itself a kind of gesture toward environmentalism, or at least toward the poem as a living organism, something with a spine. And Lawrence Ferlinghetti, who regarded himself as a disciple of Rexroth, was very much in Rexroth's spirit when he remarked, "Capitalism is an outrageously extravagant form of existence which is leading to an enormous ecological debacle unless it is completely changed."

*Fire and Rain* takes up Rexroth's trumpet and turns it into a full-blown symphony orchestra, a chorus of singular, diverse voices echoing their praise of a life lived among things, among objects, in direct, conscious relationship to what Denise Levertov called "the life around us." Here you will find extraordinarily resonant lines:

> The person you love is beside you
> and the rest of your life is a big question—
> it's something about the cornsilk
>
> of one two three hawks
> swooping low
> into the numinous.
> —Jennifer K. Sweeney, "White October"

~

> The tops of sequoia hide in the mist,
> so I look at one's fire scar, that hollowed
> center. How do they grow even weakened,
> for centuries? Do they have bad days?
> I want to change my life before
> another snowstorm hits the Sierra Nevada.
> River hike a fork of Kern River or
> sleep in the mountains surrounding me.
> I want to do it with someone else.
> —Heidi M. Sheridan, "Sequoia National Park, California"

~

> I'd filled my hand with water,
> a gift. I lifted, I sipped.
> Blue so pure it lit me up
> as though I'd gulped a star.
> —Karen Greenbaum-Maya, "Long Lake Blues"

~

> A hawk cuts across that narrow sky hit by sun,
>
> we paddle forward, backstroke, turn,
> spinning through eddies and waves
> stairsteps of churning whitewater.
> Above the roar
> hear the song of a Canyon Wren.

A smooth stretch, drifting and resting.
Hear it again, delicate downward song

ti ti ti ti tee tee tee
   —Gary Snyder, "The Canyon Wren"

Here you will find instruction. Did you know that "no other local creatures besides humans experience contact dermatitis from touching poison oak (*Toxicodendron diversilobum*)"? Kirk Lumpkin tells us this in "To Poison Oak."

And there is much, much more.

The poems in this volume demonstrate clearly that, in its wars and love affairs with language and world, poetry is like ecology in Grange's formulation—and also like living in an area where poison oak thrives! It is an art of "learning how to dwell intimately with that which resists our attempts to control, shape, manipulate and exploit it." David Meltzer puts the matter eloquently and succinctly: "the ground we stand on / constantly shifts."

~

*Fire and Rain* is a vast celebration of what the great geographer Carl O. Sauer called "land and life," of *Sorge*, of new possibilities of being human. It takes its place on my bookshelf as a marvelous extension of that California vision that George R. Stewart expressed in 1949 when he made the hero of his novel *Earth Abides* an ecologist. But I'd like to conclude this introduction with a poem that is not in *Fire and Rain*—and that is not about California—but that seems to me to express the deep spirit of this ecstatic, path-making, groundbreaking anthology: "From the Deep Earth" by Vietnamese poet Nguyen Phan Que Mai. Life, love, landscape are all there, as they are in this book.

*From the Deep Earth*

The day you arrived, the world knew how to breathe,
earthworms suddenly knew how to sing,
and the earth's surface trembled with life.

My mother had kept my embryo inside for days and months
where I wriggled, the world too small.
I howl inside my own hoarse voice.

Wind blows me into your hands, so I feel the pain pierce my
　　　　　fingers and toes.

Your gaze opens the sky.
The sun rises and forgets to set.
You place me on your lips and on your chest.

Our hands join to make a universe for the moon, the sun,
　　　　　the mountains and the vast singing sea.

Into your heart love gives birth to me,
and your voice breathes
streams of joyful thoughts
into my blood.

You will be soil and I will be soil,
dissolved into each other, quietly one day,
conceiving earthworms who know how to sing
the eternal song of emerald grass.


*Từ Lòng Đất*

Ngày anh đến, thế giới biết thở
Những con giun đột nhiên biết hát
Và mặt đất rùng mình sự sống

Mẹ đã phôi thai em trong lòng ngày tháng
Em cựa quậy thế giới nhỏ hẹp
U mê trong chính tiếng mình

Gió thổi em vào lòng tay anh, em đau thắt ngón tay ngón chân

Mắt anh mở bầu trời
Mặt trời mọc mặt trời quên lặn
Anh ấp em lên môi lên ngực

Đôi tay nhỏ bé của chúng ta tạo vũ trụ cho mặt trăng, mặt trời, núi,
    sông, cát, biển

Trong trái tim anh tình yêu sinh ra em
Tiếng anh thở vào em mạch máu
Chảy những dòng ý nghĩ hân hoan

Anh sẽ là đất và em là đất
Tan vào nhau lặng lẽ một ngày
Phôi thai những con giun biết hát
Chảy lên một niềm cỏ tươi xanh

# I

# *Coast and Ocean*

we hiked to the ocean today
left a prayer for earth
where land and sea
hug each other
　　—Kurt Schweigman, "Marin Coast"

If given a soul, I'll shepherd it
on the backs of seals
held in the bellows
of a graysound love.
　　—Jennifer K. Sweeney, "In the House of Seals"

Mary B. Moore

## Abundance

For John

The light differs here, half wild and whiter
than the tamer light that gilds the inland

cities gold. It ricochets
off silicates—mica flakes, sand grains,

quartz bits. Stasis can't stay.
Even southward off Highway One

where flower herders grow mum,
larkspur, zinnia all the way

to the cliff-edge, the rocks
beyond shimmer, jut and glint;

the chicken-wire fences catch fire,
banter, undulate, wink. Nothing

holds still. Even your hair flies every
which way in the photo, the dazzle etched

against the sea. And you poise
in your winged stance, head thrown back,

arms wide, a festival receiving
of what can't be caught.

        To catch it, the Cliff House boasts a camera
obscura that shows the shore

through a pinhole. It rotates
first to Sanctuary Rock, lighthouseless,

then to the sea whose blues vary
by depth, meet and marry

like yin-yang's mutually
fitting curves.

        On Sanctuary Rock, the pelicans,
ladle-beaked, rubicund, fly and return.

The seals sun on. Cormorants preen. Everyone
does bird-call Kyrie eleisons,

the cacophony preying and mating
make. The pelicans in bands seem to dream

and lumber even in flight.
They look sideways at the seawall

with one tear-sodden, salt-reddened eye.
Then one dives. He seems to catch a fish glint,

an eye-spark, in this place that mints
new light each minute, its gift, the unstinting.

David St. John

## Little Sur

As in the beginning the early tide at last collapses
    & recedes as porous knuckles of rock

Shoulder their way above the foam where cormorants
    drift & settle & as the day begins inhaling

These last wisps of morning fog & rags of sunlight
    lift into the redwoods rising up along

The canyon walls & in the inlet below us elephant seals
    announce their daily dawn arguments

With those lessons of pre-history & your hair floats across
    the bed as easily as strands of the ruby kelp

That just yesterday rose silently beside the kayak as you
    carved a singular quiet along the waking bay

Jennifer K. Sweeney

## White October
### Big Sur

You cannot let go the ember,
cinnamon and rust,
everything husked and shaking

paper skins, the hay-sweet
evening, auburn and cold
rooted from a seasonal childhood.

You search it in the October skyline
but the day is only white
over skirted mountains.

You could lose yourself
crawling the car around coast cliffs
and all the ways you've wished

for disappearance
lower down in veils,
take a fragment of memory or

desire back into the perpetual
dusk of ocean,
wrinkling and unwrinkling

its surf and glide.
You're searching for a little
fire, anything aglow

on the mauve-brown bluffs,
but that's not the point
this blurred world is making,

white October with its white pumpkins
and pearly pampas grass.
Thin as a plume

it's something about surrender,
how your need is a shade less
in this fieldrush of cloud.

The person you love is beside you
and the rest of your life is a big question—
it's something about the cornsilk

of one two three hawks
swooping low
into the numinous.

Catharine Lucas

## *After New Rain*

On the slope, last summer's dead—uncut fennel,
dry thistles, ghosts of rye grass—a silver scrim
like tattered fog subdues the boisterous green
called forth by new rain. Our tardy wet season has begun:
dirt paths soften that last week wore like iron under
the feet. The earth is not yet muck, so the going
is easy if you stay out of the gullies.

*Look*, I tell you, meaning the feathered gray combed
over the green crown of the hill,
*Like old men's hair*—
   Or maybe not
*What was I calling it, just now? Tattered fog?*

I seem to be revising. For you. Who are here
but not here.
I remember once, on the coast road out of Big Sur,
you turned from the sea to the sweep of brackened
hills. Nestled into crevasses, lifted on the crests:
furled wands of pampas, purple as newborns—
   "Give me some of your pretty words,"
you said. (I had thought that, like most, you minded
my constant commentary). Nice to be invited,
though it silenced me awhile—a babbling child
surprised by someone listening.

I never recovered innocence.
Often since you left, I catch myself practicing—
as if you'll come back. We'll be driving along the

coast, and you'll suddenly point, far out, to where
sea meets sky.

   "Give me some of your pretty words," you'll say.

I must be ready to describe
infinity.

Emily Grosholz

## The Gold Earrings

I thought that I would meet you here.
You stood on the pavilion beside Nepenthe
Where the view is still the same.
Nepenthe, you told me, means forgetfulness.
You reminded me to notice the body of earth
So often that our exchange
Melts back into a hundred other occasions.
Surely we admired the cliffs together
Descending and descending to the horizon
South of San Luis Obispo; singular pines;
The blue Pacific arrested in a motion
So vast and tranquil it resembles staying.
Forgetfulness pours through the enormous veins
That bind and furrow the world,
The ancient rivers of Acheron and Lethe.
Mother, souls who must begin again
Drink at those deep channels; so I began
Long ago the process of forgetting.
Not that memory grows less intense,
But the period of recollection lengthens.

I thought that I would meet you near
The lion-color mountains,
Twisted cypresses weathered to silver
Unchanged by twenty years, the cyclic ocean
Enchanting and shaming thought into reflection.
Time came round full circle like the horizon
And placed us at the center
Talking together, drunk with the blue of distance,
Your voice clear as ever: pay attention

To the lovely body of earth. Nothing endures
In the end but the colored bones,
The mantling blood of ocean flowing down,
Forgetfulness. No less intense, I swear,
Just more infrequent as the years go by.
How body wears the mind in recollecting.
Tears blinded me at the door of *Souvenirs*,
Where we chose a pair of long gold earrings
I loved and lost. The last I ever wore;
For later on, my taste in ornament changed,
And they were peerless, after their own kind.

Ann Fisher-Wirth

## At McClure's Beach, Point Reyes
## National Seashore, California

I would ask my family

Wait for a foggy afternoon, late May,
after a rainy winter so that all
the wildflowers are blooming on the headland.
Wait for honey of lupine. It will rise
around you, encircle you, from vast golden bushes
as you take the crooked trail
down from the parking lot. Descend
earth's cleft, sweet winding declivity
where California poppies lift up their
chalices, citrine and butterscotch,
and phlox blows in the wisps of fog, every
color of white and like the memory
of pain, and like first dawn, and lavender.
Where goldfinches, nubbins of sunlight,
flit through the canyon. Walk one by one
or in small clusters, carrying babies,
children holding your hands—with your eyes,
your oval skulls, your prodigious memories
or skills with the fingers. Your skirts or shirts
will flirt with the wind, and small brown rabbits
will run in and out, you'll see their ears first,
nested in the grasses, then the bob
of fleeting hindquarters.
               Now come to the sand,
the mussel shells, broken or open, iridescent,
color of crows' wings in flight
or purple martins, and the bullwhips
of sea kelp, some like frizzy-headed voodoo

poppets, some like long hollow brown or bleached
phalluses. The X X birdprints running
across the scalloped sand will leave a trail of stars,
look at the black oystercatcher, the scamp
with the long red beak, it's whizzing along
in its courtship dance. Look at the fog,
above you now on the headland, and know how much
I love the fog. Don't cry, my best beloveds,
it's time to scatter me back now. I've wanted this
all my life. Look at the cormorants,
the gulls, the elegant scythed whimbrel,
*do you hear its quiquiquiquiqui*
rising above the eternal Ujjayi breath,
the roar and silence and seethe and whisper,
the immeasurable insweep and release of ocean.

Judith McCombs


## *Refugio Beach, California, 1950*

Death march, we overheard
the grown-up words like a mysterious
tramping music, those summer months
when now and then the ambulance
came wailing up the bindweed road
to a beach house that we couldn't see,
where a man lived who had returned
from war, Corregidor and Bataan.
His half-grown, floppy St. Bernard
came charging down to roll and gallop
lonesome on the gleaming sands,
or rescue our downed driftwood planes,
then chase us through the shallows.
                                        Saturdays
we kids could ride the beat-up, rattling
garbage truck, hanging on
from the running boards, jouncing and clanging
all around our shaded trailer park,
then out through the lane by a farmer's fields,
and down to the low cliff's edge where we helped
the trash go flying Bombs away
to the long swells riding in from far-off
strange Pacific shores.
                                Most dawns
while the campground slept, I slipped away
with my smaller sister, scouting the thicket
path that disappeared above
the cave you couldn't see at all
when the highest tides came rolling over.
Inside lay shells, stones, sea-
weed tatters, cast up wet and new

on a trackless swell of sand. Abalone,
its curve of breathing holes and blackish
rainbow pearl, sometimes not broken,
from the offshore beds. Sea-blasted aqua
pieces of glass we believed were jewels
till the grownups laughed. Red turban shells
with pearly spiral paths inside,
cracked or spindly, skeletal.
The tide could trap us there, we said,
like pirates, like the luckless man
who was prying abalone from
the reefs offshore—his hand got clamped
in a living shell—the slow tide climbed,
his neck arched up, not far enough
to reach the sliding air.
                           Safe,
our best wet treasures hid, we waded
out through low-tide-streaming sands
to the fortress rocks that commandeered our shore,
each thickly hung with camouflaging
blue-black sometimes poison mussels
and wavering sea-weed slick as shower
soap.
        There we bellowed like radios
from our fortress prows to the surrounding seas:
*Dream girl dream girl*
*Beautiful Lustre-cream girl*
*You owe your crowning glory to*
*a Luh-huster-cream shampoo*
                           while waves
from newsreel shores poured around us,
foam and spray, roar and sliding
seethe that sucked the cliff and tried
to pull our stone hulls out to sea.

Kay Morgan

## *Before the Oil Spill*
### The World's Safest Beach

Belly down, terrycloth
rough against my cheek,
I try to lie still, make my body a compass—
feet point to the oil rig
closer to me than the islands
Anacapa, Santa Cruz, San Miguel,
names I love—my head aims
at the gray Santa Ynez range rising
beyond lemon groves cradled
between mountains and sea.

My brothers toss sand crabs
and seaweed pods
at my bare legs and back
until I escape to the water
to jump the waves or stand
wiggling my toes to search for clams,
while the undertow swirls
around my ankles, feet sinking
with every pull of water out to sea.

As the tide comes in, the breakers
come closer until I am hit by one,
pinned to the ocean floor,
breath knocked out of me—soaked rag doll,
bathing suit peeled to my waist—water foams
around me, recedes, reveals my skinny self.
I ignore my brothers' glee, run
to my mother to re-tie my strap,
wrap me in her towel.

Our feet, sand-covered, spotted with tar,
dangle from the open tailgate
of the wooden-sided station wagon.
Dad drives fast over the bumps, to give us a thrill;
mom cranes her neck from the front, sure
we will fall out when we cross the tracks
by the lemon packing plant. We jounce,
but hold tight; feet almost touch
the road as we bottom out.

In the outdoor shower, sand washes
through the slatted floor, back to the earth.
Mom scrubs the tar off our feet, off my belly,
the smell of turpentine
mixes with sage in the Santa Ana wind
blowing across our foothill home.
The Channel Islands are clear in the distance,
while on the oil platform, seagulls perch
and the derrick pumps and pumps.

Elizabeth Stoessl

## Ice Plant, Pacific Grove

The infant squints into the California sun
in this his first outdoor photo. The Pacific
placid behind them,
mother and child are surrounded
by a sea of succulent lushness
flowering in the sand. The mother,
native to northeast snowplow climes,
is astonished by February
purples, pinks and yellows.

For years, each time she returns
to this coast, she is newly enchanted
by the sight of ice plant, rampant
along the roadsides. Why not try
to grow it at home? Then, she learns
this exotic bloom is not benign: it
dominates and conquers native plantings.
Both shelter and delicacy to black rats,
its thick unchecked undergrowth
is a perfect fuel for wildfires,
a demolisher of hillsides.

Sad at her discovery and disillusioned
by the spitefulness of Nature,
she is still gladdened by the sight of these flowers
that bring back the memory of that newborn boy
Kodachromed among malevolent blooms.

Tom Goff

## *You, Robinson Jeffers*

should be the god enthroned on the California
state seal. In your *Selected Poetry*'s cover

photo, you sit stoop-shouldered,
your profile a Macedonian crag.

The small of your bent back
refuses all help from the ziggurat

step-stone pier compacted of rock
you hoisted to rest atop Hawk Tower.

But it's your informality, plain
in the worn trouser crease,

that most becomes your godhead.
You may look majestic and tough—

lips parted, jaw hard—but the dreamier,
loftier half's best feature is a benign

prow of nose. Ample for breathing salt.
What though your funerary cake of ash

broke long since against
the granite-rough underpinnings

of Tor House? Free from the copper urn,
something akin to your image

rills, deep black, under an oceanside
yew tree. That solemn furnace dissolved

your neural typeface along with your bones,
yet you exist. To warn: We humans

are not needed. To prophesy: Nothing
will stop our seeding development's poison,

splattering whole oceans with bitters
of oil and chemical stain—so many rotten

broken yolks. To console:
A California will abide, empty

of sea-watching houses, insect-eating bats,
white priestly egrets. To pledge:

The rock will keep its shape uncrushed
through the last noxious clouds. In

your photo, a Pacific fogbank brushes in
faint hillstrips of coastal smoke. That blackened

band, an ocean wholly of onyx, can still
set you musing upon saline crystal realities.

Your right hand holds its wonted scepter,
an unopened pack of cigs.

Trace remembrances,
like mist, soften your sunned face.

Kurt Schweigman


## *Marin Coast*

For Luci

we hiked to the ocean today
left a prayer for earth
where land and sea
hug each other
it was better than good
maybe even
gooder than better

we reminisced her toddler memories
sun melted my worries away
plants, rocks, trees, sky
kept us both in the moment
beaming smiles
as prayer and earth do feel
the simplest love
of a father and young daughter
who hold hands while hiking

Christopher Buckley

## *No Other Life*
### Douglas Family Preserve, Santa Barbara

Once in a while,
in autumn,
the architecture of light
lattices the salt air
above the cliffs,
the wind lays down,
the humming thread
and fabric of the blue,
stills, and out of nowhere,
a throng of cedar waxwings
appears and pours through
a wild pyracantha bush,
stripping, from between
the leaves and thorns,
the fire-red berries that
the universe has provided
for them...
                        Then the birds
are off, certain, it seems,
of a destination,
the next assignment
for their lives, a little dust
blowing up from beneath
the cypresses.
                        I like to
stand here and follow
the air for a while
as they lift away,
for no other reason than
this is what I've been given
to hold on to...

Jerry Martien

## *In the Pines*

For Jenny

Willow along the trail beginning to yellow.
Dry sand on the dune face refusing
to hold. Each grain separate and distinct,
wanting to be part of the whole again.

When we get to the beach we turn north like I
almost always do but then we walk farther
than I usually go because we're talking—

the wave slope at its highest accretion of sand
from all summer's long shore current,
along its edge the morning tide's
arrangement of shell and stick and stone—

and haven't paid attention to where we are
until pines appear instead of willow in the
swale behind the foredunes and pine again
on dune ridges and in the hollows between.

We stop to eat in a clearing among them:
shore pine, a hardy pioneer species
turns and twists to meet the weather.
*Pinus contorta contorta*. Each tree shaped
by light and fog and the prevailing wind.

It depends where you are when it blows.

Unlikeness like the Sierra lodge pole pine
being botanically the same as in our dunes but
here it makes another tree. A different forest there.

Yet likeness like the thing in your life you think
won't happen and then it does and it outlives
the day and all the names you attach to it.

Needle-refracted light. Reindeer lichen and bearberry
spread beneath the pines. The years together since.
Root and branch of that September afternoon.

Kari Wergeland

*Case in Point*

The sea stars displayed
in the Channel Islands National Park Visitor Center
live amongst a few fish,
including one flounder swimming flat
above the transplanted sand.
Several purplish ones,
as big as dinner plates,
show off their exotic bodies
to those considering a boat ride
to one of the five islands
hinting at what California used to be.
And a common star exists almost unattached
to the side of the tank.
It flops aimlessly in its bubble bath,
as though dead.
A second glance uncovers lively
chi, perhaps whimsicality.

Vince Storti


*Malachite*

When flummoxed by the word *Malachite*
I wandered over to my bookshelf
(that rickety shelf of knotty pine
undressed by a layer of paint
and filled with reference books
grammars and such).

*Malachite:*
a dictionary word
set between
a Hebrew prophet
of the sixth century
with the name *Malachi*
said to mean *my messenger*
and *malacology*
"a branch of zoology that
deals with mollusks."

*Mollusks*—and
I'm dredging up a picture of
bivalves on a beach: California mussels
soaked by daily tides with those beings
set in pools along the Fort Bragg bend
in a coastline bed colored brown and brined.

And—

*Malachite*—

"a light to dark green
carbonate material...

a source of copper and
for ornamental stoneware"

hinting why copper pans
and pennies turn green
when changed to a
patina.

Beyond that sea with
its waves like a prophecy
from the Bible or perhaps Greece
with Sybil or Cassandra or Tiresias
warning of dire consequence
near a shell just ready
to attach itself to a watery fate
on the stretch of coastline
beach marked by black
pockets of nested stone.

Lucille Lang Day

## *Tracking*

Point Reyes National Seashore

A gray fox leaves its mark:
twisted droppings on the trail.
No silvery back or rusty flanks
flash in lupine and coyote brush
by the path, and no short
barking yips ride ocean wind.
In daylight the gray fox hides
in its den, somewhere on
the rocky declivity, but each
four-toed imprint, capped
with claws like candle wicks,
says the gray fox walked here,
where irises and ice plant
give way to dune grass
holding sand in place. Far
out on mud flats, another sign:
deep five-toed tracks, in pairs.
Right rear foot, plantigrade,
by left front means none other
than raccoon, out in the dark
at low tide for the day's first
shellfish and insect pickings.
Triangular marks, crossing
raccoon tracks, say black-
tailed jackrabbit after
succulent grass on the island
on the flats, where I stop
to eat and make plaster casts.
Tennis-shoe prints, leading

back to the dunes, will be
erased at high tide,
and I'll take my trash
back to civilization,
leaving only these words
to trace the fact that I
walked here. I ate. I sang.

Jacob Minasian

## *Half Moon Bay*

I've never seen anything so large as the horizon
from shore, orange-brown cliffs like walls behind me.
I can feel the time in the sand; it's more real to me
than it's been before, each grain gradually reduced
to its present place and size, the wind lifting it
across my arms and hands. To see anemones this morning,
the purple spines on the urchin at low tide, a hermit crab
carrying a shell containing another crab along
the long stretch of tide pool sand, to the harbor seals
erecting their heads from the water ten yards away
(which a sign would later tell us meant we were too
close), the tide rising to raise my alarm at the evaporation
of the route back to the beach, the black rock's
disappearance into the green blue
waves, the whip of ocean air lathering foam along
its edges, was all enough to fill the entire day's
expectations, though now sitting, watching a flock
of pelicans hunting in the twilight, crashing into
the roiling surf below, tilting their heads back to swallow
fish barely visible in their momentarily stretched
gullets in the light, smaller birds
flocking to every spot each pelican plunges,
I am astounded even further and with greater
magnitude and velocity to see a thin trail of water
rocket upward on the horizon. Disbelief in magic
makes me prone not to notice, though I quickly
settle to the notion that no wind could lift water
in that fashion, in that thin a column in one place on
the ocean. More jets from surfacing blowholes commence
in a concert of fountains. One after another until

finally their heads become visible,
turning in the waves, their square
rocky brows in the water-spun
gold shimmer from the departing sun.

Elaine Miller Bond

## The Hungry Calf

Excuses
pluck another humpback from the sea.
And so her calf wanders alone,
cast to the docks,
where he sees his mother's belly in every hull
and tries to suckle
milk from wood,
life from illusion.

Pitching, splashing, plying the waves,
boats are but hollow ghosts,
and the humpback, the calf, the hungry little barnacle
tears himself away—
splintered—
back out to sea,
where once he swam
in a loving broad-finned shadow,
where he will now come to practice
the cool, liquid breaths
that dissolve the salts of surrender,
and where the great leagues of his kind
come winging back together
in another
long repeating song
of forgiveness.

Tricia Knoll

## *The Gray Whale*

See the rolling backs,
migrations passing these rock cliffs

that centuries asserted into the sea
beside certainties that gray whales

lift up their babies,
play by our boats,

migrate north and south, rise
for air, dive

for food,
survive the hunt,

and swallow sea-gut tortures
of hoses, baggies, balloons,

duct tape and rubber gloves.

Gail Rudd Entrekin

## Blue Whales

Blue whales are out there somewhere,
six thousand of the hundreds of thousands
that once roamed the planet's seas.
Now separated from each other
by thousands of miles, they moan their loneliness
four octaves below middle C, so low, so slow,
we humans cannot even hear. But on our ocean liners
and in our lighthouse kitchens, the cutlery jangles on the table,
the glass pane vibrates in its frame, and we know
something nearby is crying out in need.
Two thousand miles away, they can be heard
and answered, the loudest sound made by a living thing,
and we don't know what it says, but only that,
speeded up ten times, what we hear is a long, blue,
unearthly note, a gurgle so deep
we slip down into our own lostness,
grateful that they are carrying for us
something bigger than we could hold.

Brenda Yates

## *Dolphins in April*

>Who is the I in dreams, doing things I've never
>done, seeing things I've never seen—until now?

Our bow points to the edge  of cloudless sky
    curving into seas
          varnished the dark    bright
             blues of deep water.

Suddenly, ahead,    surface breaks, boils up,
    roiling  like a festival
          as it turns    onto an empty street.

We pick up speed, riding swells
    (bigger now)   bouncing roughly
          at a pace in knots
             that knocks us about,

pitting us against hard wind that flaps our sleeves,
    whips our hair into stinging.

          Above the gauze of foam,
darting terns    thrust themselves  into the fray;
    swivel-eyed gulls  fly beside us,   called
          to the commotion,  calling their kin
          to the waves;

companionable pelicans   dip & grab,
    circle a  pod
          of leaping,  graceful,  playful
            predators
    schooling fish    into balls of terror.

Then,     the sound:
                    high-pitched voices   drill the air;
                          birds silence themselves
                                as if    anticipating,

            & dolphins are everywhere—
                    *a thousand at least*, the captain says,
                          *I've never seen so many*
                                    *together at once*—

alongside the hull,   racing us   cutting across our bow,
            their bullet-sleek bodies
                    shoot out of the sea
                          flipping & splashing,
                                    knifing back under,

holding us spellbound…     until…until…what?

            They've  had their fill,   or fill enough
                    for the journey north?

Is there someplace to be     before darkness falls?

            Whatever the reasons,   ocean  calms again;
                    tired birds   alight to float
                          & we   turn

toward shore.         Gulls follow our wake
            as though    weeping     at what
                    the water     we churn
                          brings to them.

Ken Haas

*Otter*

Steward of a breakwater kelp state
and its thicket of parenthetical subjects
(orange garibaldi, bluish blacksmith,
señorita fish like a yellow cigar,
bat star and puffball sponge,
gumboot chiton, cabezon,
turban snail and dragon eel),

he swims for miles like a rubber torpedo
from Pigeon Point to Morro Bay,
claims his fill of escargot and calamari
leaving only morsels for the gulls. But
they also make him eat a ton of urchins
so his teeth turn purple by the time he's three.
Once in a while, he gets to drift on his back
cracking an oyster against his belly with a rock.

He's for when you turn fifty single,
cashing a paycheck just ahead of the rent,
well past the days of horses and lions,
not yet ready for the company of birds.

Thick-necked, flat-eared and side-eyed,
back East he'd be playing rugby
or whistling for a rush-hour cab.
Out here his friends wrap him
in seaweed so he can rest. Rest
from endlessly burping his oily coat
to ward off frost, rest
from mating unpleasantly, rest
from sniffing the breeze with a tilted snout
for the guns of traders
long gone from these waters.

Chad Sweeney

## Arranging the Blaze

Into the eye the light pours
           of red brick and black brick and wire draped
                against white, opaque white a surface
                        of distance the
                              irreconcilable,
of gables and doors, of the impressions of pedestrians stooped
through rain. to the blur of
the water tower over roof peaks in muted triangles.
And somewhere:  there:   the contours of sound
                        those tires now on wet
                        pavement, and there
                        a plane
                        in the pearl, the milk bruise,
                        how to say it, of sky—sounded—and
                        where do I end?

This oxygen now
by which my body burns arrived from
over the sea while I
slept all night. A great invisible
wing
dragged its mass over the water—while ships,
                      while darkness,
                      while strangers in cars
             while cliffs, while pine, while elevators and
jail beds—while tides
combed the
reef and
            lobsters moved in the living rock—
this air
poised on its axis in

time—the water, the water

in my body                          waving.

Gingko trees flare yellow
out of memory, still spark
the eye. The beach grass
                    must be where I left it
                              wrapping
the whole earth last year,
how old is it
beside the sea—to be still
making me with its arc,
its sand, its small portion
of space worn about it like a shawl?—tremolo
in blue-green radial symmetries
of the beach grass.

Block upon block the buildings
scrape against
                          hills, mounting to where eucalyptus
claims the peaks—those lights
in houses, someone chose them, and by their blaze
against this water, I am also lit. Over the empty

playground in diagonals of rain, the flock
throws itself into storm, buoys
and pivots—a wind of swallows
directed from within,
                    churns above the city
          —and is this Lebanese cedar,
center point,
          abandoned and returned toward, part
          of the flock?
                    And the shingles part?
that barge docking?

the feeling too—of joy—a thing
                        in our gravity
                over which this net of eyes casts,
      the one and the many
           —and you
    who see it, shifting,
           are you
                  part of the flock?

Susan Cohen

## Ode to the Brown Pelican

I know I am not
your equal, but
when I hike along the cliff tops
and you glide past at eye level
I feel I almost could,
like you,
make everything look easy:
the ascending, the stroking, the wafting.
You aren't pretty
or songful, and yet,
around your extrovert's beak—
hints of a satisfied smile,
as if you know
the shopping bag
you always carry with you
will soon fill.

You barely flap,
just a tilt east or west.
Your eye is not a bird's
obsidian bead
that bounces off me
like a ball bearing,
but sky-blue and fetching,
an eye that could meet mine
across a pillow or a café table
if we ever came nose to nose,
which is unlikely.

It is an eye
that knows things

about how to follow,
though today I catch you
on your own swimming the air
with the equanimity of a leaf,
immune to high ambition
but alert to small,
quick opportunities.

Yes, on land
you're comic—all lip
as if to laugh at your own
awkward punch line.
But then those spread wings,
those wings, those wings
catch the drift.

Susan Cohen

## Credo

I don't believe in God, but I do
　　　believe in godwits.

How they give up the shore
　　　to stream by hundreds,

to be one feather
　　　on the same fluid body.

How they swing over the water
　　　this way and that,

a loose boom of birds, flare
　　　right or snap left—visible,

golden, invisible, as sun catches
　　　or releases them all—

a semaphore wink from the deck
　　　of the ship

bearing no message but spark.
　　　I believe then, at least,

existence is a marvelous trick
　　　of the light

as the godwits keep flocking
　　　seen, unseen, seen.

Maureen Eppstein

## Sanderlings

No sound but the white hush of the sea
and the wick-wick-wick of sanderlings

that flow in such numbers on their rippling legs
they become the foam that edges the wave.

Nothing is precise or separate:
the birds, the sand, the water-laden air.

No boundaries visible,
all that is and was feels holy.

Eva M. Schlesinger

## In Cahoots with Coots

I liked the coots best
their flapping
cluck cluck cluck
against the water
their black wings
dipping in and out
of the bay

louder than the skiff's
purr
gliding through
blue gray ripples

## Sea Lions Lyin'

Sea lions lyin'
On piers
With peers
Sea lions sunbathe
Some days
Sun dazed
Sea lions
See lions lyin'

Sally Bliumis-Dunn

## Sea Lions

Amid the heap of them,
two sea lions mating—

the bull's penis, oddly gray,
pokes between her hind fins
at the soft and fatty split,

full as the side of a peach,
where the cleft divides.

I imagine pleasure
swimming through her body
as though through a sea,

our mammalian link,
strong in the briny stench.

After, as though
their weight
relaxed and softened,

their bodies
widen on the sand.

Andrena Zawinski

## Morning News

This morning, the heron huddled into himself,
head buried deep inside the ruffled tuft,
long bill aimed at bracken edging the bog,
thin plume arched up in victory, having had his fill
of a new clutch of downy-backed ducks.

A tern picked open a stingray at low tide
at sunset, swatch of shoreline awash in blood,
and I watched the red of it, redder
than fishers' rock cod off trawlers at Pillar Point,

merciless gulls a scramble of screeches
for castaway scraps. And just down the shore
a seal pup beached, face slit mouth to cheek,
hook bleeding the sand, flies a frenzy in its face.

This morning, life seems quite hopeless. Just listen
to the early news, how it uproots silence, sends it
wild as wing beats thrashing into the wind,
chipped by words, by the fact that
nature can be such a terrible beast.

Kathleen McClung

## Whistle Keepers, 1883

We all drown. Before sinking into earth or water we work, raise
children, sing and weep, nurse the afflicted, repair a boat,
christen it with a woman's name. My own is lost.
Yes, yes, I am Mrs. Colburn in every sheriff's report passed
across oak desks, across years of sun and fog.
Yes, yes, we have a tale. Mrs. Ashley and I have a tale, wives

of whistle keepers posted to Año Nuevo Island, ordinary wives
of quiet men, Henry and Bernard. Solemn men, they never raised
their voices, took only a drop of rum on holidays, no fog
of drunkenness, no bellowing rage, steady—like a boat
just finished, not yet at sea. Readers all, we four could pass
a clear evening in silence once the children slept, lost

in *The Tempest* or *Moby Dick* by lamplight as our children, lost
in their dreams, twitched in their cradles. Husbands and wives
swimming peaceably through pages, words like *harpoon* and *magic*
            streaming past.
Other nights, the men tended the steam whistle, raised
its blast from hot coals for ten seconds every minute into
            the thick weave of sky. Grand boats
had smashed to bits years before—the *Sir John Franklin*, the *Coya*—
            in our California fog.

We'd read the stories as schoolgirls, dreamed of gold coins
            glinting in fog,
trunks of soft pelts tumbling onto beaches, handsome sailors lost
among octopus on the ocean floor.      On April 8 our husbands
            rowed a boat
to the mainland for supplies: more leather-bound books
            for their wives,

fresh artichokes, strawberry jam, a real china doll for Ida,
    sharp razors
to scrape away their beards. We busied ourselves
    scrubbing pots, passed

the spring day as any other, industrious, aproned. Pelicans passed
low over our heads. We pinned wash on the line. No fog,
but forceful gales, tall waves, the baby colicky as the last rays
of sun drained from the sky. Did he know his father would be lost
in the morning? Did he know we women—friends, mothers, wives—
would witness the small boat whirling and bobbing
    in rough water? A boat

named *Ophelia*, full of food and gifts. Henry had painted our fine
    and only boat
before the birth of our son. It carried our men out to thrashing
    open sea, past
our island of new years, past our cries, our reach.     Wives
flow into widows every hour—some keen and howl, curl tight
    within caves of fog.
But we could not. *We must signal*, we agreed, *bring a ship to us
    or we are lost.*
First the flag. We lowered the salted cloth, spun it upside down,
    raised

it again, half-mast. Then the fog whistle we wives had memorized
but never used until that bright April day. We raised the alarm,
    beckoned
to distant boats: We have lost treasure to the sea. Find us. Do not
    sail past.

Jennifer K. Sweeney

## *In the House of Seals*

Año Nuevo Lighthouse Ruins

Abandoned on its eroded jetty,
the Victorian is gutted by windbreak,
waves and the pale ash
of salt and plaster.
A clean wind howls up the spiral
stair, rattling the vacant dumbwaiter,
the picture window, walls
bleached in sheets of raw sun.
What keeper's lantern once swung
the veranda to meet the shore-
tossed plot, what wrack
and beckon of Pacific tide
is now pilgrimage for elephant seals.
Given a home, they return
to the mecca of their kind
paddle into the blown-out façade
to birth and die
in heaps of tender slack, skin
like buckled wallpaper.
Dear sitting rooms of milk and bone:
life keens starkly forward
while the dying nurse the dead.
Who knows what will become of us
receding behind white curtains
and what bright ruins might lean
from the pitch of night to shelter us?
To be so wanted
in the work of decay.
If given a home, I'll take this home.

50

If given a soul, I'll shepherd it
on the backs of seals
held in the bellows
of a graysound love.

Paul Belz

## Elephant Seal on the Beach

Point Reyes National Seashore

Baby, you weren't dying.

You pulled your wrinkled body toward the sea
used your flippers, slid inch by inch
with rapid, shallow breaths and eyes
that seemed to plead. You were one chord
in Point Reyes' crescendo, tone poem
of wind-slashed rock with sandy deer and skunk tracks.
Forester's terns plunged for anchovies.
Two oystercatchers zipped along the shore.
Brown pelicans dipped and rose
on waves, skimming breakers.
Green anemones blossomed in tide pools,
showed their jade tentacles. Everything flowed
through this visual melody.

You watched, and heard all,
still as a gale-ripped cliff,
worn out, through with striving.

                    No, baby,
this wasn't your final solo. It was a rest,
music's break. Next morning you left a trail
that merged with high tide.

Karen Skolfield

## Ten Thousand Baby Mollusks Named Karen Diane

Not to overstate, but this mollusk owes
its life to me. California beach,
softball-size turban shells, a bunch
of young guys showing off for some girls.
Low tide and they found the coiled shell
I'd just picked up and set down.
*What is it, what is it*, they cried,
turned it over and saw the mollusk's great foot,
one giant white muscle strong enough
to resist the tides, *oh gross*, one said, a girl,
because it's a snail, really, an unlovely
gelatinous body, it eats with its foot,
moves in ripples of flesh, does not speak,
does not sing or fly or hunt in packs,
the things we humans admire, does not have
a courtship dance, does not groom its mate,
does not look eerily like us or nurse its young.
*I'm going to crack it open*, one yelled.
And the California-brown boy raised it
over his head.

Later I looked up the shell. *Tegula regina*,
the queen's turban, hard shelled
but on the inside soft, defenseless,
almost let go but not quite, the long arm
of this boy nearly a man, ashamed long enough
to put it back when I screamed no,
carefully even in the water where, in an hour,
the waves would reach. I thought at first
I was the voice of the mollusk, yelling

what it might yell, but I was my own voice
shouting over the onshore winds, the surf,
shouting at the long brown arm,
at the queen drawn back
in its stranded shell, splendid,
higher than it had ever been.

Eileen Malone

## Velella Velella

Our sunrise beach-walk finds
how overnight the furious ocean
has cracked open and cast up

thousands of squishy,
tentacled, jellyfishy quivers
of sail-like crests
cloaking the entire beach
with jellied cobalt

actually a superorganism
of *Velella velella*
also known as
"by-the-wind sailors"

a cerulean colony
of palm-sized individuals
pushed in from the open sea

refugees deposited by the tide
to shatter into a shock
of a thousand translucent
sapphire stars, fallen

to gleam at the feet of the palest
most glimmering blue dawn
ever.

Sarah Brown Weitzman

## Beach Glass

From the litter of wrecks:
cracked spectacles
and watch crystals
shattered ships' lanterns
smashed porthole windows
chips, shards from bottles
all clouded by salt
smoothed by wave swells
polished in the violent tumble
and toss of undertow

blues most common
greens and browns second
opaque whites seem like stones
from the moon
a few golden as lager
reds a rare find
beach glass reminds
us that everything recycles
nothing's lost really
only changed

Bri Bruce

## *Feel*

Like every other summer afternoon
the sails unfurl in the blue spoon of bay,
white-capped but not enough to rouse
the silty sand. A pale half moon is
held up in the sky, coerced by those laws
we cannot see. A cattle egret flies east
from the lagoon, caring little for the
shrieking company of the terns,
in from the north and sheltering in the
marshes. A plover cries from the mud flat,
thrumming of waves heaving themselves
at the shoreline. Were you here I'd point out
the coyote's tracks through the sand,
the distance between where each paw fell,
tell you he was running. I'd reveal the place
where, beneath the dune grass, the gull's
body lay torn open and hollowed, say
to you, *This, this is how I feel*.

Rachel Dacus

## Docks, Cliffs, and Tidepools

San Pedro

Old men mend nets. Young men
die on boats, lose hands and legs
in the winches, hauling tuna in and over
their heads onto the deck, thirty an hour.

On the docks, the men hunch on boxes,
torn nets spread out like water.
Today the tuna fleet's going out.
All bets are off in spring fog.

Wet and salty air
stains pavements and roofs.
Fish-weather, every man
pockets a clink of sea-silver,
to the hum of fishing reels.

A bewilder of mist pleases
the Japanese farmer,
whose hoe rises and falls
along a row of cliffside kale.

His eyes turn toward the misty light.
Clouds shade the work,
make the tourists stop
at his roadside stand
for the big vegetables.

At last a sparkling morning
makes the harbor a silver tray
of antipasto hues,
and children dip fingers in foam,
touch starfish and anemones.

E. K. Cooper

## *Where Have They Gone?*

Echoed memories of "They are like a family, you must leave the generations whole" and "Take only a few, and move down the cliff." Wisdom passed from my Dad to me when I was a child.

The ocean cliffs of Fort Bragg, California, blanketed with mussels. The oldest ones, each the size of a brick nestled among the younger generations, providing shelter and comfort. Once gathered, they were dumped in a large steaming pot, covered until the mussels opened. Each was eaten whole, straight from the shell, an orange delicious meal.

Ocean rocks covered in dark and light green seaweed. Each plant was 4 to 6 feet long, swaying with each breaking wave. I would grab a handful from the rock and pull before the next wave came in. Seaweed would wrap itself around my arm while others escaped my grasp. It felt slimy, smelled salty, but when dried, fried and wrapped in a warm tortilla, it was delicious.

These same rocks held hidden treasures as well. A blind hand reaching and feeling for a rock that is not. A piece of flat metal was used to pry under and worked back and forth, then off would pop an abalone the size of a dinner plate. It would be pounded, cut into strips, floured, and fried. A food so rich in flavor, only a small portion was needed to satisfy your craving.

Pinoleville, my Dad's reservation, has a creek that holds the best of all of them, the salmon run. The river water would be bank to bank as the salmon swam upstream to their spawning grounds. Native men would wait with spears and hooks, then wade into the creek to catch salmon for their families. Always with the knowledge to take a small amount, and leave enough for future salmon runs. Baked, smoked, or fried, the flavor always reminded you that river water held a flavor all its own.

The Fort Bragg ocean cliffs and rocks still remain but are now barren. The Pinoleville Reservation creek is now a trickle on a good day but most often dry.

I learned in my youth traditional ways of being one with the plants, animals and Mother Earth. I yearn to pass down my knowledge the way I was taught, by showing. My youth of plenty now sits with its spirit heavy with sorrow as my adulthood wrestles with a future of none.

This Pomo asks one question:

Where have they gone?

Patty Joslyn

## I Live Here

I live here
I say to myself
I say it out loud
I live here

How to describe
The smell of ocean air
Salt as white musk
Seaweeds dusk as dark and wild

Is there a word
For the ropes of glistening pearls
Snails leave behind
On sidewalks cracked by flowers

Orange poppies
Clustered and splayed

Agates washed clean
Sparkling for no reason

Magnificent Tower of Jewels
Rising above weathered fences

Here on the Mendocino coast
In a moment's time fog
Knows how to lay itself
Down like a damp sheet

Soon the wind pushes
The clouds aside

A radiant halo
Reigns

I live here

I wonder if a thousand
Is too many times to say
The same thing

I live here

# II

## Coastal Redwoods

…I have been to other forests, seen
how small trees are.
   —W. F. Lantry, "Giant Forest"

"Saving these woods from axe & saw,
from money-changers and water-changers
is the most notable service to God & man
I've heard of since my forest wanderings began."
   —Anne Whitehouse, quoting John Muir
     in "Blessing XXIV"

Marcia Falk

## Tu Bishvat in the Redwoods: A Meditation Suite for the Earth

Composed for the *Tu Bishvat Seder* at Headwaters Forest,
January 26, 1997

1

Here we are. We are here.
And why, when here, do we always want more?

2

Here you are, back
in the redwood forest—

how tall the fir trees,
how delicate the pines!

Standing on the winter-dark earth,
you suddenly know these trees

will be your gravestone.
Nothing stirs—but what

are those sounds?
You balance on the edge

while under your feet
the mushrooms smolder

and the unborn ferns
hum in their bed.

3

If you sit long enough in the woods,
nothing happens.

Just the earth's breath rising and falling
up and down tree trunks

which go copper-green in the air
as if oxidized.

Just your own breath warming a spot of earth
while your heart beats

and you begin, like all the creatures,
to repeat yourself—

the same thoughts entering your mind—
entering, leaving—

while yearnings rise and fall
like the tails of startled squirrels.

4

"'And trees—you're allowed to kill trees?'
a small boy blurted…"

5

You do not belong to you,
you belong to the universe,

and you will be reclaimed
by its constant, ever-changing heart—

your wise body
and your spacious mind,

66

whether you are ready
or not,

when you are joyful
or not,

even as you turn away—
to be buffeted

and set aloft,
a twig in the wind.

6

You take the long road on your walk today,
slowly threading back through the woods,

past the log cabin, locked and posted
"Do Not Enter"

and the posted tree
announcing its own end:

"Notice of intent to cut
growing wood and timber."

You vow that every day
you will post vigil

as the hours slowly drop
from that slender length of tree

one by one
by one.

7

In a naked slice of air,
a single blade proclaims dominion:

the silent flesh of the last living redwood
towering, alone.

Stones shift beneath the mold,
the earth's breath rises and falls.

Why has it gone so quiet?
What is left that we need to know?

*Coda: A Dream of Recovery*

The sky is soft as a grandmother's quilt,
the needles and fronds are soft, too.
They seem to heal you with their green fingers,
their heady perfumes rising.

The trees will open their arms,
the wind will catch you in its lap,
they will rock you, rock you like a baby
as you dreamed in your deepest longing,

not as it happens when you wish for it
but as it's told in an old old story,
a story you were born knowing
and later forgot.

W. F. Lantry


## Giant Forest

We camped near Crescent Meadow, where the trees
surrounded us, rising three hundred feet
above our heads. A child, five years old,
I thought the earth comprised of scenes like this:
the redwood limbs receding, greenish-gold,
into the rising mist, the endless sweet
scent of those fallen cones of sugar pine,

where ferns and mountain laurels intertwine
their fronds and leaves along the meadow's edge.
It never seemed unusual: the soft
bark of those redwoods seemed a normal bliss.
I loved to hold my childish arms aloft
standing out there amid the budding sedge,
imagining my arms could go around

those trees, rooted so firmly in the ground.
But roots are shallow: now all camping's banned
and I have been to other forests, seen
how small trees are. And yet I reminisce,
thinking of running careless through that green
heaven I was too young to understand,
and still believe all trees should be like these.

Alison Hawthorne Deming

## Poem 22 from *The Monarchs*

Redwoods. At night they take
the headlights without blinking,
their thousand-year-old patience
disturbed only slightly by lightning
or wildfire. To them the sorrow
of the celibate fathers is the same

as the sorrow of the missionized tribes.
They are satisfied to drink what rain
can be wrung in the billowing fog.
They tolerate nattering creatures
inhabiting their bark and branches.
Their hearts rise straight through their bodies

and are not harmed by hardening.
Unable to hear, see, smell, or taste,
they know when to drop their lower branches,
broaden their root anchor, when to
climb and bud. The redwoods, without
liquid hydrogen or God, have mastered time,

with their tracheids and sieve tubes,
their angel cells catch and release the light.

Robert Coats

## Logging Old Growth, 1964

Through huckleberry, salal and azalea
a D-8 Cat has cut a swath,
then gouged a deep trench into the hillside;
soft earth is piled in the bottom
as if it were a grave dug to receive
the body of the redwood giant
now destined for decks and siding.

Finally the chain-saw falls silent.
The back-cut is complete, only
a thin strip of heartwood remains
connecting stump to trunk.
In the quiet pause, the forest seems
to draw a breath, as the fallers
set their wedges into the kerf.

They begin again: a rhythmic
*clink    clink*
of steel on steel as they
drive home the wedges
with sledgehammer blows.
Another pause, the final shouted warning.
Three more swings, a sharp "crack"
and the whole tree shudders,
its top-most twigs now arcing downward.

Then, for the last time, wind rushes
through the scaly foliage,
debris falling, saplings snapping,
chaos of lichen flying.

A seismic "boom"
so loud it will echo
down the years.

Vincent Peloso

## *Wounded*

Entering these woods to meet
an old-growth redwood stump
girdled with rectangular slots
big enough for my fist,

I plunge my hand in once—twice—
my arm becomes the iron shaft,
my nails the sharpened blade

chipping live wood to hold long boards
on which two men once stood
at opposite ends of a two-man saw.

Felling large trees by hand is hard.
But seeing so many stumps like this
scattered among much smaller trunks
makes it even harder to meet

these woods unwounded.

Vincent Peloso

## *Clear Cuts*

Clear cuts bring vistas undreamt in old growth.
Geography stripped of botany's clothes
exposes itself to our view.
Topography simply glows.

Without trees, fertility riots.
Annuals pop. Perennials sprout.
Invasives exploit any advantage.
Natives fight for their home.

Resource extraction is hatching
an exurban terrestrial phoenix
in the Pacific Northwest,
third millennium A.D.

## *This Burl*

This chest-high, breast-shaped burl
corseted in thick, dusty bark
is rough and dry when kissed.

Light feeds my eyes.
The air tastes like milk.
Yet this burl isn't a breast.

Neither hamadryad
or my own dead mother
reincarnated as a tree.

Erin Redfern

*Some Knots*

in the redwood fence still weep.
Not the ones you'd think—
not the largest, but those dense
and deep, sliced eyes shut tight
against the feel of phantom branches.

In winter each rufous tear fell stiffly,
cold-stopped, suspended
as the tree's own breath. As iron
does blood, tannin turned
the dead tree's crying red.

Maybe you've seen split planks
like these, massed
under canvas flaps in the lumberyard,
missing their hearts,
or on the interstate you've passed

trailers hauling triangular stacks
of giant, amputated trunks.
Maybe your HOA paid
a careless crew to slap together
some cheap privacy. I'd rather

have the shade. It's summer now;
the sun's thermal gaze warms the sap,
blackens its slip along the grain.
Color of grief? rage? or something
more enduring, an end to all that?

Cynthia Leslie-Bole

## *Redwood*

your aroma wakes me
like a slap from a Zen master
it slices with clean clarity
from the slender leaves
growing at your tender tips

during life
you stand as a silent sentry
stolid and sure in the slowness of time
when you die
your emptied husk
nourishes the forest floor
and your love sprouts offspring
in a circle around your ghost

you are a good mother
and your steadfastness comforts me
I am compelled to bury my nose
in the clefts of your bark
and wrap my arms around you
in filial embrace

your wisdom is root-deep and sky-high
your discernment grows
as you witness creatures
living lives of frantic industry
at your feet

redwood
show me

how to slow my metabolism
so I too can feel the seasons

show me
how to accept earth sustenance
so I too can have faith
in the long-term good

Kirk Lumpkin

## The Dudley's Lousewort

For Kim Kuska and the Dudley's Lousewort

Though unfortunately named the
        "Dudley's Lousewort"
        with its population
        even more diminished
        than its more
        dramatically named
        relative the
        "Indian Warrior,"
        it's no less
        full of life than
        any other
        species.
And though not officially so
        it is in fact
        an endangered species,
        apparently failing
        to adapt
        to the changes
        our culture has made
        to the mixed
        Redwood/Douglas Fir forest
        of small parts of
        the Northern California coast
        that are its only
        home.
And you might ask,
        like the Boy Scout executive
        asked my friend,
        "What good
                is the Dudley's Lousewort?"

And I might reply,
      if not too taken aback,
      that the
      Dudley's Lousewort,
      though small and subtle,
      is a lovely thread
      in an ecosystem
      we are unraveling
      every day
      and a golden
      opportunity
      to learn
      how if we can save
      this small fellow being
      we still might learn
      to save ourselves.

Maureen Eppstein

## Red-Bellied Newt

*Taricha rivularis*

What stirs, with the rain, that urge to return?
Some years she ignores the tingle in her nose,
the scent of that particular section of stream
where under a stone she hatched into a nymph,
then played for a year in the rippling water
before crawling transformed up the bank.

Summers she hides. Home is a secret hollow
under gnarled redwood roots in the ancient grove.
Some winters too. But once in a while, when the rains begin,
she emerges to make the journey to her breeding place.
Purposeful, she crawls, the red of her feet and belly
bright against the redwood duff,

navigating by smell to the rocky stream a mile away,
not home exactly, but the place she came from,
that pulls her back as it pulled her mother back.
Here she will mate, immersed in the water that gave her life,
deposit the fruits of her procreation under a stone,
then wander off to find good forage for the summer.

For thousands of years, as the giants grew overhead,
her kind have made this journey, secure in their faith
that the stream will still flow clear and fast over rocks.
They raise a question: what pulls us humans,
and to what deep places, and what is it we deposit,
like fertile newt eggs on the undersides of stones?

Susan Gubernat

## To Return as Owl

The head swivel—I'd give up speech for that
and learn to savor mouse flesh,
leaving behind a bolus of bones,
intact, and a molted tail feather

a pellet being better than any poem, I think,
coughed up from the deep psyche
to mark the stranger's path
under the redwoods

with my imperial presence.

Harriet Gleeson

## Charmed Circuit

Quarter-mile on redwood feathers
faintly heard the ocean's roar.
Rain will bring fantastic fungi
coral, brain and dead-man's-foot.
Green translucence cool and shaded
red brown cushion underfoot.

Rain will bring fantastic fungi
coral, brain and dead-man's-foot.
Blue and purple iris, sorrel,
shy calypso orchid spring.
Green translucence cool and shaded
red brown cushion underfoot.

Blue and purple iris, sorrel,
shy calypso orchid spring.
Saprophyte transparent white
hid from undiscerning eyes.
Green translucence cool and shaded
red brown cushion underfoot.

Saprophyte transparent white
hid from undiscerning eyes.
Tread a world of modest beauty
in this brief and rounded walk.
Green translucence cool and shaded
red brown cushion underfoot.

Diane Frank

## Mendocino Late Night

After making love
in the Mendocino woodlands
late at night, walking home
through a cathedral of
redwood trees

A path I find in the dark

High branches
the shape of a rune
Osprey lifting from the Gualala River
What the owl said

An echo of white deer
running to the moon

Sometimes I feel you in the morning
silver koi under the water
of my dream.

Diane Frank

## *In the Mendocino Woodlands*

He walks into the forest
where trees are burning
finding his path in the silence.

Woodpecker, memory, larkspur
in the night of burning.

His eyes ask me to wait,
to keep the connection inside
the silent place where I find
pebbles of intuition, rose quartz.

In the morning, lupines on the trail
to the cliff where the giant trillium blooms,
kelp and seals swimming beyond
the tide pools below.

I run through Indian paintbrush,
milk maids, cinquefoil,
climbing the path where he finds me.

And what is love?
A fire walk initiation
from the ocean through a cathedral of trees,
fuchsia, wild grape, sudden
blue streaks on the wing of a moth
Steller's jay wanting to fly free.

Maureen Eppstein

## Redwood Grove After Fire

Crunch of black fragments underfoot,
faint whiff of char,
earth beside the trail fresh broken
where a burned tree fell
as they sometimes do, years later.

Cave walls of the hollow giants
gleam with fresh scorch.
Ferns have returned to the flat,
though sparser now.
More logs among them fallen.

We celebrate survival:
redwood sorrel has spread
its green salve over ashy ground,
warty and wrinkled, the old ones stand
in their accustomed silence.

Anne Whitehouse

# Blessing XXIV

The redwood trees stand
like sentinels on the lonely coast,
the tips of their lofty spires lost in fog,
shaggy trunks and fragrant needles
dripping in the rain that swells
Redwood Creek as it tumbles
from Mt. Tamalpais to the sea.

"Saving these woods from axe & saw,
from money-changers and water-changers
is the most notable service to God & man
I've heard of since my forest wanderings began,"
wrote John Muir in gratitude to William Kent
after Kent bought the land to preserve it
in Muir's name with his blessing.
"If we lost all the money we have
and saved these trees, it would be
worthwhile," vowed Kent to his wife.

Such a racket echoed through Muir Woods
the day we saw that one salmon
struggling upstream, flapping half out of water.
The sound of it drowned out everything else.
All our lives we'd heard of its grueling
uphill journey at the end of life,
yet until that day we'd never seen one
fighting the swift shallow current,
striking through the surface in great blows.
We waited on the bridge and watched it go
out of sight up the rocky-bottomed creek.

Lucille Lang Day

## Muir Woods at Night

Rust-colored ladybugs, clustered like grapes,
mate on horsetails that wave by a creek,
where silvery salmon spawn and leap
when the sandbar breaks at the gate to the sea.

The ladybugs have come hundreds of miles,
from valley to coast, for this singles bash.
The females are choosy: they twiddle the males,
seeking appendages padded with fat.

And all around—high in redwood burls,
on elk-clover leaves, and in the rich soil—
the meaning of life is to stroke and prod
under a humpbacked moon, dissolving in fog.

## Lake Leonard

For mosquitoes, whose long, delicate legs
dance in air to the hum
of high-frequency wingbeats, the ring
of redwoods on the hill by the lake
is cathedral enough.

And the sugarstick feeding on humus
on the forest floor—its single
erect stem rising from earth,
striped red and white like a candy cane—
has all it will ever need to know of Christmas.

In low trees, male cicadas create their own choir
by vibrating membranes near the base
of their abdomens, and in oblong, glossy leaves,
madrone leaf miners make
their own rich veins of silver.

The striped bass are quite satisfied
with pits they've made for spawning
in the shallow southern end of the lake.
These craters are the closest
they will ever get to the moon.

And the Western tanager high in a pine—
red head, yellow body,
black tail and wings—singing *pit-ik*
in a hoarse voice, appears
to be content with its own beauty.

I'm a creature too, with disc-shaped
red blood cells lacking nuclei
but packed with hemoglobin to pick up
oxygen in the capillaries
of alveoli clumped in my lungs.

I breathe carbon dioxide into the forest,
where oak leaves and redwood needles
turn it to sugar, but my skull
is a cauldron of yearning.
Nothing is ever enough, certainly not

my ability to describe the Indian pinks,
their scarlet petals divided
into four broad lobes with rounded tips,
or checkerspot butterflies, lighting
now on the shining leaves of the yerba santa.

Arin Vasquez

## *a new homeland*

we made our way here
out of war, out of the Spaniards
we made our way here.

my sunsets were colder than the salvadorenian ones
the sea still sings to us here, still tells us stories
of long ago, of brown-skinned gods touching sand for the first time.

we rose up out of fear and hope
phoenix from the fires of our war-torn homes
we were born from our parents' immigrant ashes.

we live in the redwoods now, say hello to the people
who belong in this land more than we ever could
touch the forest reverently—this is new life.

languages are mixed up, we say words
pulled from the tongue of the invaders
we have forgotten our own song.

breathe in saltwater air and collect shells by the shore
new roots will lower deep into sandy soil and cling
one day, our bodies will be as strong as the redwoods.

the trees have seen our story sprout from seedling
to a redwood like the others. we speak the language of the forest
it is the language of our home.

Lisbeth White

## Bay Laurel

you remember now making a crown, one
slender wisp of branch teetering with the green
slice of leaves on either side, just a simple loop
placed on the head to clear the mind and deter
confusing thoughts while you sat
in your first hippie women's circle
and learned songs to the forest, welcome
to the Golden State, but now that you are
thinking, you knew even before then about
its capacity to keep things at bay: you put that
dried arrow of leaf into a small satchel with
tobacco and angelica when you traveled to New
Orleans one fall, the streets full of bourboned
spirits stumbling down the Quarter,

and how sometimes without even thinking you
snap a fresh single leaf when you walk
in the woods, a lone brown woman with her small
brown dog, and slide the leaf into your bra on the
left side against the skin of your breast and how
your stride lengthens out, protected like that,
and once you sat with a friend in a redwood grove
the day after a new moon and wrote your wishes
with pencil on slim leaves harvested from the
ground, when you looked down for one, you
saw them littering the forest floor in plentitude,
you and your friend gleeful at so many wishes.

you remember now, walking out on the
deck after the rain has passed and the sun is

spreading out the sky, how few rains watered
this year. instead there were brush fires
along the highway all droughted summer crackling on
and on, the pungent sting of bay leaf oils as
they burn, so different from this soft ascension
after a long longed-for shower, clear and delicate
in the passage, that there will be more burn
than rain from now on, the seasons rolling
one beyond the other, sprawling loose hipped
and jilted as they are.

in this inhale of wet earth and bay tree singing
scent onto the hill, you realize all this time
you thought it the redwoods you would miss most,
their bark against your cheek, stringy coarse fur,
and how they stand sacred as monks, while the sun
pulls damp from their trunks in halos
of steam, but it is the smell of bay laurel
after the rain, opening on the air the way your own
body opens  after a good long drink, wafting fresh
and peppery.

it is the smell of this constant tree,
brimming wistfulness, this smell
that lovers have known of your skin as
you rise from their beds, this smell verdant
and penetrating, you cannot resist but to reach out,
to tug a leaf aromatic from a wet tree, to crush
and rub its shine against the pulse points
on either side of your jugular, so primal, so sweet
the vanishing perfume.

Timothy Houghton

# *Redwoods: Northern California*
### 4% left

Decay   gets woven into branches, dust
and bits of bark,

dried grasses
blown up   over two centuries

to a height where soil shouldn't be—
where needles cluster,   a fractal

plane higher
than Amazon canopy,

                        alien enough, far enough
                        from waking voices

to be the dream   where fairy tales find wings before
coming down.

~

These trees hold up,   they control
movement of water in a parallel earth:

Soil and ponds
in scaled-back versions of what we know—

fissure rivers   no bigger than crayon marks
from a child, driven
by slow drips,
                take their time in the rain.

Announcement : This brain is higher,   and more fine-tuned
because of the wind
blowing through arms on either side.

~

With so much seeding from wind
this place hangs on, protected

for now, the noise of earth movers
still unheard, despite
                              a thickening ring
                              of scar tissue.

~

Here is the floating earth where I've always lived anyway,

        the height between
        cloud and calling—

…and more than one kind of place can house a person.

This tree, for instance, swayed by wind
and sheer momentum

reveals its name if it had one:

the texture of height in relation to ground
as brokered by wind:
                        a lab-tag for bloodwork.

~

Above me—smell of burning.

Lights blink off and on
behind a door of fog
                        built from heat and wet air.

It's a dream chamber,
the slow glow

of a mind at work: Taller than me, a fire cave
smolders
where lightning hit the massive trunk,

but redwoods don't care if they burn,   they use the burn

and take their time
in the high air
                building stories in the holes.

# III

## Hills and Canyons

…I was born just in time to discover the hills
or what's left: rutted trails and barbed wire
leading to glimpses of doe and fawn paused
in such warm evening light…like a golden dream.
   —Thea Gavin, "Born in the Land"

The ancient ones who walked these lands
who made their arrows from coyote brush
knew not to make one's home on a ridge
for a ridge will insist on fire
   —Naomi Ruth Lowinsky, "Where Coyote Brush Roams"

Dana Gioia

## California Hills in August

I can imagine someone who found
these fields unbearable, who climbed
the hillside in the heat, cursing the dust,
cracking the brittle weeds underfoot,
wishing a few more trees for shade.

An Easterner especially, who would scorn
the meagerness of summer, the dry
twisted shapes of black elm,
scrub oak, and chaparral, a landscape
August has already drained of green.

One who would hurry over the clinging
thistle, foxtail, golden poppy,
knowing everything was just a weed,
unable to conceive that these trees
and sparse brown bushes were alive.

And hate the bright stillness of the noon
without wind, without motion,
the only other living thing
a hawk, hungry for prey, suspended
in the blinding, sunlit blue.

And yet how gentle it seems to someone
raised in a landscape short of rain—
the skyline of a hill broken by no more
trees than one can count, the grass,
the empty sky, the wish for water.

Dana Gioia

## *Rough Country*

Give me a landscape made of obstacles,
of steep hills and jutting glacial rock,
where the low-running streams are quick to flood
the grassy fields and bottomlands.
                                        A place
no engineers can master—where the roads
must twist like tendrils up the mountainside
on narrow cliffs where boulders block the way.

Where tall black trunks of lightning-scalded pine
push through the tangled woods to make a roost
for hawks and swarming crows.
                                        And sharp inclines
where twisting through the thorn-thick underbrush,
scratched and exhausted, one turns suddenly

to find an unexpected waterfall,
not half a mile from the nearest road,
a spot so hard to reach that no one comes—

a hiding place, a shrine for dragonflies
and nesting jays, a sign that there is still
one piece of property that won't be owned.

Thea Gavin

## *Born in the Land*

I was born in the land of promiscuous wildflowers
thick between oaks, lichen-bright chaparral
home of the cougar and grizzly bear
plenty for condors to scavenge there
plenty of stories for sisters to tell
rinsing bitter acorns up in the canyons.

But I was born too late for all of that
the grizzlies are gone like Tom Thumb Hill
erased to make room for people like me
suckers for crumbs of the golden dream.

I was born in the land of vaquero and rancho
and the missions that swallowed so many so much
home of the Mexican, Spaniard, and gringo
on the lookout for land and more room for their cattle
plenty of stories for sisters to tell
shaping fine masa for the next fiesta.

But I was born too late for all of that
the cattle are gone, though the barbed wire remains
protecting habitat—gnatcatcher—arroyo toad
and the flame-ready fuel of someone's golden dream.

I was born in the land of citrus and promise
Go West for your share of the gold and the sun
and the land advertisements made people crazy
Chicago to L.A. for a buck and a half
plenty of stories for sisters to tell
sorting Valencias on endless conveyor belts.

But I was born just in time to discover the hills
or what's left: rutted trails and barbed wire
leading to glimpses of doe and fawn paused
in such warm evening light...like a golden dream.

Thea Gavin

## *Nothing Rhymes with Orange*

Home is where you hang your head.
—Groucho Marx

Brilliant yellow mustard used to smother Orange;
they say that Father Serra planted it
to liven up the walk to San Francisco—
our El Camino Real, paved with Old World gold.

It escaped up to the hills just east of Orange,
and now the mustard elbows out the purple
needlegrass, thickens the air
with its heavy, sneeze-inducing musk.
All the honeybees (from Europe also) love it.

Where it hasn't yet invaded, chaparral
paints chamise mosaics in the foothills,
along with coast live oak and sycamore,
willow tangles in ravines and everywhere
sage and more sage reigning to the east,
a sphere of influence for hawks and rattlesnakes,
miles of hills all ready to be scraped
since people need a place to live. Can you
imagine a nicer spot than our fresh Orange?

The century turns; the Plaza gets a facelift,
again. We stroll by Old Towne's equity
millionaires, all of us addicted
to refinancing and reminiscing
about spring times past, perfumed by orange
blossoms and the aching for what passes,
unrhymable longings for our favorite shade.

Thea Gavin

## Definitely Home

*Riparian*
willow and mule fat congregations—
noon's withering glance, rebuked
in the cathedral of sycamore arches
yellowthroat choirs join in, jubilant

*Slope effect*
how green follows north folds—
no fence-line created this contrast—
half-hills quilted with laurel sumac
quail embroidering the curvaceous air

*Drought deciduous*
in dry times leaves retreat
not skeletons, but patient dancers
wait for winter's sweet beating
rain drums—who can hold on till then

*Vernal pools*
ephemeral home of spadefoot toads—
no fish survive summer's dust
just round rainbows of wildflowers
doomed to recede, recede, reseed

*Chaparral*
look out: California's wild identity
the opposite of disneyfication
old-growth elfin forests—licked
like frosting by tongues of wildfire

liz gonzález

## *Fall in the Chaparral*

Santa Ana winds howl
down Cajon Pass

I sleep on the edge
my side of the bed
not to disturb; you
snore on the couch

Gusts plow calico-
hued hillsides

Filigree bones
of a scrub jay's wing
snuggle in the shadow box
you made to save the memory

Flailing yucca swords
slash the moonlight

A battery-operated clock
glows on the mantle
(Electricity is unreliable
during winds and quakes)

Bitter breeze whistles
through window cracks

Your Granny Smith's rot
in the glued-back-together
anniversary bowl
You don't notice the smell

Brittlebrush bows
Christmas berry slants, rattles

I scrub pomegranate specks
off the carpet
before you spot them

A coyote crouches
behind beavertail cactus
ready to pounce on a jackrabbit

We waste hours bickering,
like tumbleweeds bouncing
aimlessly in the cactus garden

Dry leaves crumble so easily
veins can't sustain them

Our tromps back and forth
shake the wood floor
startle snakes
slithering beneath the foundation

Manzanita bushes thrash
as though they want to uproot and bolt

We snap our love like weak branches
cracking off eucalyptus trees
You brush shards of us
into a dust pan

Add a spark to the drying landscape
uncontrollable wildfire will result

Flames cleanse the soil
of allelopathic compounds

clear space
for new growth

Buds curl, dry on branches
Cinder does not disintegrate

We toast Thanksgiving
from opposite ends
of our new glass table

Fall quickens

CB Follett

## *Once Here*

From an article written by a man of 87
who grew up in our town, our area,
and he wrote with such poignancy

about all the bears (now gone)
in the forests (now gone),
how we used to look up at sunset
and see them silhouetted on the ridge lines
against the dusky sky.

How great troupes of elk (now gone)
used to come down to the creeks
(now gone or buried or channeled) to drink.

How the rivers (now trickles)
used to be filled with salmon (now few)
struggling their way upstream
to the source of their cycles.

How much we have lost,
and soon
will no longer even know
we have lost it.

Grace Marie Grafton

## Canyon, Santa Barbara

Inspired by the painting
*In Mission Canyon, Santa Barbara,*
by Henry Joseph Breuer, 1902

This canyon, before it was turned into town.
Now closeted in the imagination. Picture
the same stone over and over, white, slightly
rounded, unencumbered by loyalty to
the conviction that people and their shelters
deserve attention's spotlight. In nineteen-
oh-two, only the one red-tiled roof, only
the single tower among the no-holds-barred
fescue claiming the winter slopes. And
the live-oak trees never bare of black-green
leaves and the black squirrels like swatches
of laughter in the limbs. The many unimpeded
water courses, rivulets during the rainy season.
Convocation of acorns, squalling jays,
absence of sheep or car horns or streetlights
or streets. Room for moon's silence.

Ann Fisher-Wirth

## No Vow

Calm yourself, here where the blue painted saint
in his wooden shrine
presides over the hillside. The mountain lion
they saw by the barn is not, as you're convinced,
looking especially for you. Yet all you can see
is your own fear, projected on to his twitching tail.

Calm yourself, you who could not fight a dog
or outrun a rattler. There's nothing to be done.
The world makes you no vow.
Flies want what you offer.
Pray all you like, carry a whistle around your neck,
march along the trail singing.
The hay is white and golden in the wind.
The thistles, crowns of thorn, with light on every sepal.

Helen Wick

## Behind the Hill

The hill behind
your house was no more
a hill than it was an entrance
to an animal world—
chasing deer, the occasional
rabbit, practicing making
ourselves big for mountain lions.

We emerged from the trees spitting
stones and grit from our teeth,
arms of wheat and wildflowers
for our mothers.
We were finally still as they began to
groom us—picking
ticks and foxtails from our hair.

Cathie Sandstrom

## *Good Bones Endure*

Struck down by bobcat, the deer carcass
splayed in the ravine for several weeks now.
Sleek coat's gone to dulled bristle, collapsing
against stark bones the sun will bleach.
Come rainfall, water sluicing down will carry
stone, sand and seed of lupine the ribs
will hold: a small stage for spring to scribble on.

A manzanita, blackened by wildfire, arches
over the trail cut into the mountainside.
Erosion steadily bares its anchoring roots,
exposes their clenched grip on the hillside,
restraining the mountain from its inevitable
shift to the bottom of Sierra Madre Canyon.

And me shouldering my share of desire
and grief up this trail several mornings a week,
studying as the calendar rotates, my kin,
these other living things teaching me
to fully inhabit this cage of bone
before it's time to lay it down.

Erin Redfern

## California Condor

This condor is tagged and numbered
twice, once on each radius, a bright orange ember
against ash-colored wings. Her featherless head the scalded color
of pain. She flares her dark pinions and won't despair. Condor,
do you remember the pinch and grip that made you "59"
and gave a slight, strange weight to your soar and bank?

Now epigeneticists are saying that what parents endure
may after all be passed on—a codicil to the genome's intent.
Male mice smell almonds and freeze against their fathers'
shocked feet. Budding yeast carries the memory of sugar.
The Agouti mouse grows golden and round as an egg.

And so which of your single-hatchlings will be born
pre-adjusted to the snug fit of this tag? Which will gauge
from the smallest plastic flutter and bend
the import of altitudes and updrafts?
And might it someday miss this badge more
than the feathered crown your progenitors traded
for a hood of gore, the death you dip into for sustenance?

And will we, scanning the sunburned sky
for your white crossbar, look in our turn
like nothing so much as unhinged chromosomes
wandering the desert with our binocular sight,
shrugging our aborted scapula and singing
as we scavenge for water and topsoil?
Will you follow our trail of histones to the horizon?
Will you see in us potential, at least, for a good end,
a last meal, one more improbable way to persist?

Kirk Lumpkin


## To Poison Oak

> No other local creatures besides humans experience
> contact dermatitis from touching poison oak
> (*Toxicodendron diversilobum*).

You
with diversely lobed leaves
in sets of threes,
     on diverse forms:
     from little plant to bush to vine to treelet,
     at home
     in diverse
habitats
from grasslands to chaparral,
conifer forests to oak woodlands,
coastal scrub to riparian thickets,
but especially along the edges
as if guarding the borders
of different plant communities;
from dappled shade
to full sun,
in male and female plants,
from Baja to British Columbia.
You're a provisioner
and shelter
for multitudes
of birds
some that engage with you
in a gift exchange,
and for receiving your fruit,
they spread your seed;
you
are a provider of food

for deer, squirrels, chipmunks,
mice, woodrats, elk.

But in the DNA's spiraling
cornucopia of possibility,
       in the rich red whorls
       of your ancestry,
       did you have a
       genetic
       premonition
a creature would come someday
who for its self-presumed superiority

and vast
destructive impudence
it would be your destiny
       to inflict
       a small, but persistently
       irritating penalty
       or worse for those ignorant
       of your own special art
of resistance
to this creature?

Oh beautiful plant
whose fiery shining reds
are the most vivid
of fall colors
in all of California,
I acknowledge
your diverse strengths.
Though I mostly try hard
to respect your space
the fierceness of your presence
sometimes calls up in me
a similar fierceness,

and I feel the need
to protect my space
by cutting you out of it.
As one
who sprouts up even
from the ashes
after the fire
I bet you
will survive
this current round
of climate change.
I am sure
there are deep ways
that our roots are interwoven
though I dare not touch
your skin,
and wonder
what our world might be
if we were as true
to our nature
as you
are to yours.

Dolores Hayden

## *For Rent*

1

In a sheath of weathered boards, false front
on all four sides, the red house rides
a saddle of eroded ground

and leans as if it might wash down
in winter rains. But reader, here
you see the oldest house around.

It's much too high for neighborhood.
From worn-out steps long views expand,
command wide axes everywhere,

entice your kind of hairpin vision,
a swaying out and cambering in.
The city sounds don't reach us here.

2

Hummingbirds sip hibiscus cups.
A red-tailed hawk circles, plummets
into the canyon, reappears.

The mailbox sags. Century plants
split broken, almost impassable steps—
they flower every hundred years.

Yes, you know the place needs work,
ungrudging cultivation, a poet
like you to weed in noonday heat,

count pairs of small blue butterflies,
repair the broken hearth, stoke fires
with eucalyptus or mesquite.

3
Due north lie wooded peaks too steep
for cut and fill. Packs of coyotes
scavenge their slopes, sing through the nights.

Eastward sits gated Mount Olympus,
muscle-bound mansions, turquoise pools,
an acre Omega, party lights

blinking southward across the grid
where cowboy towns crowd French chateaux
and terrazzo stars spell HOLLYWOOD.

Look west, you'll glimpse Pacific swells
beyond the park where hungry men
cut whirligig toys they trade for food.

4
The old red house rents month-to-month,
no boiler plate, security,
sometimes, late summer, the well goes dry.

You think you might be interested?
Skywriting pilots buzz this house,
roaring cloud vowels a half-mile high.

Dusk swims with wispy backlit cirrus,
three-mile nouns stretch out your eye,
wild verbs advance, alacrify,

moonrise carves commas in your sky.
So, you're sure you want to sign?
Hooked on the place? So am I.

Thea Gavin

## Spinning SoCal

*Winter*
Rain taps on clay,
uncracks dry maps.
Green leaps—
photosynthesized,
or someone cuts barbed
wire fence at night
to paint the whole hill
world ephemeral emerald.
Arroyos rustle in
monkeyflower shenanigans.
Aim to photograb it all and
it escapes.

*Spring*
More rain is a gamble—
some green shooters like the odds,
throw their petal-heads back,
go all in, all out.
Press their startling inflorescences;
when the phacelia blues blanch
you'll feel guilty, although
a mariposa lily tissue-whisper
pinned to your office wall
might cheer you up
even as it fades.

*Summer*
Rain memories in fog
drip down toothy quercus

and conduits of artemisia.
O frugal blooms:
goldenbush, slender tarplant,
twiggy wreath, yerba del pescado.
Then there's buckwheat.
Oblivious to lack,
it remakes the red dust
into bouffant congregations
marching through
the hills. Fill an empty
vase. These last.

*Fall*
No blaze of color unless
the devil winds kick sparks—
who would do this—into fireblooms
of orange against the night
and the unwelcome gusts
howl at your leaky window:
how long, how long, how long—
(The curtains shudder
and you call it
earthquake weather.)

Grace Marie Grafton

## Earthquake Country

The way the land shifts and rolls,
sometimes breaks, becomes a kind of evicting landlord
to roots that would rather stay put. Flimsy grip
on what is, after all, their parent.

Meantime, since we're in the here and now,
we appreciate the leftover cracks and crevices
where trapped water has saturated seeds sufficiently
there's a spree of grasses fluffing out, rinsing air
with what almost seems like the chatter of children
running after the butterflies that frequent these
slopes and canyons—checkerspot, buckeye,
mourning cloak a brunette splotch in the blonde vista.

Sharp scent of sage startles flaccid nostrils,
breeze fiddles the live-oak leaves into a rusty
seesaw. What else is worth as much as
immersion in the water of now? The minutes
when earth stays steady underfoot and we
feel at home.

Susan Cohen

## Golden Hills of California

This light began in lamentation,
but I don't want to think
about the unmaking, the burning
hopes and homes a hundred miles
from here. This light is strangely
sewn with honey as if thimbled
from the flight of bees. It drifts down
through maples and the cedar,
burnishes our scarred floorboards
to yellow oak this morning,
our walls to butter. In the fabled state
we live in, somewhere always is on fire—
dry grasses torching, shingles searing,
latches melting, miles of forest
reduced to the single syllable of ash—
while elsewhere that combustion blends
light and gold we can savor like wine,
which also begins with crushing.

Thea Gavin

## Fire Cycle

I. *Early October 2007*

Twenty months of sun days—
the succulent battery loses
its green charge.
Prickly pear pads yellow
into thin wrinkles;
fleshy dudleya fingers
darken into talons.

The leathery ones
gathered on north slopes—
laurel sumac, toyon,
lemonade berry—
fold up some, wait
for the clouds to call.

Shorter members
of the south-facing mosaic
shrug off their shriveled
leaves—sagebrush,
mallow, monkey flower?
Who can recognize skeletons...

Twenty months—
2.2 inches of rain.
Drop, storms,
swing south for a while—
we are rattled by the Santa Ana winds.
We want our fat shadows back.

II. *28,000 Acres Later*

"Santiago Fire Scar Appears in New Satellite Image,"
headline from the *Orange County Register,* November 6, 2007

in Limestone Canyon, where the thing began—
monster-ignited, fed by the devil's breath
of shrieking Santa Ana winds—
that was October. This is June. Defeated

oaks four times my age have crumpled since;
a bleak pretense at leaves marks the survivors.
Mustard and oat grass bully their way
up exposed slopes, but if you learn to look

sweet native plants hum with juicy life:
scarlet silene and blue erigeron are stars
in the universe of dust; farewell-to-spring
spreads its lavender lament along the trail.

Benjamin Gucciardi

## Scavengers

Wildfire has scorched forty-seven acres
In the valley below the house where I am staying.
And now three slow vultures
Trace black circles through the haze,
Descend, feast, climb, repeat.

I want to combine myself
With the world that way,
Finding succor in the char.

If no clouds bring relief,
Let us place our fingers
Like crimson beaks
Into the burn of our lives
And endure.

Judith Terzi

## *The Road to Buckhorn*

> Over 160,000 acres of the Angeles National Forest
> were burned in the Station Fire of 2009, the largest
> forest fire in the modern history of Los Angeles County.

It starts halfway up. This aftermath of fire,
risen from ash, from arson. Lavender forest,
overgrowth of *turricula*—poison wildflower.

Sharp-toothed leaves & blossoms bend against
limbless poles of big cone spruce, Coulter pine.
Risen from ash, from arson. Lavender forest.

This air infused with char recalls the crime,
the feat of flame, Santa Ana's scorch & howl.
Limbless poles of Douglas fir & Coulter pine.

Saplings planted high in drought-drenched soil
are gone. Do beak-beats revive the cloth of bark?
Feat of flame, Santa Ana's scorch & howl.

Yet larkspur & goldenrod delude the dark.
And monkey flower, Spanish broom & sage.
Do woodpecker beats revive the cloth of bark?

My mind returns to clothing in the after-phase
of life. Polyester remains as if my mother
were still alive. And monkey flower & sage.

Her dresses & blouses hanging in closets lure.
It starts halfway up. This aftermath of fire,
of death. Polyester remains of my mother.
Overgrowth of *turricula*. Wild fire flower.

Bri Bruce

## Storm

Through the night the trees rocked
to and fro, boughs bucked and pitched
against one another and I remember
thinking it sounded like weeping.

At first light I left the hilltop for
the shadows of the canyon. The river
was frenzied, filled with leaves
and waves and mud. I stood for a time
at that tempest, where it boils as it greets
the sea. When I turned to leave
I found the owl's nest had fallen
from the branch that embraced it,
torn away from the old fir in the storm,
the knot of it resting at its roots.

Tonight the moon is full. I trace
its course through the sky beyond
the window in my sleeplessness, a square
of moonlight at the foot of the bed, later
waking to find it has shifted and I
am bathed in it. I am imagining the owl
in the tall four-hundred-year-old Douglas fir,
standing sentinel in the black of the night
beneath a smattering of bright stars.

Naomi Ruth Lowinsky

## *Where Coyote Brush Roams*

> Well they'd made up their minds to be everywhere because why not.
> —W. S. Merwin

We were high on the sky when we lived on that ridge    high
on the red-tailed hawk    high
on the long green rumps of the hills going yellow
while the sun did its dance from winter to summer and back   high
on our ridge after work while the fog flowed over
the darkening hills we poured red wine on the earth   high
on escape from the city's exhaust    high
on the song of the frogs in the pond
some man had made
          never mind

that the pines and the cottonwood trees
knew they didn't belong up there   never mind
that electrical towers asserted their rights
that coyote brush said the land was its own
that the ridge wanted fire and we did not
we weed whacked   cleared   cut down those pines   never mind
that we heard their cries in the night
though they never belonged up there    never mind
that the frogs went away one day and so did we...

The ancient ones who walked these lands
who made their arrows from coyote brush
knew not to make one's home on a ridge
for a ridge will insist on fire

          home is in a valley
          by a river among cottonwoods

We live in the valley now where once there was a river
                     where frogs once sang in spring

                  never mind


## *Because the Mountain Is My Companion*

Because it meanders from coyote yellow
to occasional green
Because we know that temperatures are rising—
          we never expected this sudden freeze—

Because the mountain reached into cold wet skies this morning
And gathered itself a celestial garment of snow
          as though it had ascended
          become an Alp
          a Himalaya

Because my tawny old Devil Mountain
          is a suddenly wild thing of snow and of ice
I try to put these things together—how green
          the hills glow along the freeway
On the news the leaders of nations gather
          to argue about carbon footprints

while in the city dozens of red and white Santas—
          mostly without umbrellas—
          are gathering in United Nations Plaza

Because the North Pole where Santa
makes gifts
is under water
And the Great White Bear has walked to the end
of his melting world

Because all our lives there's been some catastrophe
        just behind us
        just before us

You could hide under your desk—protect
            the back of your neck…

or you could get in your car and drive back
        to the mountain
        which has descended
to its essential coyote yellow
        its occasional splashes of green

Because the mountain knows the eons in its bones
it is a patient, broad-shouldered bearer
of wind, sun, rain, change…

*I ask it to teach me the long slow way…*

Dave Holt

## Waiting on Spring

A quiet afternoon between storms—
in the ebb of time, we discuss
the pruning of walnut trees.

"Do you remember where you saw it?"
he asked, so I led the park botanist
down the hill to Mitchell Canyon,

through a grove of Northern California natives,
black bark contrast to gray limbs grafted
onto rough-ridged trunks of walnut
by a farmer whose land became state park.

We search for the English walnut I found,
distinguished by uniform, gray trunk.
"*Juglans regia*, means a nut in the king's palace.
Something like that," he said,
"It's really a Persian species, not English."

Panic at the quail crossing,
fleeing brood of chicks,
clucking *pit-pit*, whir of wings.
We violated their path but found my tree.

Cold patch, change in the still air—
breath of chill breeze,
lift of hawk wing.

Gray clouds drift in,
covering Diablo's peak.

Dave Holt

## Volunteer Work Day on the Mountain

My car's the first to arrive in the parking lot.
Rest of the volunteers will be here soon. Jeff and I
don't feel like waitin'. We haul our chain saws
and tools up a switchback trail to Twin Peaks.

No one's walked the mountain yet.
We break the spiders' silk barriers
strung across the path at night,
brushing webs from our eyelids.

Finches from a safe perch
in scrub oak and coyote bush
call to their neighbors,
*First humans of the day coming through!*

Sunlight sneaks over the range of hills,
Diablo, Olympia, North Peak,
arrayed on the opposite side
from us on Eagle Peak trail.

We scramble up the rocky horns
in time to see sunrise arrive,
stir wind into motion,
signal the start of a race

above land, from the east,
as if a sun chariot really were starting
its run across heaven.
Hail, Phoebus Apollo!

Calling *kl-ee-yu* from a nearby Coulter pine,
lone flicker we couldn't see till it darted out,
catches a ride on the new-risen breeze.
Swoop, dip, flies like it's rowing, sculling the air.

Gentle breeze becomes strong, cold wind
that blows across the top of the world,
mighty weather engines of the planet
doing their work as we hurl along in earth's orbit.

Rain predicted this evening.
We have to finish clearing the trail today.
I pull the cord on the saw. Its violent roar
shatters the serenity of morning.

Lucille Lang Day

## Eye of the Beholder

> The symmetrical arrangement of variously shaped *setae*
> and the ornate sculpturing of their cuticle make many mites
> some of the most beautiful and spectacular of all animals.
> —Robert D. Barnes, *Invertebrate Zoology*

Scarlet pimpernels nod by a trail
on Mount Diablo, flat stars
glowing close to earth. Under a rotting log,
slime mold also blooms red,
a royal garden for the termite queen

who'll charm her half-pint king
for years, each day laying thousands of eggs
to be nurtured by workers
and guarded by soldiers, whose soft,
slender bodies shine like pearls.

Farther up, amid wild hyacinths—
tiny blue vases with fluted necks—
floating on the frozen waves
of the Franciscan formation,
a black widow spider spins her web.

Her legs are long and shapely, her body
a marble, polished, black,
with a perfect orange-red hourglass
on the belly. Complete in herself,
she'll eat her mate, savoring his juices.

Under yellow wallflowers rising in tall grass,
a wolf spider, hairy as a cat's ear,

emerges from her nest to scout the earth
with four pairs of eyes that glisten
when sunlight strikes them.

She drags a ball-shaped gray silk sac
packed with eggs. Soon spiderlings
will cover her back, and she'll chase her prey,
then pounce to feed the magnificent dress—
her quivering little ones.

Climbing past poison oak and Muir pines,
I emanate butyric acid, and to the small
creatures of the forest and meadow,
I must smell like a pot roast
simmering in fine wine.

A hungry baby finds me—a nymph
of the Western black-legged tick,
which digs its toothed pincers deep
into my thigh and expands,
a balloon filling with crimson liquid,

and all the bacteria dance
as they multiply in my blood. I am
one with them, one with the tick—
my epidermis a fragrant field, flowering
over hidden rivers, piquant, delicious.

Lucille Lang Day

## *Mount St. Helena*

Climb through the chapparal,
past oaks and knobcone pines
with cones bunched on the trunks,
past the stony opening to the old
Silverado Mine and over the lost
vein that a future prospector
might someday find. Climb
past madrones and manzanitas
with cool red bark and sour berries,
past gray pines with pale needles
and sugar pines named for the sap
oozing on two-foot cones, past rock
formations etched by the wind's
sharp teeth. Don't fall on the steep
parts of the trail. Go slowly, watch
your footing. Increase your pace
when the path levels out. Stop
to rest when your heart pounds,
your legs grow wobbly as gelatin,
and sweat pours from your brow,
but don't give up. It's too easy
to turn around and go back down.
Don't miss your goal. Keep climbing,
all the way to the top, where trees
give way to vegetation lying
close to earth and you can see
valley and bay, vineyards,
distant peaks, and the wheeling
flight of a golden eagle whose
white wing patches and tailband
gleam in the creamy light and
legs are feathered to the toes.

Lenore Weiss

## The Widow Discovers the Secret of Leona Canyon

Before dog-walkers with squadrons of panting beasts
pull up in SUVs, I arrive early—a woman without a pooch
who can be trusted to make a game of counting packets of shit

set aside for some doggie-walker's return trip.
I start early, knot a hoodie around my waist,
hiking in the sun I want to lose myself,

balance on a branch of a buckeye tree
with its candelabra of mock lilacs,
walk past hemlock that lace the trail,

everything is a blaze of white
as spring marries summer and loosens her veil.
I dip my hands in water and wash my face.

Anna's hummingbird, with her red crown and red
spotted throat, sips right along with me. Shepherds
follow their off-leash flock up the canyon.

Bronwyn Mauldin

## *Dead Snake on the Trail*

Neither long nor short, this dead snake on the trail, its chevron stripes gray-brown and iridescent dark blue. An army of tiny black ants has blazed a trail from nest to snake. Two columns, each one two ants wide, crawl the length of the snake from nose to tailtip and back again.

How much moisture does a dead snake contain? How many ant lives can it sustain and for how long in the midst of a drought that has lasted more than a thousand days with no end in sight?

Infinitesimal ants, they are as much a menace to this mountain as I am in rubber-sole shoes with neon pink laces. Their forebears stowed away on cargo ships carrying coffee from Brazil to the Port of New Orleans as the nineteenth century came to a close. In the pungent dry chaparral above the city, they crowd out native harvester ants, fiery red and nearly three times their size. Parallel columns of these ants carry the dead snake back to the nest in their mandibles. They will strip its skeleton clean, one tiny bite of snakeflesh at a time.

The stuttering rumble of a sixteen-wheeler with bad brakes startles me, and I peer down the mountain. From the Port of Los Angeles, an army of shipping containers three beasts wide blazes a trail along the length of the valley below, sunlight flashing in their rearview mirrors.

Jeanne Wagner

## Highway 80 Before Vacaville

I envy the steepness of hillsides,
where cows hold their ground

like push-pins stuck into the green baize
of lit pastures, the grass needy for light.

Those same cows, who are not even
goat-ravenous but patient as

lovers in their slow-licking foreplay.
They consume with such fastidious

calm the ragged grass-line of the hill,
even as they lean into it, even

as they loll it around in the mucousy
pink tunnels of their mouths.

If only I could watch them devour
the landscape that contains them,

sliding it absently sideways between
those great flat molars of theirs,

till the horizon itself protrudes from
both corners of their lips

like a piece of intransigent straw,
and the green gulps of light

they ingest so idly would course
through the difficult

maze of their gut like an omen
waiting to be read.

Jim Dodge

## Flux

Driven by the wild rage for equilibrium
At the dynamo core of every thermal exchange,
The cool coastal air, drawn off
The Pacific by the rising Valley heat,
Flows inland over our ridge

And the wind comes up.

Down in the garden,
The stalks of the sunflowers quiver,
Bowed seed heads
Ready to spill.

## Wisdom and Happiness

The wet crescents left by the dogs' tongues
Licking spilled cat kibble from the cabin floor;

The strand of light, finer than spider-spun,
Unspooling from the center of my chest
As a 20-pound steelhead slashes downstream
Through the celadon waters of the Smith;

The gleam of rain along Victoria's flanks
In that moment of stepping from the sauna
Into a wild Pacific storm—
Vapor-wreathed shimmer, body gone;

The elegance of an elk track
Cut in sandy streamside silt;

Red alder bud-break in early March;

Venison stew and fresh salmon,
Sweet garden corn coming on;

Jason asleep early on a school night,
His bare right leg dangling from the bed
(Geez, that boy is getting big);

Sliding a chunk of madrone
Into the firebox on a snowy night,
Damping the wood heater down
For coals to kindle the morning's fire;

The way the terriers sneeze and leap and race
Deliriously through the orchard
When they know we're headed out on a walk;

Raindrops still cupped in huckleberry leaves
Hours after the rain has stopped:

I made 55 years today, still hanging on,
And though only fools lay claim to wisdom
I don't know what else to call it
When every year
It takes less to make me happy
And it lasts longer.

Joan Gelfand

## *California Cobra*

*Darlingtonia californica* is no sweetie of mountain species
A plant as graceful as milkmaid's pitcher, she hides among tall trees
Where she munches on bugs and innocents. A slim seductress
        of the creek
She's called cobra plant; her form, compels, and then deceives.

This colorful one draws aimless flies, her flower ever enticing
Sprouts on the banks of gurgling creeks. Never naïve, this lover
        is vicious,
Attracts bugs to her sticky sweetness. Trapped, they succumb
As *Darlingtonia*'s tasty, carnivorous dinner they quickly become.

Nestled among shooting stars, hound's tongue
Leopard lilies, bleeding hearts and foxglove—
High up above treeline, near knife-sharp peaks alive
        in mountain's chill
Our darling *Darlingtonia* is the only plant who kills.

She's rare and famous, *Darlingtonia*. Feasts on skeeter carcass
While wrens steer clear and even tiresome jays traverse
Sideways, long ways, search out the furthest thermal
In northern Trinity Alps' jagged, pristine landscape.

Our cobra plant lives where angels
Swim in crystal water, shuck and jive
Where lemon sage scents the air and hummingbirds dive-
Bomb fuchsias and monkey flowers for nectar so divine.

In this pristine meadow, in this place so close to heaven,
*Darlingtonia californica*, our deadly beauty, thrives.

Steve Kowit

## *The Bridge*

Climbed up past the ridge,
slipped off my pack,
& sat there
on that viewy overhang,
that emerald vista
vast & luminous
as I'd remembered,
a pair of hawks
circling slowly far below.
The world is opulent,
indifferent, undeceitful.
Still & all, its latter purposes
elude us.
Brushing off a fly
that had been buzzing
at my skull,
I dug a pippin apple
from the pack.
At my feet, flakes of mica
glistened
in the faceted conglomerate,
& to my left, suspended
from two stalks
of mountain lilac
past their bloom,
a miniature bridge:
the swaying membrane
of a web
some solitary spider
had abandoned—
a single strand,
half glowing in the light,
& half invisible.

Steve Kowit

## Perognathus Fallax

When I went to the shed to check for water
damage after the last rains,
I found a tiny gray mouse
dead among the stacks of old cartons,
& lifting out the rags & jars,
found his mate, backed in a corner,
tiny & alive. Beside her—ears
barely visible flecks, tails nothing
but tendrils of gray thread—two nurselings:
one curled asleep by her snout,
the other awake at her nipple;
the three together no larger, I'd guess,
than the height of my thumb.
I took the box into the yard,
where there was more light,
& where the cats weren't lurking,
& lifted out the rest of the detritus—
a shredded pillow, cans of varnish
& spraypaint—beneath which I found, woven
out of what must have been pieces of cotton,
chewed cardboard & small twigs,
some sort of ramshackle nest.
With nowhere to hide, she scurried
behind it, a pup still at her dugs,
& looked up at me, into my eyes,
the way one of my cats might
who'd been cornered, or as might
one of my own kind, pleading—
her gaze wholly human, wholly intelligible.
It's uncanny, isn't it, how much alike we all are?
The next morning, when I went to the pump house

where I'd set the carton for safety,
I was amazed to see
the stunning filigreed globe
into which she had rewoven that nest, overnight:
from a small port at its top, her little snout
with those two bright eyes,
peering anxiously into my face.
I just stood there. I could hardly believe
how exquisite that nest was,
& how happy I was to see her.
The crumbs of seed I had dropped in
were gone, & I thought how good it would be
to keep them there, safe from the hawks,
feed them whatever they liked—but
for only a moment, then took out my knife
& sliced a small escape hatch in the cardboard,
an inch or so from the bottom,
& the next time I went back they were gone.
I was sorry to see the thing empty.
Is that stupid of me? *Perognathus*
*fallax*: the San Diego pocket mouse,
according to my *Audubon Guide*
*to North American Mammals*—
which was the last week of March,
the whole yard given over to mountain lilac
& sage & alyssum, & out by the wood
fence, that stand of iris,
too tattered, I'd thought, to survive
all those hard rains, but which had.
& under my feet, alive,
but so tiny one hardly noticed,
a hundred species of wildflower:
saffron & white & pink & mauve & blood red.

J. C. Todd

## Foraging

What was there we could not name.
It was too whole to be honed.
Saying *tall* omitted moss; saying *trail*
refused the intertwining canopy.
Then one of us broke a leaf

at its central vein. Remarkable,
the redolent oil of laurel in air,
on skin. For a moment it was all
there was, then there was us,
breathing its particular aroma.

The atmosphere sorted into scents
we had names for—redwood, jackpine, damsons
sweating in a pack, and the scorched sugar
we discovered was a hilltop of rye
trampled by deer. Wandering

a maze laid out by hooves, we entered the
underfoot of field—brushed against tassels,
tamped seed into turf. In the haze
we were stag, vole, weasel at work.
Lying under muslin now, home, in bed

at early light, we don't remember what
led us to the headlands, but that hunger
lingers in the pungency of leaves
crumbled among keys and coins
on the dresser tray. Scent turns us away

from insubstantial memory. One skin
is all we want. Beyond the ridge
of your shoulder, the window, wide open,
beyond its screen, the filmy, half-shut
eye of the waning moon. If we looked back

at ourselves from a great distance—say,
how far the moon has traveled from itself
when it was Earth—we could not tell
our tracks from the herd's, the headlands
from the Great Cascades, the land from water.

Jennifer Lagier

## *Last Stand*

Cypress trees stand despite scarred trunks,
wind-amputated crowns,
wrenched away branches.

Azure horizon backlights rooted captives.
Sunrise catches septuagenarians
clumped together on ridgeline.

Interwoven remnants of dwindling forest,
a fallen tangle of toppled limbs
curls around tall survivors.

Downhill, clear-cut ruin.
Twisted fingers plead for reprieve,
invoke vanquished spirits of Druids.

Mary Makofske

## *Dear Editor*

The light tracks me all day, sitting at my desk,
late afternoon now. Air holds its breath,
barely a tremble in the fountain grass,
the box elder leaning against the glass,
a small plane droning low over the hills.
Does it seem leisurely? Does all seem well?
Today I composed more and more
fervent letters to the editors
of every local paper, why it must change,
why we must think who we are, as the same
that is never the same turned over leaves
that flamed or quietly browned. What dies,
what thrives in the garden every year
is different, unpredictable. Our share's
enough, we can't change the weather,
we used to say, though now we know better.
Too late moves toward us faster
than the fast-retreating glaciers.
We keep thinking we'll advance forever.

Terri Glass

## Wind Turbines of Altamont Pass

Standing upright on barren hills
facing both sides of the freeway
catching the smog
spewing from automobiles
catching the wind in wild blades of steel
killing kestrels and red-tailed hawks
generating energy for power grids
lighting the streetlights of grimy alleyways
lighting the traffic light that turns red.
You stop breathless at these colossi
the loneliness of gray metal against blue sky
and ask what part of you
feels like this—
what part of your loneliness
churns thoughts inside your head,
kills the flight of your imagination
but lights the dark alleyways of your doubts?
What part of you
has hardened to your own spirit
longing to find the nearby delta
where egrets wade and rivers converge?
What part of you stands on barren hills
thrashing your arms toward the universe
hoping that all this thrashing
does some good in the world?

Mary Kay Rummel

## Conductor

In California, a bundled child of the cold
might think she is a goddess of color.
She might conduct an orchestra
above saffron hills, holding
her baton of lupine sky

over bee fuchsia, setting in motion
the deep hum of creation
while hills loop brown green
the way she once learned to chant
Gregorian notes, rising, falling.

Her arms become waves
showing shellfish purple tethered veins,
beaded ribs, spoon-shaped nails,
while automated tollbooths lift stiff limbs
then drop them over medians.

She spends California days
on patio, veranda, overpass, balustrade
where palm trees wear full-length scarves
concealing the nests of rodents,
trailing perfumes of fennel and sage.

A cape of dust will not blow away
will not be washed from palm or grape,
live oak or dead. No wind, no rain.
Only slow white fog brushing
piers, darkening highways.

In California, blue cornucopias
of wisteria pour over the balconies.
Bougainvillea guards the stairways.

Ancient flowers play old melodies.
Cracked with clay, crusted with brine
their scattered notes fly over the earth.

# IV

## Fields and Meadows

It is not
enough
to say
"the life around us"—
we *are*
"the life around us"
　　—Jack Foley, "Viriditas"

　　　　　　　…on that day, the blackbirds
taught me, as I stood in dry, windy, golden
　　　　　　grass, at last, what it means to abide.
—Eric Paul Shaffer, "Flight Forgotten"

Donna Emerson

## First Rain

Hurtling north, sudden rain pelts my car windows,
a cascade of pearls.
I leave the wipers off, my breath deepens, my speed slows.

When I can't see the road anymore, I pull to the side,
next to the field above Novato in Godmother's Pumpkin Patch.

I take off layers of clothes to feel the rain. Slip out of the car,
watch it land on dry shoulders, creped arms.
Cool rills bathe me, new smells of fresher air, sage,
dripping water I can feel after four years of drought.

Wet soaking deep into thirsty skin, water puddling
above my collarbone,
sheets of water gathering, until rivulets form,
running down thighs to my feet.

The surprise of this rain makes its own music on hard surfaces
around me: rocks, posts, snare drums played with brushes,
on the bending grasses, the upper strings of a harp.

Ravel crosses his left hand over his right before the glissando
in *Jeu d'eau*. Glittering rain.

Dust rising from the cracked ground.
The dirt almost smelling like earth again.

I feel lighter than before, silvery  salvaged  surfeited,
sitting down against the fence post, shaking water from my hair,
touch drops in my ears, eyes,
dry mouth open to rainwater's christening.

Patty Joslyn

## Elk Prairie

Light hit the earth
And turned to gold
Whole bags of coins
Tossed to the ground

And we said
*Look at the dappled light*
Not thinking of the riches at our feet
Trinkets for our pockets
Jingles to buy things
To make us happy or full

We saw the coins touch big trees
Again, the word *dappled*

It wasn't a word commonly used
It was a thing to be saved
*For exactly the right moment* she said
He nodded his head
But didn't say anything
Yet another reason she adored him

The coins pressed themselves
Against rock walls
And created potholes
That weren't there

What was there

Two velvet covered
Multi-pointed bucks
Standing in the light

Elizabeth C. Herron


## Fawn on Bodega Highway

Her head lolls when I lift her,
legs a spindly sway
below the roil of translucent intestine.

No odor of death, only the scent
of her mother's milk.

Take her to the dandelions and vetch,
the foxglove with their spotted throats,
under the thyrse blossoms of buckeye.

The doe browses alone now

crosses the meadow in the morning, uneasy
sense of nothing behind her,
the hollow open where light had gathered
into form and slid bloody in a sack of pearl
to the grass beside her.

Still astonished she turns, listening,

hesitates

suspended in the throb of her flanks,
the curdle of her grassy milk.

Grace Marie Grafton

## Tangle

Summer solstice

Beetles, mud, larvae, worms,
the ordered armor of centipedes,
salamanders' damp, penetrable
skin and waterdark eyes,
growth lurching
from saturated soil.

To show leaves, to court
light, wild ginger's slick
spade-shaped gleam tripling,
quadrupling above humus,
dime-sized scoops of
violet leaves, snakes of wild
grape, clinging morning glory,
bracken's rattle, rusty-haired
fronds uncurling lewd digits.

Crazy heading for sun,
these Icarus flowers,
foxgloves' deepset
eyes peering out, bleeding hearts'
flagrant dangle, larkspur's
fuzz-bedecked clitoris displaying
its alluring purple lip.

Kim Roberts

## The Invasive Weed Syndicate

*Shepherd's Purse*
A rude ring of lobed leaves cling
to the bottom of the stem, and from this stage
the actors rise in heart-shaped pods
and strip to white petticoats by the open road.

*Bull Thistle*
A ratchety stem with spiny leaves splays;
at the top of each spear, a green gumdrop
garbed in angry spikes wears a hot pink mohawk,
and the bees hone in and get drunk.

*Chickweed*
Tight oval buds covered in a coarse white beard
pop open to reveal a tiny white flower
like a loose corona following the sun.
Little prospector: beware the claim jumper.

*Fleabane*
Leaves like elongated spoons climb,
alternating, left and right, as if marching
in single file. The buds droop at the top
as if from shame. So much
is beyond our control.

*Nutgrass*
Tri-corner stems shoot from underground tubers,
a deep blackish-red, that tunnel
under the crops. This mission is a go:
pulling them up leaves the nutlets behind,
pulling them just makes it worse.

Abby Chew

## Ohlone Tiger Beetle

For Audrey and Harper

I am bright, bright green.
When you go hiking up by Santa Cruz
I walk beside you.
Hunting other bugs, seeking my mate,
just out for a stroll beside the tall grass.
If you find me, you'll find other
bright, beautiful beetles,
other hunters and walkers.
Praying mantis and monarch larvae,
they're here. Even black widow spiders!
So when you wake up early, take your dog.
Start walking up the trail. Look for me.
My bright green back and white spots.
I'm scary looking maybe, to little girls like you,
when you see me that first time.
I am a surprise.
But I am also a gift. Just like the two of you.

Abby Chew

## Island Barberry

Feral pigs give us trouble, always, always
rooting their way through our roots.
Up in Santa Cruz, where the tiger beetles live,
you can find us, too. But the search
will wear you out. Bring a snack.
Wear your favorite red boots. Be careful.
You people know of only two of us left,
little shrubs with yellow flowers—
they shine like the sun. Look in the shady places.
Come in February, when the cold
on the ferry to the Channel Islands
will chatter your teeth. And when you find us,
don't tell anyone. Walk backwards.
Keep our little secret. And scare the pigs away.

Ginny Short

## *barn owl*

it appears
in full darkness, a
white ghost that
startles
with the intensity
of its silence
passing
in a heartbeat
swallowed by
a tenebrific night

i stand
transfixed
by its glance
a look that rebounds
off my sensibilities
a look that
screams
i am the intruder

a look that
says the wildness
of a mouse screaming
in her talons
is the only reality

it leaves
an imprint
on the background of stars
a permanent shadow
on my retina

the wake of its passing
illuminates what is
written in that shadow
between the stars
between my eyes

have     you      remembered   to live?

Sonja Swift

## *Compass Point*

West: place of endings. Edge of the continent. End of the line. Dust
and cattle horns. Budweisers, Squirt cans and pistols. Feathered
sagebrush, live oaks and eucalyptus. Round-ups and farmer's
markets. Scratchy mariachi music from truck radios in the
orchards. I am ten years old running barefoot alongside galloping
horses (I think I can fly).

## *Dust*

California rangelands in the summer look like sand dunes. Like a
beige old mare who loves to kick her hooves in the water trough,
make a noisy splash and then roll, pleasurably, in the soft dirt.
Like the tawny mane of a lion hiding in tall savanna. Like dust.
Old California was full of flowers. Wildflowers. In those legendary
days before the Spanish conquistadors came with their horses and
cattle, gold lust and gunfire, priests and missions. Wildflowers
everywhere and hill slopes verdant year round. I've always thought
of California as dusty. The California I know. Born and raised
on a ranch up Los Osos Creek, named after the town, which is
named after the bears that used to roam there. Grizzly bear spirits,
they infected you when you were young. Got inside you. Etched
themselves into your very bones. So I was told once. I responded
by nodding and then staring out across thatch and stone-dry cow
paddies with a wayward, lonesome gaze.

Sonja Swift

## *Coast Starlight*

Northbound from Los Angeles to Jack London Square. Through the east-facing train car window this is what I see: Decaying fence posts. Pale yellow cliff exposed and crumbling. Four heifers trotting across a jade hill slope. Dust. Wind and dust. California flag tattered along the edge. Winds that eat cloth with invisible knifelike teeth teasing away one strand at a time. Winds that are hardly discernible through the window frame until I notice a plastic bag strung up and billowing on barbed wire; fennel and mustard in cracked arroyos beaten over, bounding back again. I read wind in the way the grass moves. The rippling grizzly bear, the state's extinct mascot, seems almost like the grass slopes. Or the grass slopes, gray-sand brown, like bear fur. Blown. Softly. Hairs, blades, in synchronized motion. Like light traversing water. Wind reminds me that the land breathes. I want to stroke the hills' soft slopes like the back of a shaggy mastiff, a husky, or a speckled Appaloosa in the wintertime when her coat is thick for warmth. A tent encampment beneath a giant gnarled oak tree and a family sitting around on blankets and crates. We pass too quickly but I think I see them laughing.

Rebecca Foust

## *Sonoma Oak*

Knee-deep in owl clover,
wild mustard, white
firework wildflower.

Three kinds of fern:
maidenhair, sword,
Japanese painted.

Galleon-girth trunk
twisted back—a god
caught surprised.

Grace Marie Grafton

## Succession (2)

Fences. Hold in. Keep out.
Stay close. Stay away. "I own this,
you don't own this." A tree
inside the fence learns about
barbs. Is this tree inside the
fence, or outside? Learning
about grow-here, don't-grow-here.
The fence has broken down. The tree
reaches out and slowly rubs
against the wire, the post.
Wind pushes the branch harder
against the dead, used wood, a skreek
sounds again and again in the air,
no one comes to trim the branch
or rescue the abandoned fence.
They've gone. The livestock are gone.
The horsetail ferns spring up, rampant,
along the fence line. Rabbits
come and go, living trees' dead branches
stick around, cover for quail
and wood mice, dying leaves mulch
into soil that bracken spores
take root in. Nothing against cows,
not to blame the humans who want
to own. They come and go.

Nellie Hill

## After the News

For Dolores Borgir

Grasses, once again the color of burnt sugar,
wave in the wind like arms of the dead,
slender and voiceless dreamy
with premonitions of music.

Among the oaks, brown birds
with one-note cheeps hop
into manzanita, coyote bush,
hot shrubs

while along the roadside, thistles
and mint nod to the new season.
Rattlesnake grass grows quietly,
daisies bow to the changed air.

I walk the roads remembering
layers of feeling, those sounds
she brought forth
from the music.

Nellie Hill

## Sunol Song Master

A quiet but forceful song
from an almost-tangible yellow breast
beneath the open beak. He sat
on the very top branch
facing the wind, like a ship,
visibly rocking, we could
feel the waves, and also we felt
constrained, curiously surprised
by the wide black band around his neck,
a natural thing, a marking,
that should have told us what he was

as should have the song, a fierce
unquiet liquid arcing sound.
How could anyone—eagle, hawk
or other male meadowlark—
contest this voice? We'd noted others similar
throughout the day, flitting through the grasses,
scattered on tops of trees with plain
and quiet brides among them.
None were like ours. We watched him
through the binoculars—indeed he was special,
so yellow, so marked around the neck,
and his demeanor toward the north wind
so fierce, so large.

Kevin Durkin

## For the Birds

I guess I've always liked the local sort,
pigeons and sparrows, crows and mockingbirds,
the type that don't require binoculars
or Peterson to be identified,
the birds you find in shrubs or shaded parks,
the parking lots of grocery stores, on lawns:
These are the kind that I can talk about
and not sound over-serious or absurd.

But I know nerdy back-to-nature folks
who pay for courses, drive to Morro Bay,
and muck about for hours on the flats
in hopes of spotting oystercatchers, grebes,
Caspian terns, and other birds that please
their esoteric tastes, though prickly winds
scour their faces and sun stings their lips.
Out there, you see, they get what they deserve.

So why should I be found today with them,
parking my car on the Carrizo Plain,
traipsing along the soda lake in boots,
scribbling loose notes, expressing my surprise
to see a sandhill crane before it flies?
Could there be some vague longing in me, too,
to spot a rarity that can't be mine
simply by looking, which must be defined

and added to my list of birds I've known?
Here comes a golden eagle with his brown
wings spread out full. He settles on a pole

beside the highway, eyes the rippling heat
for inattentive rabbits; stern and bold
in his peremptory ascension there,
he's in no hurry to give up his throne
and take his chances on the empty air.

Farther, higher up, against the clouds,
two condors ride the thermals at the brink
of their new range, circling a barren knob
where calf or antelope or rat has found
a final place to rest. They double dip
their wings, then spiral down and down and down
until their shadows sweep across the brush
and they no longer stay in sight of us.

These birds seem distant now in every sense.
Their ancient lives—evolving since the time
of dinosaurs—descended in a line
that's run for ages parallel to ours,
a time that fuels the engines of our cars
and brings us here, so far away from home,
to be reminded how the world has flown
since we've retreated to our own backyards.

Jennifer K. Sweeney

## Abandoning the Hives

From barn rafters, antique hives hang
queenless,
paperworks delicate as ash,
scaffold and cell mended thick with wax.

Wake up, the currents of bees have fled
this hour of seed
dark imaginings in their wake—
unsweet feverless drone.

Comb the hillside for sleepwalkers
drowsy on some chemical spool or
beg the swarm box to dance.
Everything depends on this refusal of happiness.

No one knows what they know.
A row of empty jars fills with sunlight.

Barbara Quick

## Cotati

All my life I've dreamed
of tilling such soil:
sandy loam that yields to the shovel
as readily as powdered chocolate to the spoon.
As receptive as the womb of a teenage girl.
Soil that wants to be impregnated
with the seeds I want to grow:
Genovese basil, twining peas and lettuce in a row.
Soil that snuggles up against the roots of heirlooms—
Black Krim and Brandywine.
Drink of me, the soil says. Cling to me.
Wrap your legs around me early in the morning
as the sun rises and the rooster crows
and the birds start to sing.

Ellen Bass

## *Their Naked Petals*

While Sophie lay in perfect symmetry
between death and life, I pictured Da Vinci's
Vitruvian man stretched within the hoop of existence.
Her blood was summoned out of her body and wheeled
through a mechanical angel that breathed
it back from the blue of night sky
to the iron red of oxygen. While she lay still—
a copy of herself—drugged beyond an eyelid's
flicker, a stray synapse firing, nothing
to waste a joule of strength,
I picked the tenderest string beans
on my son's farm, thick fringe hanging
under leafy awnings,
some green, some a purple deep
as the dyes of royalty.
When the pods are young, each is so slight.
We harvested for hours to fill a lug,
mounding the slender bodies as the sun blazed.
We dug up beets, rude lumps
the gophers inscribed with their incisors.
We carried melons against our breasts,
fragrant with sugar and time. We all know
one life is not worth more than another,
but who does not beg for mercy?
Who does not want to be the one
who slips through the fence
when the god on watch turns away to take a piss?
The phone in my pocket rang and rang,
and with each call the odds fell.
I was already sweating as I started in

on the black-eyed Susans. Rows so yellow
it seemed such brightness could not have ruptured
from the dun-colored soil.
Tolstoy gave us the scene: Levin walking the streets
the morning after Kitty says she'll marry him.
He's dazzled by everything he sees—children
on their way to school, pigeons flying from a roof,
a hand arranging cakes in a shop window.
How is it that fear can also burnish the world?
The flowers opened their naked petals, shivering
gold in the hot breeze. I cut
only the freshest, centers packed with florets.
I stripped the leaves from the stems,
set them in water. One bucket and then another.
As the day wore on, the heat mounted, the light slanted
into my eyes. All I could see was the shadow
of the jagged corolla, blinded as I was by a sun
that I, for a moment, understood was a mortal fire
that would have its own death.
I remember the tough hairy stems. I remember
the green stain on my hands.
I remember my son with his face in his hands, my hand
on his shoulder, the bare muscle of his arm, his hardened palms.
And while Sophie lay still, unknowing as dirt,
we kept on—the gleaming eggplant,
the humble cabbages, the scarves of heat.

Polly Hatfield

## Del Monte

I come from a place
where people knew
not everything
is born in a can or a box.

Grandma Louise
worked the swing shift
at the Del Monte processing plant
in Yuba City

her main job
was picking snakes
dead and alive
out of the endless stream
of red tomatoes
as they passed by her
on the humming conveyor belt

she kept a machete
hanging from a nail
where she worked
on the line
and the snakes
divided
under her sharp blade
and her attentive eyes

she sharpened that blade twice every shift

and by the end
of her shift

after standing
all afternoon and evening
in the relentless heat
of the closed-up
tin-roofed packing plant
      like a giant tin can itself

she had to walk
the eight blocks home
barefoot
her feet had swelled up
so bad they no longer fit into her lace-up shoes.


## Paraffin Moon

Floating atop homemade jelly
always Concord grape
from those old gnarled vines
luxuriating in the long
months of summer heat
against the once-white wall
of the slightly sagging
chicken coop.

Hens and roosters
gone to the stewpot
long ago
now Grandpa used
their chickenyard to grow
his prized vegetable garden
their old roosting coop
became his toolshed.
Waste not, want not.

He told me
the soil there
was hot
thanks to all those years
of chickenshit.

Too hot for root crops
they burned he said
no hope of growing
the crunchy radishes he relished so much
he loved things hot,
weather and food alike,
i watched him eat peeled onions
right out of hand
just like apples.

Tomatoes grew lush
in that nitrogen-rich pen
he paid me 25 cents
for each tomato
hornworm i found
and smashed against the rocks
in the back alley
out behind the burn barrel

& i can remember still
the scent of those
rampant tomato vines
& the way the tapwater would flood
the white enamel sink
green
as the water ran down my sun-
browned arms

when i went inside the house
to wash up
finally
at the end of the day.

Candace Pearson

## *Alfalfa Light*

Light over the stockyards
filtered by the cows' ancient breath.

Light rising from oil fields at night
misty orange in the steam.

Tule light, thick as cotton batting,
divided by the slats of a boxcar.

Light reflected off silver underbelly
of cottonwood leaf, trout skin, catfish,

shed in the feathers of a white heron.
Almond light, apple, grapevine, pear.

Light of the valley.

Summer sheen, seared, electric,
slivered through cracked ground,

aged in a cropduster's plume,
unwashed by irrigation sprinklers.

Truck light, twangy light, echoing down
the highway, dropped by steel guitars.

Light I tried to leave.

Drawn back by river light, metal cool,
nickel flat, wanting expression,

gleam from grasshopper, waterstrider,
dragonfly, cast in a raccoon's eyes —

alfalfa light, green as new limes
warming to yellow,

the light inside my fingers
finding this page.

Nancy Sue Brink

## On the Day He Left for War

Twenty-thousand snow geese rose outside Merced and circled
over fields of sandhill cranes picking through corn stubble, red
heads flashing on thin gray necks.    Geese calling.    Cranes
answering in creaking purrs.    Then they took off, too, thirty-
thousand birds deafening the air.    Clouds of blackbirds
(red-winged, tri-colored, Brewer's) twittered    swirled
like iron filings drawn by a magnet over fields of glass.

On the day he left for war, a San Joaquin kit fox (endangered)
slipped up to a levee, trotted in the open for more than a mile.
A great blue heron gulped down a white-footed mouse.
Rattlesnakes hibernated.    Widgeons called like squeaky toys.
A loggerhead shrike filed its captures on barbed-wire spikes.
A ferruginous hawk, grown-up russet and white, soared to a
phone pole, where she perched and hunted all afternoon.
She was trapped, banded, released, that day.

On the day he left for war, wise councils failed to reach agreement.
One country launched a missile into open sea. No one knows
when the fighting will begin.

Eric Paul Shaffer

## Flight Forgotten

On an August day in the great Sacramento valley,
                    a hundred red-winged blackbirds burst
from a California live oak. Leaves become birds

        and fly. As a human, I know what departing
blackbirds see: a world rushing toward them,
                    opening like a book with pages of earth

and sky, as the horizon draws wings into distance,
                            a new landscape in every moment,
and the reason for flight forgotten in the leap

        into the new, but on that day, the blackbirds
taught me, as I stood in dry, windy, golden
                    grass, at last, what it means to abide.

Barbara Crooker

## *Leaving the White In*

To get true white in a watercolor,
you have to leave blank spaces, let the paper show
through, paint around it. Here, in the San Joaquin Valley,
the irrigated desert stretches into row after row
of orange trees, almonds, grapes, to where
the foothills of the Sierra sleep, tawny animals,
in the dusty golden haze. I'm visiting a friend
from college, twenty-five years rolling back,
and we've stopped for vanilla ice cream, sit in dusty mauve
booths that could have been painted by John Register,
whose picture *Waiting Room for the Beyond*
we talk about, all that cool glowing space. She tells me
why she's always tired, her white counts rising—

The heat is on us now, like a hard-breathing animal;
the light's of pale gold olive oil, iced tea.
She shows me recent paintings: El Capitan in Yosemite,
a stark white wall floating on a sky of cobalt blue;
she is glazing it over and over, working it up,
building the layers of paint to catch what the light
does to granite; in another, she's painted an old man and his dog,
the plaid of his shirt around his full beard, the folds
and creases in his worn denim overalls, the dog's soft fur.
The white isn't paint but paper; everything glows.

She steeps green tea in hot water for both of us,
here together, two old friends from Jersey,
drinking and talking by the sun-dappled pond.
She paints the light, the California light,
that dances off the Matilija poppies, the desert flats.

She wants to paint the world, the entire edible world,
full of pomegranates and eggplants, before her blood tires
of the virus in its sluice.

Now night falls abruptly, its inky wash covering the sky.
We do yoga, eat bowls of rice, drink more tea.
Jasmine fills the air, the moon floats up in its chalice of bone.

Jan Steckel

## *Atascadero*

Our wheels got stuck between
the San Marcos Pass and Salinas.
Dead fennel lined the shoulder.
"Lettuce romaine in your hearts," said
the side of a truck full of iceberg.
We crashed in the Motel Inn on Baseline Avenue, off
the Senator Vernon L. Sturgeon Memorial Highway.
Giant plywood cutouts of happy Hispanic peasants
tilled the spinach fields. Paint peeled off
the south side of the water tower.
I filled an ice bucket at the rattle-machine,
fixed myself a jack and ginger.
Prickly pears by the propane tank sang
"luna, caballo, guitarra, cuchillo, amor."

Andrena Zawinski

## Women of the Fields
### For Dolores Huerta

The women of the fields clip red bunches of grapes
in patches of neatly tilled farmland in the San Joaquin,
clip sweet globes they can no longer stand to taste—
just twenty miles shy of Santa Cruz beach babies
in thongs, Pleasure Beach surfers on longboards,
all the cool convertibles speeding Cabrillo Highway
women line as pickers, back bent over summer's harvest.

The *campesinas* labor without shade tents or water buffaloes,
shrouded in oversized shirts and baggy work pants, disguised
as what they are not, faces masked in bandanas under cowboy hats
in *fils de calzón*—

   the young one named Ester taken in the onion patch
   with the field boss' gardening shears at her throat,
   the older one called Felicia isolated in the almond orchard
   and pushed down into a doghouse. The pretty one, Linda,
   without work papers, asked to bear a son in trade
   for a room and a job in the pumpkin patch,
   Isabel, ravaged napping under a tree at the end of a dream
   after a long morning picking pomegranates, *violación de un sueño.*
   Salome on the apple ranch forced up against the fence
   as the boss bellowed *¡Dios Mío!* to her every *no, no, no.*

The *promotoras* flex muscle in words, steal off into night
face-to-face to talk health care, pesticides, heatstroke, rape,
meet to tally accounts—forced to exchange panties for paychecks
in orchards, on ranches, in fields, in truck beds—to speak out to risk
joblessness or deportation to an old country, a new foreign soil.

Women of the fields, like those before them, like those
who will trail after—*las Chinas, Japonesas, Filipinas*—
to slave for frozen food empires in pesticide drift,
residue crawling along the skin, creeping into the nostrils
and pregnancies it ends as they hide from *La Migra*
in vines soaked in toxins or crawl through sewer tunnels,
across railroad tracks, through fences to pick our sweet berries,
for this, this: *la fruta del diablo*.

Jack Foley

## *Viriditas*

For Adelle

Viriditas—
the dream
of a green
world

It is not
enough
to say
"the life around us"—
we *are*
"the life around us"

it is not possible
to *be*
apart
from
nature
("*natura naturans*")

      the conditions
      in which
      consciousness—
      "this"
      consciousness—
      happens
      are serious, tentative, and limited
      this dream
      of green

I *am* that flower
you hold
in your
hand

we are
light
coming to consciousness
of
itself
men & women
of light

what is mind
but light?
what is body?

"Make LIGHT of it,"
writes my friend
James
Broughton—

Walking,
I vanish into light—

        Kora—the seed—
        above ground—under—
                the need
        to follow her—down the rabbit hole
                    following the
        idea
        of resurrection—
                seed-

      time vanishes/returns   we grow
      in branch and root

in winged or finny stuff
or cloven hoof
in bird-
sound, animal alarm or
pleasure
(describe a scene—
scene vanishes—
mind appears—)

Kore     woman
under
ground

                  No need
that is not satisfied
of food
or sex—

...

greenness, love:
as you lie in this moment
of danger,
as you sleep
wondering if the next sleep
will be death,
"this greeny flower,"
this green
comes to you
the power of life
Viriditas

# V

## *Desert*

This is a big place, and if you feel small
you may as well leave.
   —Nancy Schimmel, "The High Desert"

There's no debate—science
claims most desert forests
will succumb in this century.
   —Cynthia Anderson, "Joshua Tree Weeping"

Jennifer K. Sweeney

## The Day Everywhere and White

Spring in the desert and the world
is only a little bit dead,
but here we are

throwing away the dust.
Cast the eye cleanly
against the horizon, a snow

of cottonwood
hazing the plumb line.
March is a fly-by-night bird,

her eggs hidden
in tiny wells.
*My thunder My thunder*

Swing low when the moon is void.
Soon the heat will go platinum,
novice lizards dropping from the sky.

What good then, this huddle
of poppies drowsing the nothing
hillside. What good,

with moss on our hands.
Here where we need to water
down the water,

let's make a tree from a tree.
This yellow leaf
is just a little clue.

Joshua McKinney

## *Point of Reference*

Still early and dawn sows its first handfuls of light over the ridge, kindling to gold the tussocks of bunchgrass scattered across the scrub. The dust is down, still damp with the night's light rain, the sage musk and petrichor so fresh and sharp he has to stop and stretch his lungs with it, while his dog trots among the shrubs and stones, tracing the faint missives of woodrat and hare.

He tells himself he brings her here to remind her she's a dog—a mongrel pup his kids saved from the pound (a little setter, perhaps some hound), and even then so beaten down she cowered at the slightest word. His kids have gone to college now, so he brings her here, where he remembers walking as a boy, searching for arrowheads with his father, the petroglyphs they chanced upon at the base of the escarpment, the figures etched in rock by a people long since erased, and how he felt he could almost read those shapes. There were mustangs, too, and from the ridge he used to watch them grazing on the plain below and name their colors—bay, buckskin, pinto, palomino, roan—all shining in the sun.

Hushed, he'd watch for hours, until some presage startled the lead stallion and the herd would thunder off across the desert and the sound of their hooves would rise with the dust and fade away and then only the dust remained. Bound by so much absence, he finds it hard to move. But what stops him now is that the dog, always aquiver in her quest for a sign, is doing something he's sure she's never done before: she's frozen, standing stiff, right foreleg cocked in mid-step, tail straight up, nose thrust forward, her whole body aimed toward a juniper thicket he calculates is maybe thirty yards ahead. It's clear she senses something there, and is by sense compelled to adopt a posture dredged from blood, a silence and a stillness bred to signal presence.

His eyes dart to the dog, then to the trees and back again, but he cannot see beyond the thicket. All attention now, he scans the silhouette of dark limbs for any sound or movement; but his straining senses fail, fold back upon themselves. Under the weight of his listening eyes and looking ears, his sounding breath, he feels his own inflection in the world's flesh, feels he is perceived. Charged by vague encounter, changed by what he cannot name, he stands there waiting with the dog, whose gesture he understands, in a distant sense, without knowing the nature of what it points to.

W. F. Lantry

## Sailing Stones

The unimagined weight of sunburnt air
compresses, below sea level, all winds
and traps this heat in incandescent wheels,
spinning above the boron flats and salt-
strewn plains of painted clay. Nothing reveals
what's underneath, dry geysers, salt fountains
of unknown origin. No waters flow,

no springs, no river traveling below
this salt-crust landscape, where a sailing stone
moves silently across the sun-caked earth
without visible force. Rounded basalt
or cubes of dolomite, whose greatest worth
is mystery: their impulse is unknown,
but we can see the track, measure its length,

and marvel at the unrevealed strength—
enough to move a stone no man could lift,
across the valley floor, marking its trace
always in silence, underneath the vault
of constellations. Some have called this place
magnetic, others say the faultlines shift,
and some believe unnoticed sheets of ice

pick up the stones and fling them, like cast dice,
across the desert valley floor. I know
only what I have seen: the shadows cast,
marking the progress of the brittle spalt
of hillsides, give some movement in this vast
unmoving silence, where even the slow
progress of stones reflects a whispered prayer.

W. F. Lantry

## Ocotillo Wells

White exoskeletons of scorpions
litter the ground, shed skins of rattlesnakes,
a tarantella's cast-off carapace:
the signs of transformed life are everywhere,
even in this scorched-stone-cindered place.
The dried stalk of a bloomed agave shakes
its seed in pods, but at the narrow tip

small plantlets form, and when the east winds whip
their stalks diagonal, they let go, sail
a little ways, and land, setting down roots.
Here every seed and stem falls on the bare
infertile stone, yet walking cactus shoots
rise tall as men, until root frameworks fail,
but where they fall, rent branches send out growth

which thrives and flowers here, confirming both
the death and resurrection of the lost.
Thorned ocotillos lift their slender red
blossoms, like trumpets, through the desert air,
and even in the worst heat, merely spread
their arms a little wider; when they're tossed
by winds, the long hands barely move, endure

both drought and frost as if they were a pure
image, now rose and green, once scaly gray,
of what will be again, if we could gaze
outside of time, if we could, patient, stare
across the winter's heat and summer's haze
and wait, persistent, for that single day
when ocotillos' flowering begins.

W. F. Lantry

## Anza Borrego

Our evening desert swells with life, barred owls
emerge from shelters their own talons scraped
into the barrel cactus blossoming
with every thunderstorm, with each flash flood,
even if years apart. Their waters bring
successive changes to these rock flows, shaped
a thousand years by only wind and rain,

where stone and sand define a harsh domain.
Here, where the jumping cholla seem to leap
across the air, to catch on skin, and split
in sections, their spines cling, swelling with blood,
and burrow into flesh. If you permit
those barbs to rest within you, if you sleep
even one night, they'll work themselves to bone

and give more pain than you have ever known.
Steel yourself. Have courage. Quickly slide
a stick between the cactus and your skin
and as a gardener removes a bud
with a quick movement, leverage each pin,
each blood-filled barb, away. If you've applied
the proper force, the whole segment will fall

back to the sand it came from and will sprawl
wind-driven from your feet. With this technique
and others, you'll survive this withered place,
cauldroned dark sand, or rain-scalded to mud,
although each passing windstorm will erase
all hints of journeys, and the wells you seek
are only found in rifts a coyote prowls.

Susan Gubernat

## *In the Desert*

Anza Borrego

Off-trail through whiteness, dazzling, blank as the wafer sun
that bore down on us, I lost my footing among the cacti
and one sprang out at me, spearing my knee.
So a plant can leap, sensing trespass. I screamed
twice: first at the violation,  and then, when you eased
the huge thorn out. And why couldn't we keep
to the path? I was livid, awkward now, scarf
tied around my leg, blood-soaked. We don't live
as others live, I thought then. And still think so
as we blaze and bushwhack our way to old age
where no garden awaits, strung with sweet peas,
wisteria-hung. It's red rock and lizard-rich,
dry as the bones we will someday become.

Karen Skolfield

## The Mating Habits of Humans as Interpreted by Death Valley Pupfish

If I stay in the current, I am staying in the current,
I am freshed out of river, I am beside someone's footprint.
Wriggle-go-lightly where waters coolest,
I am muscled scale and mute. If I choose
a side cove where the water goes slack
I may be looking for you. I may, manner of speaking,
call your name. I brown to your blue. I chase
to your slim finning. I may expect this inching,
suitor my way on by, pretend not to notice.
I may noise loudly, for what I'm worth.
I may lose sight for what little sight I have,
I may despair if you slip pondly, if you choose
another, if the muddiest bank calls. If you let me
press my dorsal to your dorsal, my adipose fin
to your adipose fin, my gills to yours,
if you promise me the want of your streamline
then I will give you fry of my longing,
I will pupfish frenzy, I will lair this one hot canyon
into a fold of our bodies. I will no longer wonder
what is upstream or down, I will true to you
in ways no fish trues, I'll flare fondly
and icthyologically, I'll fish out of water,
if you have me I'll landwalk.
I've heard what love makes possible.

Helen Wick

## Super Bloom

Death Valley

Sandpaper eyes scrub the glass
of its edges.
Do what you will to the world—
I am still in the belly of the fish.

~

The spring will forgive us everything,
the flowers nod in agreement
with the breeze.

This is the unlearning—
unearthing the yard
wild with weeds.

~

We are enemies to our fate—
the apples of our cheeks blushing
towards the sun.

~

Think of springtime like this—
the tedious movement of the water to seed,
the intricate growth up, the painful break
through the soil.

Cracked like a skull, the seed spreads open,
grows a tail, penetrates the earth—
all the while the expanse,
then release from its prison.

The flowers repeat themselves
over and over on the desert floor.

The seeds wait for years under the
earth, yet the desert is alive
for just this moment.
It is a slight to know you slightly.

~

We call them by their colors
yellow, violet, white,
then remember how Eve
named the flowers in Eden.

We begin again—
fox paw, wild grape, moon glow.

~

The leaves from the lemon tree,
waxy and thick, greener than grass.
If you love me, you'll leave me be.

~

The movement of the wrist as it writes,
I know this well, the delicacy
of the muscle practiced over and over.

I will always know how to hold you
the way the desert floor dries
after a storm.

~

Our fingerprints resemble a wave,
the lines gather and fold into each other,
fold into the blue.
Up, searching, gone.
Left sucking salt from our fingers.

~
You could be someone
else,
or you could be
the flowers nodding,
yes, yes
to the breeze.

Bonnie Mosse

## *Desert Sunflowers*

Alone on a tall stalk
a desert sunflower stands
above mounds of purple verbena.

Trumpet-flowered white Datura
float like white ghosts
among Lenten vestments.

I follow a quiet road
to dunes rumpled
with acres of yellow-orange

just as the incoming coolness
of evening pulls honey-musk
from massed blossoms.

Swooning to drink in
this sweet cream for dry senses,
I bend down on one knee.

Ruth Nolan

## Ouroboros—Amargosa River

*...a circular symbol depicting a snake,*
*or less commonly, a dragon...*

Undrinkable, this midnight
snake, slowly moving south
from the bomb test site
at Yucca Mountain
to curl its way across sand
marking midnight trails
across dry skin
drifting into white noon
lifting into desire to flow
to places below sea level
rising to meet the dawn,
having traveled west,
then bending north
ending at Badwater
deep in Death Valley
to sleep beneath the sea.

*...swallowing its tail as an emblem*
*of wholeness or infinity...*

Caryn Davidson

## *Among the Tortoises*

I

In the desert, I saw a gaping burrow
and craned my neck for a glimpse
of the tortoise that had
carved this crescent into the earth.
*Show yourself!* I called, breaking
all wilderness etiquette. I was
tired of finding so many
empty holes, so I crawled into the burrow and
felt myself drop, slowly, but with an
irresistible heaviness.
I landed in a cavern filled with
thousands of unsmiling, unblinking
tortoises. They seemed to
disdain me—maybe it was the
papery pink skin or the
lack of a sturdy carapace. Perched
precariously on my two legs, I must have
appeared timorous, weak, and
improbable. As my eyes
adjusted to the dim light I
could see them slowly moving,
as though the delicacy of each
moment required their careful
study and calculation.
They were soundless.

II

My life among the tortoises
has been good. When the

earth has absorbed enough of the
sun's warmth to rouse us from our
sleep, we emerge onto the surface and
browse on beavertail cactus, carefully avoiding
the tiny glochids that might lodge in our tongues.
The desert is brilliant after a long brumation
in the burrow; one cannot imagine the
depth of hunger we feel after not having
eaten for months. The desert dandelions taste
like soil and fire and exploding stars and
we cannot eat enough of them. But we
take our time, chewing and watching and
absorbing the great solar goodness of the day.
I will return to the burrow as the great shadow
falls on the ricegrass and the purple verbena.
As the great shadow falls on the
hardy forbs and the galleta, on
the woolly daisies and the goldenbush
I will crawl back down into the subterranean
world where the deep hum of
the sheltering roots soothes us back
into our sleep.

III

What is that shrill whine echoing through
the ground? I cannot place it; no hummingbird
or tarantula hawk has ever been so loud.
The pitch is singularly piercing:
It could rattle the scales off a
healthy turtle or deafen any
thing that hears. The sound is
growing louder. Is it getting closer?
Now it seems upon me, the earth is
caving in all around me, it is hard to breathe
and if I don't get more air I will suffocate.
I have become the soundlessness.

IV

In the desert, I saw a concave,
bowl-shaped pit. The geometric hatch marks
of a dirt bike tire adorned it like the wax seal
on a secret document. It almost looked like an
inverted grave mound, collapsed or
upside-down. I wonder why the earth was so
unstable there, what made that shallow
depression? This land holds many untold
stories, layers of lives locked under the sand.
I lie down and a thin voice seems to rise
through the granular throat, sighing,
saying something urgent and sorrowful.
What does the desert want,
what does the desert urge us to know?

Judith McCombs

## Pictures Not in Our Albums

Mojave Desert, 1948

Somewhere it is still
a dream of safety, our young
parents hauling us up the dark pass,

Father blocking the wheels of the trailer
while Mother lets go the emergency brake
and eases the Ford into low, pulls forward
and slows, pulls forward and waits.
As if I had watched from a roadcut

I see the small oval Ford
pale in the shadows, our gray-blue trailer
weighing it down, the asphalt road
falling away on all sides into blackness,
the curve ahead climbing to blackness.

Across the vast basin of desert,
the night-drowned ridges and foothills,
a coyote howls and is answered. There are
no lights but ours on the earth,
no farther lights except the slow stars.

In the back of the car, in the warm
nest of children, I drift
from sleep to waking, breath
to breath, as the car labors
and rests, labors and rests,

and the night outside is a slow swelling sea
lapping the mountains, black waters

so vast that a ship could founder,
a thousand lit ships go down,
all lights but our own go under.

## Ruth Bavetta

### Kramer Junction

Stop for an Astroburger.
Stare at the desert
across a table that's almost clean,
see the power station, with its huge inexplicable
contraptions. Get gas at the Union station,
buy a melted candy bar. Sandblown
pottery sits on the corner
under a hand-lettered sign.
Trucks downshift, then wind up
and away. Watch the campers,
trailers, station wagons.
The wind is always blowing.
The train is always passing through.

Mary B. Moore

## Economy

Even the Mojave has plenty—dunes
moon-white in moonlight, indigo space
so full of stars they powder it like tunes
from planet radio, prayers from Grace
Cathedral, Shao Lin. Perkins sells
desert seeds, outwitting water-storing lizards,
whose tail-flick zigzags electrical
blue, and sand-camouflaged mice with built-in
backpacks. He's frugal, selling a drought garden's
worth in biscuit-colored canvas sacks—
like lava bits, pepper motes. Avid dust.
He can hear a snake ripple the slough
of wheat-colored sand, a hawk ride updrafts.
He banks on the given: unowned, shriven.

Susan Glass

## *Fainting in the Mojave*

April, and the hard scent of creosote
sears lungs.
Can the running skinks smell it?
Or the cactus wren stuttering
his broken motor song?
In part, you've come here for him,
for Gambel's quail, and loggerhead shrike and roadrunner.
You hadn't counted on your body's innocence,
your dizzying nausea that buckled your legs like a colt's,
dropping you face down in the blackbrush and greasewood.

The singing black-chinned sparrow nests in a barrel cactus,
and only now, pressed belly-flat as a rattlesnake
and cooled by your classmates' shadows,
do you see him,
a message folded among spines
that store water for a hundred years.

Ruth Nolan

## Ghost Flower: Mohavea Confertiflora

For Mary Beal, mid-20th-century botanist

shivering by day
and glowing at night

blooming only
in March and April

this flower marked
by splotches of red

in its white heart
attracting lovers

through mimicry
not producing nectar

named by a botanist
who worked alone

in the deep Mojave
to render it bold

this small flower
speaks with a lisp

on the rocky lips of
forsaken canyons

flourishing where
no woman should go

forever hard to find
unless you tiptoe by

Ruth Nolan


## Black-Chinned Hummingbird

A small hummingbird of the Mojave Desert

I cut fresh sage at the mouth of Wildrose Canyon
brought it home to dry on the old wood stove.
I want to burn the damp, string-wrapped bundles
so I can remember you, so I can forget about you.

The kitchen table is full of stems and memories
things you left behind, and your knife has dulled.
I've been hiking old Death Valley trails alone,
the hills, the dunes, the intrusive new solar farms.

I had to go so far to find this year's crop of sage.
Drought. The sky, blinded by technology's stare.
You once tried to mend the broken furniture
but wouldn't hug our daughter or braid her hair.

Outside, the black-chinned hummingbird builds
its tenaciously tiny nest in the blades of a palm tree
weaving together dried grass and other lost things,
threads of your flannel shirt that I still love to wear.

I wonder how long it will survive in the next hot
windstorm in a season without rain, a summer full
of mirrors and blades, if vultures will eat its tiny eggs,
if its young will hatch strong and yearn to fly away.

Ruth Nolan

## King Clone

King Clone is thought to be the oldest creosote
bush ring in California's Mojave Desert
and one of the oldest living organisms on Earth.

Start from the tight-knit center,
from a seed excreted by a condor
then watered by a droplet
off the back of a saber tooth tiger.
Suckle the melting blue waters
from the thaw of another Ice Age
when it tunnels, where it flows.

One day they'll measure the
aridity of where you've been, the
depth and range of soils you've
romanced for so many millennia,
your underground love sheltering
generations of desert tortoises,
jackrabbits, bobcats, kangaroo rats.

It's then you'll feel and know
that your name is King Clone.

Noreen Lawlor

## Creosote

She said she could smell the rain
in the creosote
put some slender branches
behind her ear
tiny gray-green berries fell
stuck to the strands of her hair
she grew up in the desert, says
*it only shows itself to certain people*

I do not smell the rain in the creosote
I smell its tenacity though
how it stands up to windstorms
its roots suck water out of sand
it puts on yellow flowers in the spring

there is a living ring of it in Mojave
that is carbon dated to be
11,700 years old
since the last Ice Age
one mother plant cloned itself
they are all connected underground
take 20 years to grow a foot

in Joshua Tree we have a forest of it
they want to clear cut
put up a gated community
with 248 densely packed houses

I do not think they smell the rain
I think they smell only money

Stephanie Schultz

## Holy Saturday in the Desert

After three hours of Los Angeles traffic,
everybody in a hurry to get to the middle of nowhere,
a rest stop is calling me in from the heat.

Sunbeams in a cloudless sky beat like a bass drum
on my Midwestern skin. Each stomp, each kick, each new melody
vibrates through my bones.

Joshua Tree is a real desert town like none I've seen before,
shadowed by a national park with a visitor center on the edge
of a street corner between Joshua trees that grow only here.

I bet there are locals who can't name the two deserts
that meet in this very spot. But I brushed up
on my geography and history, as if I might fit in.

I long to know this place, to experience the highs and lows,
to live like a nomad in someplace warm, possessing only nature.
Most who come here barely see the land.

It's the day before Easter.
Hot and tanned trashy folks in cut-off Coors T-shirts
hold open for me the broken automatic sliding door.

The AC inside the gas station is a welcome comfort
after the topless jeep ride here, a sweat I couldn't overcome.
It's a stark contrast, an unknown forecast, of my desert night ahead.

Cynthia Anderson

## Joshua Tree Weeping

After a photograph by Beth Moon

Shoshone call them *wicobah*,
broken ones. They give easily,
bedeviled by heavy branches
that collapse at critical mass.
But this ritual sacrifice is not
why the Joshua tree weeps—
it's the final death underway,
species loss due to climate
change—too much heat,
too little rain, choking smog.
There's no debate—science
claims most desert forests
will succumb in this century,
that nothing can be done. In
some places, infant mortality
is already complete. Yet as long
as its weathered trunk remains
upright, this tree lets the sun
turn clusters of spiked leaves
to silver. That's how it would
be remembered—not fallen,
not bent with grief.

Heidi M. Sheridan


## Desert Snow

My neighbor and I were eight when snow covered
            the high desert, making white
dunes in the field of cactus, tumbleweeds.
            Only yuccas pierce through.
Last night's coyote howl, now a calling.
            (Something happened).

It was easy to play the hours,
            run over what usually pricked:
a hundred spikes in the left calf,
            (mother tweezing transparent,
yellow splinters)
            a sidewinder come around a Joshua tree,
a scorpion ready for an ankle.

We reached into the unknown
            for snow packs, unscathed,
faces blushed with joy.
Our mittens white with wet.

Laurie Klein


## *Return Engagement*

With thanks to the Irvine Ranch Conservancy

Come back, refugee cactus wrens,
with your reedy, one-note chorus:
*cha-char, cha-charrr*. Test drive
our latest eco-brainwave,
high desert thickets of PVC cacti
hectic with needles and wire:
home sweet chollas, nine feet tall—
vinyl mea culpas. They creak,
and yes, they look like robots gone bad.

Please, little birds who love thorns,
while covert iPods air your song,
return with ribbons of litter and
brave the unknown to build
those multiple decoy nests
so that this time, the real ones
prosper, and make us ponder
what we fake, and why
what we return to saves us.

Ruth Nolan

## *Old Woman Springs*

Each April you plant yellow daffodil bulbs
between the yucca and beavertail prickly pear.
Fat desert quail hold vigil on your porch
while kingsnakes and rattlers eat bird eggs
and haunt your careful twilight tending.
Every year you keep the garden, protecting
baby rabbits from the claws of hawks,
knowing the June sun will burn the flowers
while coyotes mourn from the jagged rocks.

Nancy Schimmel

# The High Desert

Honey, I know a thing or two about the desert. I've chased those rainbows, seen the crumbling shacks and windblown signs and settling adobe walls. I don't know as much as the people who live here, but I know they wouldn't live anywhere else. Or maybe couldn't. I know there's more to the desert than you can see driving through. I like rocks, and the desert has good ones, and you can see them from your car window if you feel like looking, but if you get out of your damn car you'll see that there are people and critters that live here. That are dug in here, where it's dry enough for their lungs or quiet enough for their minds or big enough for their egos. This is a big place, and if you feel small you may as well leave. People come looking for gold and stay for the place, come looking for emptiness and find all kinds of rusted-out gear and desert sun amethyst and horned toads and desert rose—desert rose, that's rocks, the flowers out here ain't roses, they are cactus flowers, prettier than roses or lilies, bold and tough like flowers should be, no wimps. Pebbles, glass, sand, thorns, all hard stuff, but it all gets soft as feathers in the dawn light. You fall in love out here. You fall in love with the earth. Mother earth mother-naked, no redwoods, no oaks, no invasive dried-up grass and thistle, just pure sagebrush, well spaced, been growing here since dinosaurs, I guess, and if you are lucky you see dinosaur bones too. Everything out in the open. Except water. That's hidden, mostly, down in the ground. I remember going to Old Woman Springs with my folks. I remember standing on the tan-brown-red desert and looking down in that hewn hole, that blue-tinted rock and water deep down in the ground like a different world, but it's all one world, all the desert.

Steve Kowit


*Raven*

Squawks from a raven in what used to be Jack
Funk's field over the fence, scolding me
till I look up & see that the hills
are still there, that the day
couldn't be lovelier, sweeter. Susan Green's
little girls are chatting in singsong
up in the treehouse
in what used to be Dempsey's old place
to the west. Mary, who will stroll over these four-
point-five acres of rolling high desert chaparral
when we two are gone? — The tin barn,
the pumphouse & shed. That underground
stream from which we've been drinking
our fill these eighteen years.
Who'll own all this dusty blue mountain lilac,
the aloe & roses & pines & bright orange ice plant?
Who'll walk in the shade of that live oak
under which Ralphie & Ivan & Charlie,
& Eddie are buried? Who'll watch the quail
flutter out of the brush in formation,
& the rabbits scurry for cover? Who
will these granite boulders & lovely agaves
belong to when you & I, beloved, are buried
& long forgotten? — Forgive me,
sweet earth, for not being shaken more often
out of the heavy sleep of the self. *Wake up!*
*Wake up!* scolds the raven, sailing off
over the canyon. *Wake up! Wake up! Wake up!*

Laurie Klein

## *In Conflagrante*

I

Mile after mile, the torched chaparral:
its sole pulse, an itinerant cricket.

Arson and ozone,
the tarry smolder of the creosote bush,
the broken family of mesas.

II

In the time it takes to smoke
that menthol superslim,
eucalyptus passed into memory.

Colorless, mostly crystals, a mild anesthetic.
Buzz those cold receptors, under the skin.
Menthols: the price of cool.

III

Maybe the ground remembers,
like the scored rind of a melon.
"Take what you need," it says.

> And what could be sultrier
> after—ooh-la-la—forbidden love
> than rain. Rain, don't go away.
> Bare limbs recall joy they were shaped for,
> while eighteen threads of April
> tether the sheltering motel eaves
> to the patient soil.
> This is what we were made for.

Afterglow is an eye in the dark,
the shared cigarette, obvious as
that creaking sign: vacancy.

IV

Mojave, 2008:
Heat rips through the chamise,
flickers up the canyon:
fifty tongues funnel into a roar,
ravishing in its concentration.
One live coal in the hand—not yours
this time, not mine and yet,
somebody lit that streambed's wick.

V

Seen from the chopper,
kissing the fire scar: spits of rain.
And terrain, like the wrong side of a blanket.

      In the time it takes to raise a child,
      the ex-chaparral lurches onto its thorny feet.
      Between the sheets of cheatgrass,
      hummocks of red brome unravel,
      a downward chill
      fleecing mesa mint and sugarbush,
      even the sage of its room and board.

      Where is the bunchgrass now?
      the scrub oak?

Land again, in see-through fingers of rain.
And that cricket—a pulse,
a plea: Oh world, these feet of clay.

CC Hart

## Halfway to Keeler, California

At
Bodie,
caught by dusk's
decrepit light,
Esperanza stops,
faces West, her
gaze fixed on
hills burned
in
June sun.
Keeler seeks
ladies to teach
miner's camp children.
Never did she think
of fleeing her
parents' home,
queer as
rain
stalled. But,
time won't wait;
unwed, fifty,
virgin, she wills this
wild desert life.
Xeric, she
yields like
zinc.

Nancy Sue Brink

## Have I Told You About the First Time
## I Saw White Pelicans Over Manzanar?

This was out in the Owens Valley, east of the Sierra, near Big Pine,
           in the middle of the afternoon. I was standing
on a slab of concrete left from the internment camp, it radiated heat,
           heat tore me down. This was many years ago,
just a plaque and remnants of bungalows crumbling
           to ground while grains of sand were bonding, rising,
scraping the voice from my throat—creosote, mesquite, tumbleweed, sage—

           they tell me flowers are stunning here in spring. I'd like to see them—

have I mentioned mountains? Sometimes I see a white pelican and forget
           there were mountains—I don't understand—
they disappear into indifferent white steaming flatness, I have to
           will them back, push them up once again from molten earth
           to crack open sadness—

           flat white sadness.

Tall tall mountains push up so hard so harsh behind me in
           front of me when I reach up and trace peaks my hands are sliced
           and bloody when I pull them back to my lap—

           I hardly noticed it, then.

That was the first day I saw those mountains, even though I forget them
           beside white pelicans and Manzanar and the desert—

           that sad bright desert.

I think deserts are beautiful and should be left alone to remind us we will die.

My friends fear I spend too much time with ghosts, I write too much about
          ghosts and maybe I'm doing it again—ghosts
of sand crystals, exhausted ghosts lying dormant underground—

     a poem about ghosts, sad ghosts made of sand.

At that time, that first day of white pelicans, I didn't believe in ghosts but I believed
          in heat, sucking heat with alkaline claws, I believed
in passage of geologic time, in desiccation of bodies that do not get water,
          I believed in sun-bleached bones—but I know more now

     and nothing. Nothing and more.

But I was telling you about the first time I saw white pelicans rising
          over desert, over Manzanar, a poem about white pelicans rising
          over desert, when I sat down on concrete, weary—

     maybe you were expecting a delicate poem about flight.

A poem built of words and images that could be pulled apart, removed,
          misspoken—
delicate words, fragile, but strong words are just as likely to fail.

     They are just as likely to be beautiful.

You told me you've seen white pelicans today, too, for the first time.

     How many?

Strangely beautiful one by one or a few at a time but that first day over Manzanar
          a spiraling column lifted from sand and circled above mountains—
slow in heat, pelicans don't flap, they arc their wings and catch thermals that form
          when cool and hot of earth and sky try to resolve their differences.

On that first day I saw them I thought heat was driving me mad or maybe ghosts
          that I did not yet believe in were begging for faith—
          a column of white big birds with black-tipped wings rose
          against unbearable blue sky.

Then they were gone. All of them.

I looked around, hard, my eyes dug through sand, scoured peaks,
       I rubbed my eyes.

       Once again, suddenly, they were there,

perfect in spiraling white wings against blue and again, suddenly, nothing—

       I had no reason to doubt what I saw—but now

I doubt every day as it turns one way and another, all the days, all time
       turns, time and truth—maybe
time can change, maybe something in time unlocks
       once it passes, maybe
birds carry time with them, lifting ghosts from sand from burning
       surge of mountains—

pelican spiral—appearing disappearing not there there not there there
       appearing disappearing, spiraling, one around another.

Ginny Short

## Strange Reefs

An epochal history of Simone Pond
from the water's point of view

Floods have come and gone.
Warm seas, shallow seas.             Strange reefs.

The floods receded.    Volcanos arced.      The earth
wrenched apart, dropped below sea level.
The Sea of Cortez sat on my doorstep. Then receded.
A mollusk graveyard    in its wake.

A salt flat full of cataclysmic debris.
Detritus of dead volcanos. Detritus of meandering rivers.
Detritus of invading seas.
Mud hills rising. At my feet.

Jungles of cabbage trees. Giant sloths. Warm salty seas.
The sea retreated.    More than once.    More than twice.
Water locked in glaciers. Locked behind volcanic hills.
Locked in subterranean vaults
Ancient Waters that still taste of ferns and dinosaurs
and volcanic ash.
The cabbage trees retreated with the retreating waters
the earth cooled
then heated up again
Only these remnant trees remain
Caught in tectonic cracks between tormented plates.
Along the mud hills. At my feet.

People came. Collected fruit. Wove huts of palm leaves.
Sang in the shadow of these hills.

The people retreated scattering remnants of their life—
ollas, metates, manos, pipes, broken pottery bits,
trails that echo still the song of thousands of feet.
Ghost songs.
Ancient graffiti etched in ochre on stone.
Their unpretentious huts too soft-bodied to fossilize.

The miner, the homesteader with parched footsteps
in this desiccated land,
now a dune sea that laps at my feet, tongues that lick
in sleepy waves against the hills.
The mud hills. At my feet.

These people retreated. Their shacks abandoned. Their tools
rust in the desert sun. Miner's scars that never heal,
my wrists slashed.
Desolate bones strewn like orphan boulders across
the parched desert floor

And a remnant stand of Cabbage trees

Now thousands of People come to gawk and stare.
At the relict trees. At the water leaking tears out of the torn earth.
At the blue sky and drifting sands.

With each proclamation of love
With each step of discovery over virgin desert, across my brow
They are loving the land to death.

In a thousand thousand years
their touch will not recede.
Not until the mud hills melt. At my feet.

# VI

# *Rivers, Lakes, and Lagoons*

I am at this place
where the water comes from darkness
with the winter hummingbird
    —Ursula K. Le Guin, "The Spring at Sinshan"

Listen deep. In the quiet
beyond thought—ancient stones,
creeks, rivers, roots, wings
and open branches
will sing you home.
    —Elizabeth C. Herron, "Who Remembers"

Brenda Hillman

## from *Hydrology of California*

An ecopoetical alphabet

There's a river   of rivers   in California   beyond   all earthquakes
bringing   coiled water   from the north  It is grammar when we are anxious
in our days   bringing tumble   from freshets   north   of Klamath   where
redwoods   release fog drops
ceaselessly from filtered tops   Steelhead   Coho   salmon the few that do
to Humboldt   past dams   hereafter   known as  /  where streams  /  like
colorless   green ideas leap furiously/ where the Eel River flooding 753,000
feet per second / sees
fewer eels than before
Future of poetry   there's a stream   *between   a & b* as i write this   a dream
of a west   that would outlast us/   if we were life   which we are   drops
from Trinity   ice storms   to Smith River   & down   North Coast regions
brighter   seaside towns with
two waitresses named Pam
Future of poetry   i   saw a black-faced gull   a juvenile   awaiting neap   tide
We use the word *neap*   to mean   purple runnels/   Banks gathered wild force
at the edge of names   Mattole   Navarro / Hearts   gathered wild force   electrons
trading energy for food
Future of poetry   Let's move   between emotions in hydropoetics   for i   am a
pilgrim with no progress   recalling rivers   when we were anxious
past   wetlands needing   every turning time/   more than people   need
little dams for arugula
Many had lawns   They had to shower/ They had to eat   i said to main brenda
Now don't start   just ignorantly criticizing state   dams   the whole time
You drink gallons of it you know you do / We followed creeks   through decades
left of where eagles
can eat whole   deer
Stopped   near Fort Ross   We looked up to redwoods   releasing beads   fog
drops   The women so kind in Mendocino   They took the beyond   & ran
with it   You wrote on the memory tablets/ Blind sticks arranged themselves
Water-bearer was your star
Our settlements   didn't last
nor should they have   nor should they   There were economics & lifestyles

after   explorers made possible the cogs/ .00001 percent in rain fell
down /We stood & loved   south/ of the delicate eerie lighthouse at
Point Arena   where griefless
the sea lions loll

There's a quiver of rivers   the Sacramento   We saw a pleasant pheasant
near a pylon in the Delta   its back a walking rainbow   in 100,000 acres
they saved   the *they*   who can save\ We don't hate developers or do we
We hate their greed
those butt-ugly buildings   Actually
butts are adorable   compared to   Gated communities/ the poor buildings
can't even cry   though wild radish loves them   *Raphanus raphanistrum*
"common in disturbed places"   Maltese crosses each flower a shadow/
violet   in its means/
We ran near   why-worry
levees & one   time one of the developers said   Well   you wouldn't want
to   live in a tee-pee   now would you brenda   Future of poetry   we saw
*Dactylis glomerata*   Leaves of grasses\ i don't honestly mind the word
*introduced*   as in introduced species *between c & d* dogtail grasses *Cynosurus*
*echinatus* Near the Capitol
assemblymembers were drinking Fanta
near a fanning flood-plain/ coots with white beaks east of Feather River
*between e & f*   trace horse gold rush \boys picking pyrite   from   the North
Fork & 2 waitresses named Toni   Gold   must be so glad in heaven
glad & gold are
brothers w/ different mothers
The lovely   & a bit dammed   American River\ mergansers & brome/
buffleheads like reverse Oreos   rice fields\ algae from phosphates   Such
afternoons   might seem owned   O unrushed dream of time i saw some
earthly flapping   in the
rushes/ swallows eating pounds
of gnats/ & both shall row   My love & i leaned   on our tailbone   The
Giants were ahead   for a change in someone's earphones   A fundraiser for
fucked-up rivers   History   turned half our faces   golden   for a change\A
day so bright
we could not hear
the paradox   set up   by   Being   Then Gary yelled Hey   & a tall cloud
passed by   like a yoga teacher   Inside each seed\   didn't look like
competition   but   floated   forever   from us to you   Future of poetry
We wanted not   to fear   human life   to know as molecules   know   like
water from a book

There's a shiver   of rivers   north of Shasta   that melts   when we are faster
storms split   the plus signs   lava   flowed from night caves   marshes
with magpies   that dipped like punk nuns   we kept the word "beauty"
in mind for Shastina
that upside-down bride   75%
of H$_2$O slides     from north of Tahoe\ 1685 feet deep *high into nothingness*
Twain wrote   where some say   the dead sink frozen in their costumes
Future of poetry we entered   the howling edges of a dream   looked back to
Celestial City   texted each
other & soon   whole
words will be gone   c u l8r   will remain   But rain loves the day like haiku
River goes out   river comes in   like a cat\ googled *eutrophication* for June   so
that   no word should   die   New words shall sprout in dreams beyond time
Trout spawned   *chasmistes cujus/*
We saw some types
of knotting   in nature *between g & h*   What should we call those   silvery
gray parenthesis-type things   hanging off   lodge pole pines Don't colonize
that tree by naming it a nameless poet said   Lucky   he doesn't   have to
hunt for his food
a naming poet said
The pine   at the end   of the mind   Life from Life   Form   from   Form Be-
gotten not sprayed   Of one being   with the Mother   Through Her   rough
cones were made \We hiked   Desolation   noted streaky granites   moraines
condensation   infiltration evaporation chanted
Byzantium past Shirley Lake
You pronounced it *Byzanseeum*   needleminer moths   *what peeves you* David
said a fly-catcher said perched in blister rust   bitterbrush needing mouse-
shit for its pilgrim's process/   under fluttering twisted braids   cirrus clouds
Leaves of grasses' panicles
reduced   in mountain air
slowed down *between i & j*   Ice Age relic trees *Populus tremuloides*
we worried less   Glaciers beneath   Boreal & Tui chub   melts down to Walker
Lake *Pelecanus erythrorhynchos* if not too salty for them   if not   but extinction
lasts forever   in its
rivers from a book

Eric Paul Shaffer


## River Eye

When I stood on the deck above the rivers I loved, felt
the wheel turn in my hands, and stared down at the shifting,
murky, muddy curtain where the Sacramento and American

became one, I was happy to be where I was. I spent days
alone on the deck of the *Damnation* or drove the *California
Kid* against the current into sunset, watching

red-shouldered hawks in cottonwoods overhead. If I did
anything right in those days, it was finding the right things
to love and loving them till they were gone. The world

is no better or worse for me passing through, or for passing
through me, bent like the rays sunk in deep water
and glimmers of golden motes in the clouds of silt, soil,

and mud stirred by the flow moving the earth. Everything
escapes me now, so I drop a line into the river, catch what
I can, drag snapping, quicksilver muscle to the deck, and

stare for a moment into the cold and tilting, silver-rimmed
darkness of an alien eye from the river bottom before
I release at last what I never meant to catch and cannot keep.

Florence Miller

## Upriver

I jump ashore
tie line around the cottonwood

Dog jumps in water hyacinth
thinks it land

Water riffles
tules form islands

We catch a mess of catfish
fry them on the gimbaled stove

## Delta Afternoon

Delta afternoon
silver leaves
of cottonwoods

Raft inches
on the green current
cicadas shrill

A carp jumps—
flash of
kingfisher

Red-winged blackbirds
wheel out
of tules

A great blue heron
lifts

Carol Dorf

## All That Remains

We listen for chords
    of the missing frogs
        that scudded along
           this river.

Last night
    beside the water's edge
        pink traces of twilight
held the hour
    then vanished.

Ursula K. Le Guin

## A Grass Song: November

Very quietly
this is happening,
this is becoming.
The hills are changing
under the rainclouds
inside the gray fogs,
the sun going south
and the wind colder,
blowing quietly
from the west and south.
Manyness of rain
falling quietly,
manyness of grass
rising into air.
The hills become green.
This is happening
very quietly.

Ursula K. Le Guin

## The Spring at Sinshan

I am at this place
I am at this place now
where the water comes out of the rocks

This is the water
this is the spring of water
between the dark rocks
between the blue rocks

I am at this place now
I am at the beginning of water

With me at this place
the hummingbird with gray breast, green tail, red throat
the hummingbird at this place
hunting, drumming

I am at this place
where the water comes from darkness
with the winter hummingbird
that hangs bright-eyed over the water
not moving, drumming

Ursula K. Le Guin

## A Song Used When Damming a Creek or Diverting Water to a Holding Tank for Irrigation

To the ousel, to the water ousel
may it go, may it go.
Tarweed, the corn roots
need this water also.
Buckbrush, the bean leaves
need this water also.
Way of the water's going,
we do not wish this!
Let it go to the water ousel,
to the waterskater.
Let the wild goose's wings
carry it upward.
Let the dragonfly larva
carry it downward.
We do not wish this,
we do not desire it,
only the water we borrow
on our way to returning.
We who are doing this
all will be dying.
Way of the water's going!
Bear with us in this place now
on your way to returning.

Elizabeth C. Herron

## *Who Remembers*

> Here is the song of the neglected yellow moon.
> —Jack Crimmins

Stones beneath the hawthorn,
rounded and whaled up
amid the sea of yellow leaves.

Who remembers the songs of stones,
the river that rolled them,
or the hawthorn, whose berries
healed hearts for generations?

Who remembers the songs
of pale alder, favorite of beaver,
yellow willow whose roots make baskets
fine enough to hold water,
or red-stemmed dogwood and wild currant
where sparrow, warbler and wren
flutter and feed?

Canada geese glide down
to the winter pond at dusk, the marshy
muddy smell of home. Heart
by wing the geese know
where they belong.

Listen deep. In the quiet
beyond thought—ancient stones,
creeks, rivers, roots, wings
and open branches
will sing you home.

Susan Kelly-DeWitt

## Egrets Along the Yolo Causeway

Every day I watch how they float
into the wind; how they stretch
their legs out behind them

like burnt matchsticks,
then fall, heavy as drugged
eyelids into muddy browns, crushed

iris blues; how they plunge
suddenly as danger
or stupor into the shadows

of a ditch. Often, climbing up
out of a shadowed place myself—
out of a muggy airless wetland

where thoughts grow dark
seeds like wild rice—I spot one,
a loner, drifting below the causeway,

wading the weedy edges of slough
grass, his yellow beak gleaming
like a cutlass. Focused

on the task at hand: Beauty
is not even a vague
idea to him, or truth. He'll stab

whatever helps him
live. Every day as I travel past them

from the prison where I teach

       men to uncage hope, snap
open the hinges, I watch how they lift
    from the rich delta plowlands,

       how they glide free—a wholeness—
like one white feather, unlocked from its body,
    shiftless and holy.


## Bliss

    Lost Slough, Sacramento River Delta

Not bliss exactly—heat and mosquitoes
    rising from the reeds; still,
       a day afloat

in glimmer. Egrets, kingfishers, plush
    hunters all, lift our spirits
       like two cumbersome

wings; the morning gathers us
    into its murderous beak—
       holds us gently (for a time)

dazzled there. A great blue heron
    slips from the sedges
       like the Fisher King

himself, the one and only
    wild blue god.

E. K. Cooper

## Salmon Time

I learned about salmon time from my dad when I was 10 years old.

My dad sat under a tree in our yard preparing his long spear and gig. His long spear was 8 feet long with 2 small sticks tied on the end. The sticks were attached to the pole with a length of leather. Placed at the ends of these sticks were metal spear tips, each held on by a piece of leather string that was tied with a slip knot.

When the spear was thrown, the tips would lodge in the salmon and come off the spear. The leather string ran the length of the spear and was held onto when it was thrown so the salmon would not be lost in the river when speared.

I remember he would take a file and sharpen the tips. He said salmon skin is tough like the salmon. Their fins and tails are sharp and they will cut you as they fight back. You won't get a second chance to spear them, so you have to be ready and strong.

He ran his hand up and down the pole checking for cracks and rough spots. He told me long poles like this were a gift given between Native men and they were to be handled with care. A well-cared-for spear can feed your family for many years.

His gig was a slightly shorter pole with a very big fishhook on the end. I remember the hook was put into a cutout on the pole so it would not come off when you gig the salmon. It was secured into place with leather strings.

I can still remember the look of excitement on his face when I asked him when the salmon would be here. He replied a couple of days, the river is getting to the right level and the salmon are eager to spawn.

It was around 2:30 a.m. a few days later when he woke me up. He said it's time. We drove up past the old lumber mill where he and most of the local Native men worked and then took a dirt road. We parked behind some trees, and with my dad carrying his long spear and me the gig, we walked to the river.

When we arrived at a spot on the river, we walked up the river a short distance. I then saw a couple of men by the river and my dad said hello. I was happy to see that it was my Uncle Willie and Uncle Dush. They too had long spears and as we huddled together, I felt so grown up and eager to fish.

As I stood there, the morning air was cold and the river made a loud constant rushing sound. My dad said the salmon come in waves like the ocean on the beach. We will be able to get some for us and some relations.

Then I heard my Uncle Willie say, here they come! I looked into the river but could not see anything. My dad knelt next to me and said you need to look at the top of the water, the salmon will make a ripple with their backs. It looks like water is running over a rock in the river. I saw a ripple that was weaving back and forth in the river as it swam by us to the spawning grounds.

I could see a few more as my eyes adjusted to see rocks that move. I could see more and more as my dad and uncles waded into the stream, spears in hand. I heard my dad call out to only take a few this time and wait for the next wave.

Then with a strong, straight throw, into the river his spear went. He pulled it back with the leather rope. At the end was a very large gray salmon, flopping back and forth, trying to work its way off the spear tips. My dad dragged the spear and salmon onto the riverbank and stomped on its head. He then pulled out the spear tips, reset them, and back into the river he waded.

I watched as my uncles did the same until there were 12 salmon on the riverbank. I remember the sun was starting to come up as we placed our salmon on long twigs and walked back to our cars.

Salmon time on the Pinoleville Reservation, a tradition passed down from father to son for many generations.

A feast shared among families for as far back as can be remembered.

Susan Kelly-DeWitt

## Salmon

They came up the river like a band of slick
thieves. The water was thick with their leaping.
They climbed together the ladder of rapids,
hurled themselves and scraped their bellies.
The dead ones floated like pickerel weed. Many
fell out of the river of time, littering the rocky
banks, drawing the rats, raccoons and badgers.
They filled like windsocks with death.
We came there. We carried our eyes
and our baggage of witnessing. We carried
our awe like a causal fin. The willows crept
down to the river's edge and hung their heads
like sad old men, trailing all their living
silver green leaves, their dusky olive leaves
the color of salmon skin. The beached ones dried
in the sun; they poked like stiff flags from the weeds
and the light passing over them seemed dis-
embodied, preternatural. Somewhere
in the worlds between this one and the dead
river of salmon ghosts, we heard a howling.
*O Coho, O Kokanee, O Chinook.*

Joshua McKinney

## In Earnest

Fall's gold is gone. The American
will reek another week or two
before the circling birds stop
dropping black along the river's edge
to feed upon the rotting fish.
One marks this season by the stench
of kings—some picked to bones,
some bloated in the watery sun,
some carried home by fishermen.
A couple's lab has slipped its leash;
it runs and will not be called back
until it rolls in what remains, to mask
its scent in throes of primal joy.
A pack of boys casts stones at one
that offers now as evidence
its last thrashing in the shallows
near the shore. I leave my footprints
with the rest. Along this edge
death is success; and its resolve to live
nowhere in earnest, now here in every
phase, is almost nothing, almost all.

Jerry Martien


## Afternoon River Ragtime

> Mattole Valley

When we walk up to the bank the turtle on the rock
slips over the edge and into the river.
Somewhere in the world above a spirit decides to go swimming
and we dive in. On the bottom a mud-puppy
feels the shadows coming. Slides into the shade of a rock.
Everything move over for everything else.

There are a finite number of keys. Ten fingers
moving up and down the scale of what we know.
Up on the one hand, down on the other. Back and forth.
Sky is composed of cloud and the absence of cloud.
The river bottom of gravel and rock. Standing
in the water you can see the rocks move upstream.
In the wind the ripples of light
on their way to the sea. The rocks will heap up
and make mountain. The light sail out in dazzling boats
to meet the setting sun. Move over.

Yesterday the ocean winds brought fog.
Today the wind from up the valley
brings mist but not quite rain.
We try to tell the weather. Make a choice
and from it, consequent, the choices tumble after.
It is dog days. River days. Days of so much to do
there is nothing to do but go swim and watch the
day change and come home and make music so
rock and sky remain balanced in the
push and pull and the fingers stay
moving a moment ahead of the notes and the

coming to life at least keep up with the going away to
one or the other end of the scale. Gravel and cloud.
Sun and rain. Mountain. River and ocean.
The chords our lives learn to play on.

From the hills on one side of the valley
to the ridge on the other, upriver
a rainbow. Fingers moving on the spectrum of light.
Eyes, ears, heart. Move over.
Move over.

Jerry Martien

## Losing the Lines

At the summit of the coast range the fog stops. We go on. Out of
        Mad River drainage, down into Redwood Creek.
Up again to follow Willow Creek to the Trinity.
We cross over into another country. So long salt, greetings
        mountain air.
At Burnt Ranch we drop down, cross to the north bank, head
        upriver. Good-by redwood, hello mixed conifer &
        serpentine. We can't get enough of the difference.
At 6,000 feet it is spring a month ago. At the top of the Pacific
        Crest Trail: tiny heathers & violets.
Ah, but then look around. North of us the green of Scott Valley
        borrowed from rivers gone dry this year.
Off to the east massive clearcuts in the public forest.
Down in the Trinity steelhead can't get past the dam. In the
        riverbed rusting iron and mine tailings of a century ago.
This country as damaged as the one we have left. We are still in
        the beautiful land of the resource extractors. We can't go
        anywhere anymore.
And we can't remain in place. Even the trees. The very rocks can't
        stay put.
Refugees everywhere line up to leave home.
Not river and ridge. Not watershed. Not nature's lines between us.
        New demarcations of plenty and famine.
Nothing goes anywhere unless it follows money.
Drugs. Guns. Viruses. Global accountants.
There is no more away. No place is here. We flee the ruin. Arrive
        at ruin.
We have crossed over into an earth without borders.
I give you this to remember where we are. Hold on to those
        little violets.

Mary B. Moore

## Ecology of the Siskiyou Watershed

1

Of the fields I remember a flurry
of lilacs, whole meadows of thistle,
orange and magenta,

and on the slope up back
near the path of last year's
burn, dogwood bloomed,

the voluminous cupped petals
moon colored,
like some hothouse hybrid or
transplant from the South, our
Western lotus.

And at one or two,
the old bear would grumble downhill,
nightly to feast on grape, on dill,
his fur gilded, the dew
beading up…

2

…and gathered
we imagined into cumulous, stratus,
and dumped again in the Klamath
to wind through green layers
of serpentine, laden with silt and pebbles
of mountain jade,

through the nets of Hoopa,
Karok, hard by
the rock face, under
scrub oak and white pine,
to reach in the end
the sea.

3

And in November, when even
Orion is drawn toward the quilled
incense of cedar,
the brown bear, fattened
on salmon, his fur matted
with river silt, petals of blue
flowers and
fragments of bark
winters under the hill.

His bones are quartz,
his breath, dew.

Trina Gaynon

## Landscapes: San Fernando Valley

*Late Winter*
*El rio de los angeles*
runs brown and fast,
half-filled canal,
river straightened,
cement-lined arroyo,
no sluicing of earth
to allow sunlight's
reach for visions,
rock narratives.

*For a Moment*
Raindrops slide
down the window,
pound the roof;
wind flitters
locust branches
against redwood needles,
green,
deep.

*Rain Ends*
Canal waters

                                         slow,

green muck growing on top thick enough to support
a tennis ball. At the locked gates to the paths along

our concrete rivers, shopping carts line up:
Home Goods
Petco
Toys 'R' Us

some clean
some filled with construction waste.
Are the roads filled with unpiloted carts
after dark? Walmart is a long haul from here.
It's a long way to come for a soak in the canal
or a lift home in a rattletrap truck.

*Unmapped*
Passageways in every dimension,
the ones in the sky not visibly marked.

But the crow, more mobile than

the wood dove who sings the same
song in the same place all day long
or even the woodpecker who hammers
his way through the neighborhood,

knows how crowded the sky's roads are.

*790′ Above Mean Sea Level*
heat instigates
jacaranda explosions
petals underfoot
prompts ants to trail up
yet quiescent sweet shrubs
glare through open shutters

searching for the old desert

*Ahmanson Ranch*
Rattler survives
wildfire, later
summer heat draws
him out of grass
to the dirt path.

Wildflowers cover
the charred land
except blackened
trunks of oaks.

We could stand up
to our knees in
their dry savor.

We turn back.

*Ruelle*
Sycamores leaning—
one season, green leaves unfurling,
then deep shadow and tall dried grasses,
next leaves that span two hands' width

                                        falling,
ending with broad sculpture of trunks and branches.

*Dawn: Marine Layer*
Cottontail bounds across the soccer field.
Possum is last night's road kill.

*Bird Count*
In the canal:
three mallard hens,
two crows,
one mallard hen with six chicks.
Will they find their way to the jacuzzi like last year's brood?

*Green in Its Season*
The garlands of algae succumb to the heat, revealing
sand bars forming in clear canal water.

John Brantingham


*Your Story of Water*

You move east of Los Angeles
when you're four years old,
and even then something feels off.
Where you came from,
you stomped on the edges of rivers and rain puddles
and watched bugs walk across the skin of water.
The desert was a far-off dream.
When you move in,
you stand in your parents' backyard,
tilt your head back,
and watch the wind blow dust
across your new sky.
Your mother comes up behind you,
jokes that it looks just like the end times.

When you're eight,
your first drought starts,
and the governor tells restaurants
to stop serving water.
Your father takes you up
to the reservoir
to point out the bathtub rings climbing the valley wall.
That night, your mother reads *Revelation*
out loud after dinner.
She raises her eyebrows specifically at you.

El Niño years come and go.
When the torrents start,
you ride your bike in the rain
and imagine your body is a dirty flatland,

your pores sucking up moisture.
You stand on the bridge
over the concrete river
and watch the thirty-foot trench fill
and drain off into the Pacific.
In these years, when you dream of *Revelation*,
Death rides a white skiff.

When you move to London
at the age of twenty,
the river becomes your fetish.
You come from a city of salt water,
and everything is fresh here.
It flows through the downtown,
and the misting rain is a constant.
You stare at swirling eddies
until your professors
ask if everything is all right.
When you finally have to move back home,
a tiny masochist part of you finds
a relief you don't discuss.

You spend your adulthood trying to move away,
but at cocktail parties and coffee houses
in distant cities,
no one understands you, not really.
They like you
but can tell you're off
even though you don't talk about water.
The drought has moved inside of you
as it has with everyone else in the city.
You carry its lack with you,
the way you carry
your mother's dreams of the end of the world.

T.m. Lawson


## droughtfall

> A hike through the Santa Monica mountains to a well-known
> watering hole

a journey through thistles, through brambles, to come to a wall
        of stone; where
had the water gone? I touched the trickle left behind, the dried moss
        on rock
and the stagnant water pooled below like blood; where had
        the water
gone? I looked at the abandoned swing over the shrunken pool,
wood wilting on the rope; where had the water gone? I knelt
down in the dry riverbed, crushing the silken dirt; where
had the water gone? The other visitors gazed on
the waterfall's dust; Santa Monica, forgive us
—where did the fall go? Did the water run?

Robert Hass

## Abbotts Lagoon: October

The first thing that is apt to raise your eyes
Above the dove-gray and silvery thickets
Of lupine and coyote bush and artichoke thistle
On the sandy, winding path from the parking lot
To the beach at Abbotts Lagoon is the white flash
Of the marsh hawk's rump as it skims low
Over the coastal scrub. White-crowned sparrows,
Loud in the lupine even in October, even
In the drizzly rain, startle and disappear.
The bush rabbits freeze, then bolt and disappear,
And the burbling songs and clucks of the quail
That you may not even have noticed you were noticing
Go mute and you are there in October and the rain,
And the hawk soars past, first hawk, then shadow
Of a hawk, not much shadow in the rain, low sun
Silvering through clouds a little to the west.
It's almost sundown. And this is the new weather
At the beginning of the middle of the California fall
When a rain puts an end to the long sweet days
Of our September when the skies are clear, days mild,
And the roots of the plants have gripped down
Into the five or six month drought, have licked
All the moisture they are going to lick
From the summer fogs, and it is very good to be walking
Because you can almost hear the earth sigh
As it sucks up the rain, here where mid-October
Is the beginning of winter which is the beginning
Of a spring greening, as if the sound you are hearing
Is spring and winter lying down in one another's arms
Under the hawk's shadow among the coastal scrub,
Ocean in the distance and the faintest sound of surf
And a few egrets, bright white, working the reeds
At the water's edge in October in the rain.

Bonnie Mosse

## San Elijo Lagoon
September 11, 2016

An hour before sunset
a lone white egret
straightens his neck over the water.
He watches for a fish to wash by
with the rising tide.
I wait a while with him.

Alongside the causeway
that leads into the middle of the lagoon,
an even series of ripples
moves against incoming waters—
the wake of an unseen creature.

A tall tan curlew,
with feather-brushed dark markings,
pokes his long, curved bill
into the muddy shallows
brings up wriggling prey
ingests it with a swift gulp.

From the corner of my eye
I catch the egret crossing low
over the lagoon,
then his dignified upright landing.

Four small sandpipers
forage among muddy islands.
A brown duck in off-season plumage
cruises into their midst. They scatter.

From weighing down a tall sedge blade,
a small black bird suddenly darts
over the water into the grasses
—pursuing prey, watching a nest?

Walking east, I see a shaggy hawk
in stone-like profile
talons wrapped over branches
of a gray-dead tree.

Overhead the egret commutes westward
toward a yellow-orange sun
as it slides into the ocean
through gray-blue ribbon drifts of cloud.
Two ducks, arrowheads extended in flight, follow.

The chattering chaparral quiets.
Colors recede into silhouettes
backlit by the mauve dusk.

As I pass by to leave,
rapid flapping stirs the brush,
a flock of small birds flees to the hillside.
I imagine one looks back over his wing
calling out, Why are you still here?

Stephen Meadows

## Waterhole

A reedy place
full of grasses
and tules
fronded
toad colored
by the bay's
curved edge
ancestors
accustomed to moist
pliant ground
came down
the long swale
for their water
a day at a time
stepping soft
in the wet mud
knowing
they would slip
just a little

Richard Michael Levine


## Turning Seventy at a B&B on Clear Lake

Suppose for a moment I hadn't turned seventy that day
And the jagged hills didn't monitor my heart
Nor the grebes on the lake float their separate ways.

Lost friends and lovers flitted through my mind
Like the yellow-bellied warblers in the sedge.
Suppose for a moment I hadn't turned seventy that day.

I was reading a book about Caravaggio
Short-lived sinner/saint of light and shadow
As the grebes on the lake fluttered their separate ways.

Then two of the birds paired off, their fluid necks
And pressed breasts forming a heart that soothed my own.
Suppose for a moment I hadn't turned seventy that day.

My wife and I held hands and stared in wonder
As the mates dove down for some grass to offer each other
While the rest of the grebes floated their separate ways.

They rose to their feet and skied off together so fast
And so far they left a wake of winking water.
Suppose for a moment I hadn't turned seventy that day
And seen the grebes on the lake dance away.

Iris Jamahl Dunkle

## *The Laguna de Santa Rosa, Prelude*

Begin by walking the cracked, chamomile-paths.
Let the path stretch across a wide stubbed field.
Fill the air with the sounds of birds.
Fill the air with fat bees and the machine hum of insects.
Post appropriate markers that mark miles but not the whole truth.

Try to contain the fissures of time in each quick step.
When you walk under the lone oak that constellates the field like
the last visible star, smell smoke. See the ghosts of hundreds
of other thick oak trunks that once crowded this space.
Hear their lost leaves whispering.

When you reach the man-made lake constructed to replace
the natural lake, walk the perimeter.
Observe the cattails that cage the floating bodies of seven white
pelicans that have stopped here to rest on route back to the sea.

Look out across the drought-dry field and imagine
a chain of hundreds of lakes linking their way back to the sea.
Drain them for the good soil underneath.
Fill them with soot.
Fill them again with feces and urine.
Cover what's left of them in brambles.
Get tangled in the sticky blood of berry juice.

And when you near the last of the water, the floating pontoon
bridge, and the sounds of children playing baseball in the dirt
on the chalked diamond, let a red snake T-bone the trail.

Let it open in you a wound that, at its center, is a mouth.

Iris Jamahl Dunkle

## Lake Jonive

The largest of the lakes were made into
resorts. There are photographs of young
women with parasols, sitting erect
in boats afloat on the large lakes; wooden
docks where bodies hang and thread arms against
a weightless dark. All was for the taking.
Until 1895 there was great
bounty and no limits. Any man could
pull a hundred fish from the Laguna's
chain of lakes. San Francisco was hungry
for fresh game. A bushel of mallard ducks
brought a gold nugget. For those who stayed to
farm, lakes on their land became land reclaimed:
drained for the rich soil that waited underneath.

## Laguna as Sebastopol's Sewer, 1906

As the town grew, so did the waste. Buildings,
still sticky with pine sap, were built in a day.

Hope packed incoming train cars from San Francisco.
Soon, Sebastopol became known not only for its soil
and plentiful game but also for its smell.
Raw sewage filled street culverts, and dripped from
gutters, until sickness descended.
City officials were pressured to find a quick solution
and giant cesspools were dug out and filled
with all of the waste Sebastopol had to offer:

urine, feces, apple skins and cores,
animal remnants from the tannery,
peach skins and pits, rusted cans and broken bottles,
even the giant skeletons of cars.
All piled up. Formed a dam between
what was waste and what was not—
time circling the Laguna
in the body of a white egret
waiting for a chance to land.


## Moon Over Laguna de Santa Rosa

A rueful moon drifts over Laguna de Santa Rosa tonight—
river that flows both ways carrying history heavy on its back.

Those who first recorded what they saw were in awe
of the wooded plain, ripe with water and animal life.
But change was quick and drastic. First, the cattle ranchers
cleared and burned the live oaks leaving their blackened bodies

to girdle the golden tule fields. Then, the Gold Rush
increased the price of game—white and gray geese, ducks,

deer, antelope, elk, even the few grizzlies that had survived
were caught and sold on the docks of the Petaluma River.
The remaining oaks split and corded, or reduced to charcoal.
Then, channels were dug to drain the cattle farms. Then,
the sewage ponds dug and filled.
Today, the moon hangs low in the sky. Not full, just a fingernail
illuminating a single path back, past the remaining oaks,
        past forgetting.

Iris Jamahl Dunkle

## The Nature of the Place

> The nature of the place—whether high or low, moist or dry,
> whether sloping north or south, or bearing tall trees or low
> shrubs—generally gives hint as to its inhabitants.
> —John James Audubon

Today, on the Laguna, one can still see
the shock of a white, plumed body
punctuate the space between raw, golden field,
and the open question of sky
because somehow, the great egret, the snowy egret
and the cattle egret have survived.

Once, the Laguna pulsed as the heart of the plume trade.
Desperate hunters climbed high into scrub oaks and willows
to raid the egrets' giant stick nests
for *aigrettes*, white waterfalls of long, thin feathers
used to adorn fashionable hats
because an ounce of feathers was worth
double the price of gold.
Soon, spotting an egret became so rare
sightings were printed in the local paper.

Until the Audubon Society was formed
to rescue these ghost birds from extinction,
to slow the pulse of plume trade, so slowly
the egrets numbers could begin to rise.

But, the nature of the place—
the lack of steelhead and salmon
swimming in the deep, green lagoons,
the felled oaks and cleared willows,
the waters gone thick with sediment—

tell the story of its inhabitants
not just of the birds, but of us.
We are stewards to the destruction
we've caused forever.
So when you walk the smooth paths of the Laguna today
and sight the white arrow of an egret piercing
the camouflage among what is water, earth, and sky
remember the hunt that still pushes from the ground up,
and how beauty must survive.


## The 100 Year Flood, 1986

> But people are like that about natural disasters. Everyone
> believes that the history of any place began the day they arrived.
> —Gaye LeBaron

Memory is as uncertain as islands
that rise in a flood—you don't know what lurks
underneath. A silver boat can split this
seam of water: even gone muddy, gone
untold for so long. Disasters rise and stay
like high water marks in the unconscious
and each day after is checked against it.
*What do we have to fear? The worst already
happened, couldn't happen again.*

But the river, like a muscular animal,
overtakes the banks, chews up asphalt, rises
more to fill stores and homes. Until
the whole Russian River Valley is filled
with her muddy, pulsing body
regardless of what history you remember.

Joan Gelfand

## Russian River Watershed

Russian River floods, then trickles
Rushes, ebbs sprung
From Mayacamas
Through ashen haze
Flows west, always west.

Until the day word spreads:
Volcanic soil makes very good grapes.
And, the best news? They sell
Higher than Pink Ladies, Braeburns,
Gravensteins, Warren, or Taylor's Gold.

Vineyards.

Apple trees topple like mown weeds
Their imperfect limbs ripe with rosy fruit
Luscious walnuts, apricots, plums
Pears and figs enough for all plowed.
Northern California tills as the world
Clamors for Cabernet, Pinot Noir.
Farmers gird for a second Gold Rush.

Vineyards.

Trees pulled as fast as oil spilled
From southern deserts,
As violently as veins were mined.
Merlot, Chardonnay, Sauvignon Blanc
Replace apple's knobby arms, the shady glen.

Who's to sip this pricey lode?

Blue-black oak-studded hills fade
Replaced by purple grapes hanging ripe.
Scatter them. They matter to birds
And children and all of us
Craving sustenance.

Jacob Minasian

## Wine Country

History is written out of itself.
The Napa River spins, crosshatched
in the December wind. Scintilla
sitting on a timeline's shore. A blue
heron wings wide from its jutting
riverside roots. Sandpipers
feathering through puddled
mud. Loons dip their heads in
reflection, and the homes of swallows
stucco a bridge as I pass underneath.
Barbecue and gelato line banks
where bars and jails arrived before,
living arranged so minorities flooded
first, down in a channel now filled in
to forget. Bright buildings hide the
hangman's rope. My kayak cuts
across surface. My oars source rings.
History is written out of itself.
A lichen rust on tree metal.

Susan Kelly-DeWitt

## Flood Plain

A mile from here the levee holds
back the Sacramento's rushing
tons; no oil slick of sun floats
where it coils in its depths.

This valley was all water once,
a rich inland soup of sea,
a tidal broth. The river wants
to reclaim it—

the shiny tract houses, those
debtors in arrears, that line
the lanes and cul-de-sacs
like coins lining an ancient purse.

It wants to snap the purse shut.
It wants a return to the old flesh-
eating rituals. Don't let the heart-
shaped leaves of the cottonwoods

planted so fluidly in rows fool
you as they sift the morning light
along the levee; as they blossom
with branches of swallows and lift

your weary spirit with their jitter
of birdsong and green shimmer—
they have nothing to do with that
other cold heart, the river. Time

to grow gills or gull wings, walker—
learn the jackknife, half-twist, pike.

Susan Kelly-DeWitt


*Valentine*

All winter the earth
was this dark, wet

envelope. The tides
rose, receded, rose

receded...
The river took

a long time
to say what it needed.

The water was the color
of oolong tea, mixed

with a little dirty milk.
The city and all its fortified

levees were only cracked
vessels that could not

hold it. The rush
of current broke

free, swallowing
people, cattle, houses,

trees. Now this
delicate fringe of redbud

blossoms lacing
the river's dry edges—

Jacqueline Marcus

## *Waiting for Winter Rains*

When the sun lit the leaves of late autumn,
the trees were unprepared for a long winter drought,
fields, hungry for water, absorbed what they could
in the dark hour of the sea.
Lack of rain left the herons homeless.
The pond dried up like a bowl of wind.
The pines contemplated the weather.
There was a silence that reigned among the birds
not easily translatable, some kind of warning
where tides rise above the estuary.

Kathleen McClung

## Gualala Winter

Keep dreaming of gray deer asleep in woods
as sheets of rain claim every living thing—
tailor bees, bracelet cones, chipmunks, hawk broods
high up in nests that sway but last. Each wing,
leaf, stem of fern—soaked through, wet to the core—
endures these January storms we track,
evade behind our screens, our twice-locked doors.
Nervous, we curse old roofs, new leaks. Come back.
Mend quietly what's torn. Listen to wind.
Confuse it with Pacific surf close by,
cars crossing flooded roads. Gray deer may find
logs hollowed out, may curl inside, stay mostly dry
under mossed bark. Or not. Our sun will rise,
night storms will end. We animals open our eyes.

# VII

# Sierra Nevada and Cascades

to save the griz
            is to save ourselves
from what we've made
    —Eric Paul Shaffer, "Dreaming Back the Griz"

It is seductive, here in the wilderness, to believe
        in revelation.
The lake speaks to me at night, the granite murmurs,
the fire cracks and whistles its prophecies.
    —Dane Cervine, "The Only Truth I Know"

Robert Hass

## To Be Accompanied by Flute and Zither

We live on a coastal hill with a view west onto a bay, a mountain, a rust-gold bridge, and the sea beyond them. There are several sleeping islands on the bay, dark with chaparral,

And east of us in summer gold hills of wild grasses with a scattering of oaks on the hillsides a green so dark they are almost blue, and with madrone and laurel in the canyons,

And east of those trees a wide valley, hot and flat, the remnant bed of torrential glacial rivers, once an immense lake, and then a bog and then a meadow so thick with wildflowers in the late spring you could hear the bee-hum before you crested the Coast Range hills to look down on it, colors so thick and variegated that they seemed to be breathing,

Breathing, O Elysium, and now farm country mostly, industrial farming, with a strong smell of onion fields in summer, and river towns along the sloughs, and an endless rosary of shopping malls built to collapse in a generation or so, with parking lots full of empty cars and car windshields glittering in the midday heat,

And east of the valley the slow rise of red earth foothills, oakwood giving way to pine, and then a gradual climb seven thousand feet to the mountain massif of glacier-carved granite, mountain lakes blue-green with snow melt, and lodgepole pine, Jeffrey pine, sugar pine, incense cedar forests that smell of pine sap and pineapple and the scintillant high mountain air and, even in summer, snow patches in the saddles between peaks,

And among the cols and tarns of the mountain escarpment, O my love, there are immense lakes turquoise blue to the depths, with emerald green at the deeper shorelines, and small lakes, ice-blue in the afternoon when the sky clouds up, and small meadow valleys that must once have been lakes, long ago, where small streams splash down a canyon, some small Squaw Creek to water a meadow, a ski resort now, a bit indolent and full of tourists in shorts in the summer,

But there are paths out of that valley under the pines, the loud jays of the mountains squawking and squawking, and scarlet gilia with their little trumpet flowers and the dangling intricate red and gold flower of the columbine, and red also for Indian paintbrush,

Because the mountain is kind to hummingbirds, which can see red as the bees can't, and for the bees the brilliant blue of the larkspur and the fuzzy soiled white of pearly everlasting, and for everyone the bright yellow monkey flower that likes the spray of plunging water,

It breathes well there, breathes, O beloved, and that may be us standing in the trail above it under the sheered granite, you among buckbrush and huckleberry oak with the field guide in hand naming the flowers—

Have you noticed that this is an anniversary poem? and a medicine bundle for the hard stretches when we carry what we've glimpsed into the grinding days down the trail there which we'll be walking, muscles a little sore, as that breeze comes up and gives its lightness to the summer air.

James Toupin

## *Saturday, Midsummer 2010. Driving 80 Eastward.*

To come again into these mountains,
riding the freeway's magic carpet macadam,
is to reenter a terrain of pasts—
manicured forests whose trim tops
overgrow and recall the scars of fire and use,
rock sheered at road cuts insisting
on the other age the range has risen,
road crossings disclosing rails that hardship
and ingenuity worked through rock,
sign posts to places that mined played-out hopes,
routes of pioneer starvations.

All times incommensurate...
I do not know if he made his way
inland, our first San Franciscan,
who crossed oceans to be written down
as street peddler in that first census,
merchant ten years later, picking
a living out of gold's afterthought.
The mountains, to his offspring in
the coast's gray, seemed as far away
as the main chance to a wage earner,
or wages to a child let loose to play.

But one week a year we ventured the trip
into needle-forest altitudes.
What stopped us midway, years running,
can now only be reconstructed.
The freeway, unfinished, deposited
the high-speed traffic into redlight-greenlight

stop-and-go and, of course, our car,
and parents' tempers with it,
boiled over in trapped valley heat,
a last more vivid upsurge of
the day-to-day before the week's retreat.

The transient tan of leisure attained,
the banker's allotted loss sustained,
we would make our way back on schedule.
Somehow, heading home, we never broke down,
as if the car, before we could, were a horse
scenting its stable. We did feel it, in our time,
before water was sighted, the cooling air to which
we were glad to return, into the days of
"fog near the ocean extending inland
night and morning," where we, near the ocean,
gave no thought to an elsewhere.

Now I am the only one remaining
to report himself this year of census.
Decades removed, car rented,
I have driven into the mountains.
The interstate swept through the halfway city,
a skimmed landscape of signs and roofs,
as the adamant future bypasses,
though I cannot, those vanished lives.
I must not think the playing work
that lays these lines could construct
causeways through the impassable.

J. C. Olander

## Sierra Foothill Birding

Rufous-sided towhee's quizzical—
  cool man!
Solid rock kicker
  digs detritus deep
    feather flash jig-dance-scratch
  six kick out sticks, yea!
Under bush
  up wet, slippery slopes—
    slips into
  seed nursery's paradise
gets down in roots, man—
  in blue, black, live oak
    dig it!
Listens to insects:
  springtails and the mulch munchers
hoe down at the root ball—Yea!

Nine golden-crowned sparrows
  align sticks
    stacked angles
  in brush pile—fat
fluff wind ruffles—
  flock over leftovers
    over all ground—
everywhere!

Large live oak umbrellas
  early morning glow puddles
    on gravel driveway—
Two Steller's jays squawk-squack
  migrants of pine forest
    east of here

make winter residents'
   acorn pickings good—
Four scrub jays squeeeech-squawk
   back yaks and yaks-yaks-yaks-attacks!
Even resent tourists
   taking acorns:
picked crackerjacks
   at gravel pools
      in leaves and silt
         soft shelled, swelled
leached—
   edible acorns.

Anarchy's anarchists
   in red-capped
      harlequin masquerades!
Hey, acorn woodpeckers
   three, dart down
      perform panache chatter raps
         between yacks
snatch up snacks
   checker flight
      black-white
         back-forth
elevating acorn stock
   in tall snagged gray pine
      cache stash!

Gary Snyder

## The Canyon Wren

I look up at the cliffs
but we're swept on by downriver
the rafts
wobble and slide over roils of water
boulders shimmer
under the arching stream
rock walls straight up on both sides.
A hawk cuts across that narrow sky hit by sun,

we paddle forward, backstroke, turn,
spinning through eddies and waves
stairsteps of churning whitewater.
Above the roar
hear the song of a Canyon Wren.

A smooth stretch, drifting and resting.
Hear it again, delicate downward song

ti ti ti ti tee tee tee

descending through ancient beds.
A single female mallard flies upstream—

Shooting the Hundred-Pace Rapids
Su Tung P'o saw, for a moment,
it all stand still.
"I stare at the water:
it moves with unspeakable slowness."

Dogen, writing at midnight,
"mountains flow

water is the palace of the dragon
it does not flow away."

We beach up at China Camp
between piles of stone
stacked there by black-haired miners,
cool in the dark
sleep all night long by the stream.

These songs that are here and gone,
here and gone,
to purify our ears.

Stephen Meadows

## *Drought*

Hot breath
on lupine
on sizzling
Sierra
parched grass
the seed pods
tick soft
in slow wind
on the skittle
this summer
madrones
are bright
yellow
ponderosa
brown needles
low water
sucks
the stone

Stephanie Noble

## In This Land of Wind and Tinder

My scoop of ice cream crowned with a curl of black ash
drifted down from the forest fire fifteen miles away.

Cafe owner says 14,000 acres burned so far today.
Next morning 44,000, uncontained, heading this way.

Ranger says to evacuate, so we pack up and
drive down through smokey Angels Camp where

we pass fire engines from the southern cities
of Indio and Palm Desert rushing to aid.

Achy heart holds them tender
in this land of wind and tinder.

Next day at home, again a fiery red sun:
to our north Middletown burns to the ground.

Along with my donation I send blessings
in this land of wind and tinder

where the oaks and laurels on our hillside
go almost yellow with the strain

and I pray for calm air and rain
in this land of wind and tinder.

Ruth Nolan

## Mopping Up

It's the most unraveled and well-paying job I've had, fighting fires in far-flung, fiery wilderness areas all the way from the San Bernardino National Forest to the Panamint Mountains near Death Valley, the Southern Sierra close to Yosemite, the San Gabriels looming above L.A.

Most of the time, I was the only girl on the crew, cutting fireline and sucking down smoke, and after a fire had laid down across ravaged meadows and once-forested slopes, our job was far from done.

We hiked in baked-potato-hot, ankle-deep ash that blew eerily in the wind like shed snakeskins to finish off dying wildfires by stirring and cooling the molten detritus with the sharpened shovels. To finish the job, we sprayed dribbles of water from the fat bags that sloshed like heavy vertigo on our backs.

We struggled to keep pace in the slowed-down underbelly of burned-up things in cherished, if little known, Golden State geographies with lonely names: Rattlesnake Mountain, Horse Thief Spring, Last Chance Range, Toro Peak.

Above us, the whispered remains of familiar forest trees, lurking black and tall and jagged, stripped of the dignity of their given names: Jeffrey pines, ponderosas, Western sequoias, California black oaks. At our feet, the complete bequeathing of the ladder fuels: Manzanita. Western juniper. Coyote brush. Poison oak.

We could never be sure the fire was completely out, so we stirred ash, sifted through what had been scorched and watched each unearthed ember spark hot and red, then whoosh unto its puffy last breath.

This is what I remember most vividly from my firefighting days: the mopping up. Making sure the fire was put to bed. Soothing the feverish brow of forsaken landscapes to cool them down. That, and how often the guys on the crew asked me why I'd left behind the apron of my domesticity to flirt with flames instead of them.

Tom Goff

## *The Work of the Monitor*

Malakoff Diggins State Park, California

This side of a twisted manzanita gorge
the monitors once forced wild mountain runoff
through blunt iron nozzles. Water blasts dislodged
cliffsides' impacted gravel: ridges torn off:
tons of rock, ounces of gold. That wide red ledge,
hawks' eyrie, rootwoven earth and sapling, shorn off.
One miner's one-day's work could silt or sludge
whole rivers to swollen. Now the noon sun, flung off
spurs of eroded granite, stuns, bruises our eyes.
That faded museum video displayed the device:
The last of the aqua-cannons, filmed still roaring
its water-breathing-dragon act, keeps pouring
pummeling imprecation through its snout.
Most of the rock's gold fire's long since put out.

Karen Greenbaum-Maya

## Long Lake Blues

So obvious, my discovery:
postcard Mediterranean
and glacier deeps
light up the same blue.

Glaciers loom ancient, yet only recent
as Lascaux bison stampeding on stone,
ice ages still piling and ebbing,
futures our bodies try to remember.

This year, two miles into mountains,
nothing but the drift of sun-dried scree.
Thirty years back, I'd stopped
and stepped over the shoulder
right onto a glacier's latest snow,

soaked in that blue made of air
fled from cities, lakes, lungs.
Outside turned inward,
most private blue on earth.

I'd filled my hand with water,
a gift. I lifted, I sipped.
Blue so pure it lit me up
as though I'd gulped a star.

Ken Haas

## *Birthday Poem*
### Truckee, California

This year's has fallen
on the day heaped snow
is slipping wholesale from pines
by dint of earth's mood and spin,
as when something that is meant
to happen sometime
happens now.

White pads tip off in sheets,
chunks quit their cradles,
then a pause, after which
more concert of mists,
tails and stag cascades,
old trunk knots and bark nobs
fleeced, branches freed
by the same law that bowed them.

How still life must stand
to animate the cold,
hold for a while the sky come down
then let it fall again
to suckle the root,
turning frost back to forest,
as if these were still
last year's woods.

Eric Paul Shaffer


## Dreaming Back the Griz

A song for Doug Peacock

The deer and all the other animals move through
with the exception of the grizzly bear; grizzlies
are now extinct in California. We dream sometimes
of bringing them back.
    —Gary Snyder


a griz 8 feet from the lens
            scares you
                        less
than the auditorium
                full of us come to see
a man who claims standing on the hood of his pickup
in Manhattan
            seeking the North Star
for direction to his hotel and drink
                                before running
            the bear film tonight

        "My film is not a film.
                        It's just a bunch of footage."


Tonight, you bring along the bottle,
and I'm damned
                if you don't drink the whole fifth
                                in front of us
        while your film runs
                        your voice through the dark

        "I call this guy 'Happy Bear.'
                            Always playing.
            One of the happiest critters I ever saw."

bear on his back in a green pond
                          ice in paws
            over his head looking at himself

sniffing griz scat
                          bursting
            into a stiff-legged spinning
dance of recognition

thrusting his head
            into the ribcage of elk
                          shouldering the earth
reveling in the smell of rebirth

the griz dances over our heads
                          in the dark
      a dream we all consent
                          to dream together
            of a return to wilderness
            we would recall
                          California

the footage runs out
                  the bears gone
now in complete darkness
            voice steady in the buzz
                          of the projector
            you speak

      "Well, that's it.
                  Except—remember
      to save the griz
                  is to save ourselves
      from what we've made.
                          Griz is
            what we've lost.
      You can turn
                  the lights on now."

Dane Cervine

## The Only Truth I Know

Dan and I with throats burned dry and souls that cry
For water, cool...clear...water.
—Folk hymn

I open the door to the outhouse in the Sierras,
find a Jehovah's Witness *Watchtower* perched on wooden beam.
With the forest in front of me, I sit, turn the pages,
read of God's plan, the end times, remember
that sense of mission, of surety, as a boy
when all I needed to know was in that one black book.
It is seductive, here in the wilderness, to believe in revelation.
The lake speaks to me at night, the granite murmurs,
the fire cracks and whistles its prophecies.
But the young ranger, who speaks reverently
of the hungry bear roaming these woods,
says it had to be put down. It wasn't afraid
enough of humans. I am afraid,

which is why I love the woods. For a moment,
forgetting politicians who believe in Armageddon,
the ideologues who are happy to oblige, trigger-happy cowboys
of every ilk staring towards the horizon, revelation
gleaming in their eyes, fingering destiny. Absolute surety.
It is a feeling I would give almost anything

to regain. Place the pamphlet, instead, back on its perch,
hike back to the lake's edge, remove my clothes,
stand naked to the only truth I know.
Jump into water so cold, so clear.

Joyce Schmid

## At the Treeline

We've talked before.
But suddenly, tonight,
your words go lucent
and I find myself inside
your wilderness, at Echo Lake.

This lake, as ice,
once carved a glacial bed,
then melted into it
and gathered cozy clouds
to make a nest to tempt the sun.

We take a small canoe
among the trees
that glimmer by us,
and we come to ground again,
in needled stands

of scraggly lodgepole pines
inhabiting the soggy earth
where other species drown.
We walk on slabs of rock
where Jeffrey pines and red Sierra junipers

absorb their life from stone.
We scramble over granite, over scree,
to hike this stark moraine.
You have allowed me this, your wild terrain,
and I melt into it, amazed.

Mary B. Moore

## Rock Is the Premise

      these ancient pines stand
on and for. Mother sun flare

and father ice-blow bend, warp
and singe them. Lightning hones

them; they're toothed, fire-blackened,
like Lear's ruined diadem.

But even so, the stumps
bear blue-green needles in

bundles like hardy stars,
jagged points of faith and resistance.

      Quartz spark, mica glint,
sunlight flickers off rock;

even those that staying
stains and rusts with lichen

craze in sun and split when ice
calcifies here: granite's

salt-and-pepper look
scatters;

whole talus-slopes
skitter down-creek to make of havoc

waterfall ledges April
run-off leaps and quarries.

      The lake quakes in its Alpine
bowl, since sky's azure

balm and earth's under-fire
both house boom and rage.

But in summer sun, the lake's
all turquoise shallows

and fjord-blue pools.
And the way wind chevrons

lake-wide ripples, a skin
of slippage over larger, tidal moves,

moon-pull's lapse and surge,
testifies: nothing's still.

      Imagine its depths:
Whole cities, boulder built;

rock-jumble piers;
transparent fish with stars

for teeth; dinosaur-bone
ship hulls; spars of pin oak,

Bristol pine. It stores molecules
of air millennia cold.

Surfacing then, you'd find
the land-bound house-huge

boulders no surprise,
nor granite stairs climbed by

ice-bonzaied Jeffrey pines.

       The casinos, neon-signed
all-night ladders of lit cubes,

can't displace the lake's
hoard of sapphire, starred

even by day. Besides, space
is no mere dome, abstracted,

cut from different rock;
it's only as blue, as chill

as the lake whose maker
slaked the ache for shape

with quartz, fire, ice.

                 *Lake Tahoe, California*

Ann Fisher-Wirth

## Light. Olympic Valley, California

In memory of Zdenek Sirovy

You bring your grief to the mountain. Lay it down.
The shaggy mules'-ears dance in this clear light
and the shadow of each long leaf joins in the dancing.

Blue lupine, speckled alyssum
sending off sugar and heat, the poppies' furling gold—

what do they know of desolation? How could the ragged daisies
stop plunging in the wind,
or dust and day relinquish their bright unfolding?

The pine mat manzanita, low mariposa lily,
a junco's click and trill,

or that skinny brown horse in the stableyard,
one ear cocked,
softly whickering, shifting his haunches,

and all the light you will ever need.

Heidi M. Sheridan


## Sequoia National Park, California

The tops of sequoia hide in the mist,
so I look at one's fire scar, that hollowed
center. How do they grow, even weakened,
for centuries?  Do they have bad days?
I want to change my life before
another snowstorm hits the Sierra Nevada.
River hike a fork of Kern River or
sleep in the mountains surrounding me.
I want to do it with someone else.

But now it is Tuesday, and I'm back from the park.
What of hibiscus and fuchsia?
Will the hydrangeas and the new myrtle
make it past September? Of my mini-fruit trees,
one orange grew in New Jersey, four limes,
many lemons. All taken into the sunroom now.

And then it's all moss and shadows again.
Time. Explosions. Logging leaves stumps
bigger than cars or pools. Now,
I understand the power of passivity.
Last week, a sequoia fell across a major access trail.
No one knew what to do. Build a bridge
over it? Cut a hole through it? Go around?
The sequoia's bark even resists fire.
How do we start if we begin with fear?
So much taller than me, soft yet splintery.
If you pull bark off you can see its blood sap.

Rebecca Foust

## *Seeds of the Giant Sequoia*

come cone borne, encased
in diamond-hard coats;
something secreted
encrypts them against
climate and time,
lets them wait out
the cold-ground
generations of winters
for that lightning-crack
thunderbolt trunk-split of fire
to fissure them to life.

Dull glitter of years
layering down.
But when the firestorm
comes, the ground melts
and boils like stew,
swells each seed
from germ to koan,
seeks meaning
from rain, memory
from pain, how it feels
to feel anything.

John Brantingham

## *Up on Whitney*

From up here,
you can see out across to the next state
and who knows
maybe the state after that too.
You look over Owens Valley,
which was once a lake,
and Death Valley,
which was once a sea,
toward the Petrified Forest.
It's there somewhere
either that little piece
of tan desert in a world gone tan
or just the other side of the curve of the earth
where the ozone
has grayed out our eyes.

All this life, not gone but changed
from seas and forests into deserts,
but life is always there,
and you realize
that the ancient forest
is really a creeping thing
climbing now over the range,
a giant creature that's
amusing itself here for now,
waiting for the Ice Age to begin again,
so it can cross back to Russia
and play with its old friends
who are wandering
through Asia or Europe.

For these millennia, it's content to slide down
this massive mountain,
to ride the wave of erosion
and have its tectonic fun.


## Alta Peak

This year, I was likely the last person
to hike up to the peak.
I came down on a Tuesday,
and it filled with snow on Wednesday,

and that summer world is gone
for nine months of ice.
Up there, it's winter most of the year,
a winter that no one will ever know

because it's too steep and too high
and the foxtail pines stand lonely
for thousands of years
in their secret world.

I think about that cave
up above the trail
that I climbed to
and was tempted to enter.

It was maybe four feet high
and the blackness just past the opening
looked deep somehow
and maybe it was.

If I were a different kind of person,
I would have crossed into it,

but I thought about Plato,
and I didn't want to be chained up,

and also there might be a mountain lion,
and then I was sure that one
was watching me
even though I don't think they like caves,

but once an idea like that
is in my head, it's stuck,
and I imagined a giant cavern system
where I would be chained toward a wall

and pumas would stalk
behind me throwing shade.
That whole invisible world of my mind
is buried in six feet of snow now,

and that cave, which is unknowable,
is even more unknowable in the high-altitude winter
that begins this year in September
and that is the beauty of everything, isn't it?

Dreams of the deep caves
of this world are as real
and as accurate
as my imagination

of what life among the foxtails
must be right now.
It's all one thing now,
and it will stay that way until summer.

Tasha Cotter

## Solar

For Mom

Disregard the glittering iced coffees, bought on the golden chain
highway. The world, back then, was hot. A hundred degrees by
mid-afternoon, you locked the pool. Locked the door. Took a
wrong turn toward Oakhurst and circled back. Pointed out the
mule deer eating what remained of the Nevada blue-eyed grass
in what remained of California in its four-year drought. Tuesday
was Half Dome. Wednesday was Mariposa Grove, where a circle of
sequoias stood in prayer deep in the sanctuary of Yosemite. *This
is the last thing we'll ever do together*, you said. And so I defied the
bucking yellow-tinged landscape. Braved the white-hot mesas and
blistering heat. We stood at Glacier Point, Curry Village at our feet.
I was thinking about the solar panels on the property, arranged in
careful tiers, the occasional square spectrum of black nests on the
ranch. How, at first, I didn't know what I'd been looking at. I saw
them and then I stopped seeing them. Days passed. I thought they
were bleachers. *That's what powers this place*, you said. *The sunlight
feeds the place we've been living in.* We stood there, our heads drifting
to the blood-orange horizon. I want to be back on the light-buff
granite, staring down the side of a mountain.

Susan Gubernat

## *Yosemite*

A coyote, many deer came.
But the bear never appeared.
How I longed to see his face,

the dumb muzzle; feel
a paw land on my head
—the heavy priest's

in absolution, then my skull
torn open, orange peel
scattered on the trail.

Shelled, unshelled, what
mattered to the Steller's jays
was what we laid out

near the creek that fed
the lake. Caught in the lens:
pert black eyes and head,

feathers raffish—they were punks,
they were church ladies.

Patti Trimble

## Above Isberg Pass

Each summer I am voyager to the unknown meadow
high in wilderness, walking, sailing on that green beloved sea.

My heart spins as a gyroscope along the wide view trail
where river runs from cloud. I must go there in fragile months,

to memorize the flowers as they hang from threads,
blue columbine, cinquefoil, the tiniest of daisies.

I have always thought the sky was trembling and the boulder
shivering for multitudes of gods in search of home.

But now I think they shake in fear of me, as I see behind me
deepening troughs and trails across this Earth I meant to love.

W. F. Lantry

## Tehachapi

Maps fail here. No human hand can draw
the sheer cliff faces of this mountain range
lifted by earthquakes from the desert floor.
Knife edges of cleft granite, wind-honed rock
cutting azure to bands, slicing the core
of sunlight into ribbons, tying strange,
tight labyrinthine knots of figured waves,

prevent all climbing here where light behaves
like water, cresting, breaking, plunging down,
and pooling as moraine along the base
of every mountain, where each granite block,
veined with rose quartz, extends the interlace,
as if a woven fenceline could surround
this cordillera, and there's nothing left

except to walk around it, find a cleft
or find the southern curve, and then turn west,
walking without a shadow, where once gold
lit up earthlines, where coal seams interlock,
as if their layered patterns could enfold
at once the valley floor and distant crest,
and if we trace those lines, if we pursue

the curving seams of anthracite clear through
the convex hills and sunset light, reweave
their patterns through this vineyard's corridor,
as if they shared a single stem's rootstock
but pushed their vines across the veins of ore,
then we could find a passage, and believe
the truth ancient mapmakers, sunblind, saw.

Rafael Jesús González


## Bajo Monte Shasta

Bajo el monte sagrado
cuyas nieves cierran
los Prados de la Pantera,
poniéndose la luna temprana
tras los pinos y los cedros,
las galaxias giran sobre nosotros;
se desprende una estrella
brillante y fugaz.

Somos tan cabales
que ni se nos ocurre
　　　　pedir un deseo.


## Below Mt. Shasta

Below the sacred mountain
whose snows close
Panther Meadows,
the early moon setting
behind the pines & the cedars,
the galaxies spin above us;
a star breaks away
brilliant & fleeting.

We are so complete
it does not even occur to us
　　　　to make a wish.

Lynne Thompson

## Shasta

> Echoes are real—not imaginary.
> We call out—and the land calls back.
> —Terry Tempest Williams, "An Unspoken Hunger"

Even on a hillside covered with narcissus,
day opens its throat
to sing to the constellations: of thunder
and its lover, lightning;
of the wingswoop of a Cooper's hawk.
Every light has its own melody:
dark in places not yet shadowed,
a full palette for the artist who thinks she is
if she could only recall the last time
she told herself that it is true.
Day's song returns again
and again whether or not we listen.
We are calmed by it. We are reminded.

Perhaps you remember the song of Castle Crags
whose granite spires look down on *Úytaahkoo*—
the White Mountain renamed *Shasta*?
The mountain—formed by the fury of a volcano
two hundred million years ago—was the site
(like almost every other whose native name
has been erased) of a battle between inhabitants
and settlers who drove the locals away.

No matter.

If you climb from the trailhead and go through
the mix of pine and fir and cedar, you will pass

Root Creek Trail and its eponymous watery bed.
Climb a little more, a little more. Amble among
boulders, over the flat rocks. Listen for a soft
breeze through manzanita as you gain elevation.
Call out *Úytaahkoo* until nothing's left but the timbre
of voices. Call her name. She will never forget you.

Laurie Klein

## No One Wrings the Air Dry

Burney Falls, California

1

Seeping, like swollen eyelids
behind Burney Falls,
a dozen nests daub the cliff.
Mother Swift is a black knife
thrust sidewise, the maul of water
rent. Shred-by-strand,
her cargo of moss jeweled
by the mist, she stalls
mid-air: Stone Sweet Home,
slicked over with spit.

2

In the streaming darkness
the slow, exacting language of eggs.

3

No lulling pulse, or voice—
chicks in their shells wake
to endless tumult. Pure roar.
Where warmth hovers,
each day's solace is juiced
with spiders and gnats,
bees, beetles. Whatever it takes.

4

Hour by hour, the breached
torrent. The killing cold.

For each shivering life,
she is the preening beak.


5

First hop's a doozy. Readied
for iridescence, her offspring
brave the shock of quiet,
dry air, and daylight. They carry,
from this flight forward, night's
living sheen in their hollow bones.

A. D. Miller

## Apocalypse Is My Garden

The breaking up and down of things

Sitting on a lava block, this rock,
a reminder that other times meant other things.

While farmers in Europe plowed their land,
that was not theirs to waste with ruin,
Lassen erupted and for seven years
the mountain shook.

The world shook.

Europe stayed revolution by starting
a war. What revolution had earth planned?

The mountains just needed to break out,
magma jetted through vents skyward,
plague of flowing stone and fire,
incinerated cedar and redwood,
tephra cone volcanoes,
flaming rocks and mushroom clouds,
house-sized boulders tossed
on Devils Postpile, reshaping
land, raising here, leveling there.

Tehama, an acid factory, burbling
under our feet, sulphur and nitrate explosions,
smell of gray scent, rotten eggs.

Embedded in lava pockets, squirrel scat,
staghorn lichen, seeds and dust.

A rain and something new will grow.

Tobey Hiller

from *Interlope*

*#2 Status Report*

There are no wolves in California.
OR7, the lone wolf tagged in the Wawona Range of NE Oregon,
came down here, or so they say, but left
again for Oregon—what did he know of
all those storytellers hoping for a native
to reappear
despite guns
and poison
and stories
of the little calves
and lambs
picked off
by his Grimm majesty,
the lone wolf?
Dressed to the teeth
in grandma's
bedtime story?

In Wyoming
where we have leavened lèse-majesté
and ignored the vulpine insult
to our flocks and fields,
to release a few
of those gray marauders—
ruthless shepherds
with their Arctic eyes—
back into the wild,
a strange cascade
brought
balance
home:

wolves killed deer,
coyote too:
fewer deer,
more grass & scrub,
some trees
returned,
birds & beavers—
fewer coyote:
more rabbits, foxes
badgers, mice.

And more carrion:
raptors circled,
bears
ambled in.
Beavers built
& willows grew back
along the rivers
which began to
wander proper,
given sand & shallows,
and then
the minnows
found
the shadow eddies
to shelter in:

the fish,
the river,
fields
and forest,
the brother animals,
they need

the toothy one,
the howler,
longtrot gray ghost—
wolf.

*#5 Red*

At first it looks like weather.

Great plumes & fluffs of cumulus—no, white smoke
bellies wide behind Mt. Shasta. Red
haze bleeds up over Mt. Eddy and the Marbles, spreads. It is
a Turner sky, scorched into
dreamy rose.
Below, inferno. Char, flake, ash
blacken the hoods of cars.
Sky billows thick
blushes
and falls
on roof tree bush shoulder barn:
all that waits and runs and stands
here below.
Beyond the ridges,
air baked into
smudge and glue.
Animals run.
Brush darkens
in the crimson, shimmers,
trembles
into cinder.

Roar of fire
tornadoes up the canyons.
Whirled
cauldron. Pines
explode. Nitrogen
flies free.

The West Coast's on fire,
north and south, and we are tinder
prophesied
in this red future's unhoped
—and shall we call it healing?—
breath.

# VIII

## Cities, Towns, and Roads

...I crave the pure,
magnificent, bloody beauty of a smoggy sunset.
—Ruth Bavetta, "Oranges and Pomegranates"

The mountain lives so close to us. Visits us
with eagle and owl, with snake and rabbit;
why not coyote, tonight, in your garden?
—T.m. Lawson, "Brentwood Coyotes"

Jane Hirshfield

## Today, Another Universe

The arborist has determined:
senescence      beetles      canker
quickened by drought
                                          but in any case
not prunable    not treatable    not to be propped.

And so.

The branch from which the sharp-shinned hawks and their
        mate-cries.

The trunk where the ant.

The red squirrels' eighty foot playground.

The bark   cambium   pine-sap   cluster of needles.

The Japanese patterns      the ink-net.

The dapple on certain fish.

Today, for some, a universe will vanish.
First noisily,
then just another silence.

The silence of *after*, once the theater has emptied.

Of bewilderment after the glacier,
the species, the star.

Something else, in the scale of quickening things,
will replace it,

this hole of light in the light, the puzzled birds swerving around it.

Jeanne Wagner

## *Prunus Subcordata*

Western native wild plum

The plum trees are effervescing again,
nudging their ruction of buds
too close to my window,
pushing at me with a promiscuous beauty,
ravenous as fire in its own way.
All the visible fissions of nature at work.
I can guess why my neighbor wants me
to cut them down,
the cells in his blood, called blasts,
indecently raging, while he talks about
how the trees draw lightning;
last year an acacia fissured down the center,
exposing what used to be symmetry
into a splay of roots so unseemly
he could barely stand to look.
Now he tells me how I should give
all my plum trees the chop;
they've become too crazy, too rife.
Spring spreading its shrapnel of blossoms,
but in a few months, mark his words,
there'll be wild plums so small
they're passed off as cherries, skin broken
and bitter-sweet,
their juices smearing the deck,
whole families of deer gorging on windfall.

I want to tell him I'll miss the way such fullness
makes the slender limbs loop down.
Trees so rampant with crimson they blaze,

their branches bursting like the shivery plumes
of those fireworks they call *Peony,*
*Ground Bloom, Willow,*
as if even our gardens combust.

Maureen Eppstein

## Calypso Orchid

*Calypso bulbosa*

From a grove of firs on Woodstock Road,
the goddess of hidden places,
bright pink on her tiny stem,
stepped to the verge to greet me.

The next day, orange traffic cones stood guard.
Two trucks hunkered where the lady stood
while workmen felled and dragged fir branches
grown too close to power lines.

I could have yelled at them but did not,
knowing I was complicit
in the ravages we humans undertake
in the name of warmth and shelter.

Today I passed again and marked
the truck wheel's muddy indentation.
Less than an inch away the orchid huddled,
battered but preparing to set seed.

Further in the duff, untouched, a sister
blazed brilliant pink above her oval leaf.
I paused and bowed my head, acknowledging
the grief I felt for being who I am.

Cathy Barber

## *Return*

This is a neighborhood of war streets—
Trenton, West Point, Lexington,
Bunker Hill, Yorktown, Forge.
Here sprinklers fight desiccation.
Brown needles, tinderbox hills, crackling grass.

Suburban, no view of
neighbors in driveways after work.
No outdoor chores,
just weekday Latino crews
with rackety leaf blowers and floppy hats.

This area was wild.
Once there was a fawn cuddled
next to the house, no doe in sight.
Opossums, raccoons and skunks
owned the backyard, peered through
the doors, tiny paws quivering.
Coyotes yammered in the canyon.

Evenings, deer galloped up Lexington,
charged up Tarrytown, took each hill,
destroyed flowers in watered yards—
white and pink impatiens, azaleas.

The coyotes live beyond the highway now,
its tall steel bridge of rumbling autos
that separates humans from open space.
The land preserved but for the paved trail,
and the fence to keep us from reaching the reservoir,

from dipping our cupped hands
into that expanse of water and
taking drink after drink.
From skipping stones and scaring ducks
just for fun,

or crossing, near the three-mile mark,
late in the summer when the last rain was months ago,
the water thoroughly defeated
and a land bridge appears slowly,
like invisible ink heated by a flame.

Cathy Barber

## Scrub Jay

A scrub jay hops near in that low-to-ground
way it has, from branch to fence, walk to dirt,
tossing this and eating that morsel down
in rapid fire shakes, eyes agog, alert

to all, especially me, sweating
at my scraggly garden plot on bent knees,
troweling holes for impatiens, plucking
snails from their hiding spots and pulling weeds.

## The Waiting Season

The waiting season has arrived—
waiting in cars for children to appear
at the end of each day,
waiting for the change that will not come.
Here, in California, leaves stay put, stay green;
the certain rains of winter soon will bolster
their livelihood and their hold.

Five liquidambars bolster me—they live by Eastern rules.
Their leaves darken satisfactorily, predictably,
then clutter the ground and sidewalk.
Their little stick trunks cluster at the
corner by the neighbor's house, against
the backdrop of California oaks and Monterey pines.
I will think of them fondly as
the winter rains sound loudly on the roof
and I wait for respite from the storms.

Lynne Knight

## Small Deer, Small Lilac

Towards dusk I came down to a clatter
on the deck as a deer leaped for
the acanthus border, the back slope.
He'd topped the lilac in the wooden tub.
A small lilac: they don't like it here,
where their roots can't grip enough cold
come winter & their only extravagance
is leaves. Now the leaves were a crown

of mashed tips, saliva. Usually, the deer
go next door, where the neighbor has more
to offer—gentler slopes, with exotic shrubs,
a knoll for sleeping. Maybe our white
plastic deck chairs had looked like
salt licks from there. Maybe if I'd
waited for morning before coming down,
I'd have seen the deer at the patio table,

elegant legs crossed, elegant neck bent over
the morning paper as it sat digesting
the rest of the lilac, star jasmine.
Every green or flowering thing gone.
*Look what you've done!* I could have cried
then, wakening to no deer, no damage.
What relief I would feel—flowers & greens
where they belonged, & you not gone.

Lucille Lang Day

## Naturalists

For Devlin

Two years old, he takes my hand,
leads me to the blackberry vine
growing on the fence in his backyard.

*They're not ripe yet*, he explains,
then points to a small hole
in the earth. *The ants live there.*

*I need a digging stick*, he announces,
holding up a fragile twig and shaking
his head. This one's no good.

I hand him a thicker stick. *Perfect!*
In a shady corner near the patio
he digs and makes a find.

*It's a roly-poly in a ball*, he says.
I hold out my hand to receive
the woodlouse, a terrestrial crustacean.

Gretchen and I called them pill bugs
in first grade when we found them
with ants and Jerusalem crickets.

*Careful!* My grandson warns.
*A pincer bug! It will pinch you.*
He points to an earwig, an insect

with cerci: forceps on its abdomen.
It's had five molts before
becoming an adult. Someday

I will tell him this, and that females
have straight pincers, males curved ones.
Today, though, he's the teacher,

and I'm his eager pupil, standing
in light while blackberries ripen
and a woodlouse unrolls.

Patti Trimble

## San Rafael, California

In the 1960s, two-lane highways and wild valleys, we could walk
most places then, and on the rise above this marsh my sister caught
a tiny mission blue. She opened up her hand; a secret flew.

I shoved a purple lupine close, made her breathe the scent of now.

Today there are eight lanes, a nice hotel, banana trees, such industry!
And vanishing the species of the children walking railroad tracks
and California fields; we who knew which butterflies will worship
at a bloom; we: demanding lupine overwhelm us, sweet and bitter.

Judith Offer


## Strawberry Patch

The strawberries don't remember.
I planted them myself, only three years ago,
Forcing them into the hard clay of my unused side yard.
The swept streets and graveled roofs
Have seen only fifteen years;
Could tell of just one generation
Kicking cans home from school.
Most of the people, too, were nowhere near
When the ground darkened with
The black husks of walnuts every hot October,
Before the saws were sharpened and bit.
Perhaps there is someone who can tell you
How before that they chased jackrabbits and rattlesnakes
To plant the little walnut trees,
And built the house themselves out of cinderblock,
And cried for joy the first Christmas,
Even the tree was oak, not pine at all.
The Indians, who might remember something,
Are not here either, having been cut down
Like the trees, without grandchildren.
So. There is only the land,
Dozing like a toothless old lady on a sunny front porch,
With nothing to say, nothing to say,
And all her memories, unspoken,
Underneath a lap full of ripe strawberries.

Tiffany Higgins

## There Is One Lone Hawk Who Seems

to do just fine over the city I catch
its upturned V cresting below wires
above apartment buildings at first
I thought it was a drone so perfect
is its flight that driftless soar &
circle what must it search for
here amid cement gardens the vole
absent me at my little table
threading lines while it is doing
the tough work of living perhaps
a mouse a rat some blessed carrion
the luckiest kind of dying
it has chosen to take up residence
here bordered by boulevard
& urban lake every
time I happen to look
up from my tapping to eye
it who moves like no other
I feel a timber
of me go off and lean
with it into the cindered wind

*Oakland*

Gail Rudd Entrekin

## The Fittest

All summer a dead vole, or mole,
or pointy-snouted mouse turned up
on the doormat every morning,
often with its guts spilling out its neck.
Jack liked to bring them in through the cat door
alive and kicking when possible, when avarice
and battle lust hadn't made him bite down
too hard, split the thin skin like a juicy pear.

He liked to put them down good-naturedly,
let them run around on the deep green carpet,
let them taste hope, make a real run
for the baseboard before he grabbed them
on the fly, tossed them into the air by their tails,
held them down with his soft-whiskered
cheek, pressing his huge golden eye
to their terrified faces, until he grew
bored and weary of the game—
the same pathetic attempts to flee,
the same ridiculous tiny squeals—
and bit their heads off, dropped their bodies
just outside the door,
                    and probably
when the coyote stepped out of the woods,
grabbed him up by his fluffy throat
and bit right through, if Jack had a moment
to reflect, he thought *damn*
and then he died.

Ellen Bass

## *Taking My Old Dog Out to Pee Before Bed*

Dew is already deep in the overgrown grass,
the air damp with a salty tang.
Zeke's hips are too ground down
to lift a leg, so he just stands there. We both
just stand, looking into the darkness.
Sometimes a moon silvers his thinning fur.
Sometimes it's clear enough for stars.
Orion strides across the heavens, his dog
trotting at his heel. A great live oak reaches over
from the neighbor's yard, dense black limbs
silhouetted against a paler sky, single voluptuous
remnant of forests. Can a tree be lonely?
Zeke tips up his muzzle, scent streaming
through a hundred million olfactory cells
as he reads the illuminated manuscript of night—
racoons prowling down the street, who's in heat
or just out for a stroll. Handsome still,
he reminds me of an aging movie star with his striking
white eyebrows and square jaw. He always
had an urbane elegance, a gentleman
who could carry off satin lapels and a silver-tipped cane.
Tonight an ambulence wails. Someone not so far away
is frightened, in pain, trying to live or trying to die.
And then it's quiet again. No birds. No wind.
We don't speak. We just wait, alive together,
until one of us turns back to the door
and the other follows.

Susan Glass

## Chance

A new Bewick's wren is trying his latchkey voice,
not his father's song,
though that's been nearest
since he splintered the white, purple-flecked shell
and lay blind and down-wet naked
in spider casings, Irish setter hair,
and fern fibers.
Faithful to his species,
he auditions the tunes of his neighbors:
a liquid, cascading curve from the male in the oak,
a stammered trill borrowed from the guy on the fence,
and oops, the buzz of scolding mother he hadn't quite intended.

His is not the only voice
to come of age in late July's temperate safety.
Fifteen well-lit hours per day
allow for stuttering new goldfinches,
and kingfishers, clumsily hoarse.
But it's the wren I notice most,
popping and flitting between branch and ground and glade,
and only chance to warn him that a hawk's shadow is not
            a passing cloud.
Beware the leaf blower! The amber cat,
the stunning window glass bare of decals.
Mind the viral mosquito
and the kingsnake.
Take none of these for granted,
but preen,
and sing here
next spring.

Judy Wells


## Tenants in Common

The squirrels
are at it again
in our attic
rebuilding their nest.
Gnaw. Gnaw.
My God,
they are pests!

Last year
one persistent female
in the midst of El Niño
created a warm, smelly nest
which vibrated behind our wall.
In January, she delivered
dos o tres niños o niñas
and all was quiet
for several months
except for a persistent
animal smell in our house.

Come spring
the juveniles
are scampering around outside.
Come fall
they're all rallying
round the nest again
with nuts in their mouths
building their inaccessible condos
in our house
fooling the biologists
and critter controllers
who can't find their holes.

No, I will not
call in Rat Patrol
to blow ammonia into their nest.
I want those squirrels
to pay up all their back rent
and ante up a cleaning deposit.
Then I will decide
whether I'll let them stay
as roommates.

My imagination swirls
as a colony of squirrels
sets up a commune
in our attic.
Now they are smoking dope!
Now they are having
Grateful Dead concerts!
Now they are wearing tie-dye
T-shirts stolen from
Louie Cuneo's tie-dye stand
on Telegraph Avenue!

My God!
What is Berkeley coming to?
The Naked People are supporting
squirrels' rights
and letting the squirrels
nest in their hair!
My God!
The squirrels are having us evicted
under an indigenous animal rights law!

Squirrels—
I give
I give
I give up!
Take our house
and shove it!

Evelyn Posamentier

## *Peanut Shells*

San Francisco

scorned city birds
pigeons shouldering bleak insults
bad-tempered jays swooping irregularly
spikes on the gates windows roofs
get out who is that aged opera singer
feeding them feeding them the peanut
shells the landlords cringe anger anger
merchants wringing their hands
i know you

a pet shop burned to the ground
some years back they say some parrots
escaped & colonized the palms
along dolores street

i am telling you secrets
a telepathic communication across the city
as maniacal as those green birds
mad as the tropics

the city
the city must figure in this
a great cloud over everything
the city did buildings emerged
in the mist colors exchange meanings
i was meant to figure this life but it didn't add up

that night
the local t.v. news

close up on big cat
lion oh pussycat
i would say meow
not do the right thing
when facing the big cat
who has done nothing
but come down from the hills
it's thirsty the grainy footage
the cat bewildered by estates
and landscaping and idiots
like me wanting to kiss
the sweet mountain lion's head

Rachel Dacus

## *Bowing to the Gods of Upheaval*

During the Loma Prieta quake,
      Earth grew into a tall woman,
            swayed and dolphined
   underfoot, breathed
          her songs in moth-wing heat.
               Buildings commaed
         like new moons.
      Timbers did the rhumba
in our molecules.

Bridges waved
    and oceans flipped.
         Every day on Earth, a quake
somewhere makes bookcases
           shiver and walk, pages
     in books
           flutter their fragile wings
and lets us know the way off
    this jello planet is to roll
       with the rocking
           as they did in San Francisco
     in 1906, when the sea
           shimmied and swallowed beaches
     and the spilling bay
overturned like a coffee cup.

Now our towers shimmer
    in the sun, undulate
        and prepare for their shatter,
        and for the fires
            with water jugs, prepare

as when you say
                is it best to separate, I toss away
    what I can for a journey into the fault.
But the ground coughs me up. A shiver
          and I straighten,
                and then again bow
                    to all the gods of upheaval.

Patricia Brody


## Demeter Shops Local

I know that place, curving into Stinson.
We slid down the damp dune
                    Oh yeah, I was there
                              young as no summer
the fog rolls over,  bringing *Brrrrrr!*
Chill wind instead
my boyfriend from Vienna sent for his smelly sheepskin
I had nothing warm enough for Northwest summer. Later later
                                        summer again
my daughter, two,  and I pick blackberries
along the brambly road to town. Our rented house, as you
describe
eucalyptus, squeaky gate askew.
                              Sharp Pacific gust sneaking through.


At a hippie thrift shop  I buy her a baby-hippie jumpsuit ripe-
purple as the fruit in her pail. No other partner needed—
                              we two,  dressed alike.

Zara Raab

## The Sawmill Smokes Above the Village

houses hide behind their shrubbery
and jostle for place on a pebbled street
stretching out almost a mile
to unfenced pasture and forage.
Yards might descend of a sudden
to embankments and rushing creeks,
where berries grow thick and jumbled.
At dusk the mill hands come in
to sleep unwashed on tousled sheets
and dream the night of fire and blade.
The sawmill stands like the Mayacamas'
looming presence, smoke rising
over the town, where the highway
seams the land of the San Andreas
and brings only tourists passing
to the redwoods or Trees of Mystery.
In the rain-drenched glen, we tent
our umbrellas and peer from the rim
spoked like a high spinning wheel.
Each nod of greeting is a script
started by codgers in the old-time,
some kind, some more cruel,
name and lineage at every entry,
the lot bound by milk and semen,
and the sticky, untapped sap
of pine growing high in the valley—

Eva M. Schlesinger

## Egret's Egress

That egret
white and still as bone
stilt legs on triangle of grass
freeway's edge
stands proudly between two signs:
Pedestrians Prohibited
and
Wrong Way

Deborah Fass

## From the Freeway

You would never know
that beyond Silicon Valley,

beyond glass and concrete
offices and townhouses,

Alviso Marina, abandoned boats
moored in green reclaiming

reeds of tule and sedge,
beyond salt ponds with eroding levees,

saline red and brackish blue,
clear creeks and sloughs

emptying into
the bay—

along the edges, mud-brown
sandpipers feed.

Carol V. Davis

## On a Stretch of Coastline

Squeezed on both sides by four stripes of wire, barbs snapping
in the wind like the wicked fairy's come hither,

the lane collapses into the largest lagoon in the lower 48
where forty years ago the water rose, tracing a figure eight

through downtown, sweeping eleven people out to sea.
Even now the town drowns its sorrows beneath a battering of rain,

families split raw between developers and nature lovers,
while an endangered butterfly (the lotus blue) hides in stretches

of drying bog, or (depending on your beliefs) is now extinct.
At sundown fishermen haul up half-empty crab cages,
        then disperse to rundown bars

to drink their way through another punishing winter.
Ink-stained clouds push against the mountains like children

shoving on a playground. I swear I wouldn't be alone if I
        escaped here too
into the forest to pick wild blackberries, leaving no
        forwarding address.

Judith Terzi

## *Rearrangement*

Return-home feeling at last, like
                    cruising the Coast Highway

in a convertible after years of absence.
          Glitter of sea, liberator of my losses.

Or a return to stability after illness,
                 bouquets of well-intentioned

roses no match for this jolt of color—
           yellow flame of Spanish broom

flanking the mountain highway. Nostalgic
                aroma slopes through the senses

like a prom corsage. At Charlton Flat, only
           snow plants burst the monopoly

of dun earth, blackened bark, arm of pine.
            Splatter of blood, species

of red grenade that births on pillows of fungus,
          pine cones, mountain exhalations.

Scalloped candles for waxy stalks, or soap
               spires on bathtub ledges,

pining for skin, for rub. And further into
           the trail, a seahorse appears,

its displacement, char of shape jarring. We
                imagine this used-to-be tree

nose-diving into the trickle of creek, holding
            its Big Pine breath in the savage

heat, its ego writhing against the betrayal,
                the realignment of being.

Sylvia Ross

## *Cultural Capitulation*

below California's cold white sun
and the swooping crows,
skaggy branches reach for my old red truck.
i like this truck's gaudy color. maybe the trees do too.
these gray trees long ago pushed past fence lines.
brooms of eucalyptus branches
scrape the windows. sickle leaves block my view
along the easement road.

i drive ahead and don't see the snake,
but the truck's wheels bump twice over its length.
In the mirror, the banded king lies in the ruts,
now only fit for crows. my foot on the brake too late.
it's time to evict these blinding foreign trees.
i can't worry whose property they're on.
oak belongs here, eucalyptus doesn't.
i have saw and shears and axe.

i could strip this alien arboretum down
to the ground and take a native's revenge.
my killing of the harmless snake
the trees' fault. but the intrepid crows,
longer residents than my indigenous ancients,
wheel in the air, squawk and scold over the truck.
crows live in these dubious trees,
mate, nest, adapt better than i.

it's time to go home, to the sofa,
to a cup of Columbian coffee, to a consideration
of snakes, Australian trees, and the
essential dominance of crows.

Jan Steckel

## Santa, Santa, Santa

Before we leave, my father intones
towns with In-N-Out Burgers:
Buellton, Santa Maria, Paso Robles,
like listing missions for bygone travelers.
We hit El Camino Real, the royal road,
its rusty bells ringing Santa, Santa, Santa.
Santa Rosa Island with a fog lace collar.
Snowy egret aloft, legs stretched behind.
Inland we ride, through San Marcos Pass.
Hawk on a line. Hawk on a post.
Hawk on the crux of a crucified grape vine.
San Luis Obispo's Madonna Inn,
where guests drink pink martinis,
wash pink cake down with pink shakes.
Buzzard spirals in the sky.
Oak and sage, interloper eucalyptus.
Dry river beds. Crows on dead citrus trees.
Llamas laconically stretch their necks.
Black cattle seated sedately like library lions,
goats, roan horses and ponies.
Rusted train tracks. Santa Margarita.
San Anselmo, San Miguel, San Juan Bautista.
Rolling hills ribboned and posted.
Road to Mariposa Reina, the Butterfly Queen.
Arroyo Grande, Pismo Grande. Pismo Beach,
home of giant clams. Yellow-flowered ice plant,
ubiquitous oxalis. Little lemon trees.
Stooping brown-skinned laborers,
trailer parks, their tiny yards beautiful,
leaf blowers busy borrowed from work.

Sand-colored tract housing, red-tiled roofs,
round about planted with palms.
Higuera, "fig tree," Los Osos, "The Bears," Prado, "Meadow,"
that once were here and are no longer.
Hometown Buffet, Margie's Diner, IHOP, McDonald's,
In-N-Out Burgers like rosary beads.
This is my own, my native land. Santa Maria,
pray for us now and in the hour of our lunch.

Christopher Buckley

## *Drought*

Late afternoon, nodding off
on the chaise longue,
the yellow pad slips off my lap…
and I'm riding my red Schwinn again
through the tunnel of camphor trees
on Humphrey Road, sitting among
jasmine and pittosporum on the cliff
above Butterfly Beach…until
sun-flashes off windshields
of cars on the hill, or a breeze
fingering the newspaper
wakes me.
        Still, each day,
I feel I need to take up my work,
place myself before the sky
and try to see what all the speculation
has come to? But more and more
I doze off thinking
I can hear the rain
in one of my old poems…

Winter, 80+ degrees,
all the roses cut back to sticks
as if we could forecast
some bright future,
some hopeful outcome months away.
The liquidambars are nothing
more than a scribbling on the air,
the neighbor's tangerines have gone
brown and hard,
as we will all go in time.

There's no
predicting the winds, slapdash
west or east, so I accept any
fanfare in the boughs, wishing
I were as nonchalant about
what's coming, or not…Nothing,
of course, saves us in the end,
and this far down the path to dust,
the little thing you choose
to hold onto is as good as any other.
I choose my cat who naps with me,
the white crowned sparrows splashing
in the shallow bath…none of whom
see the least foreboding in the sky.

What few clouds there are
enter a new world each day,
unaccountable for any part of the past
as they pass us by—the cool mercies
of morning evaporating in no time
through the leaves…
little more
to be done than lean back and,
insofar as I am able, love whatever's
above or before me, the sky indistinct
all year now, and be content
with a great blue absence
of memory, not much left
on my mind other than the
little hoppers on the rose canes
waiting their turn in the bath.
And this could be instructive,
as above us, the patient stars
and the dust we're made of, burn
away in a white, invisible sky…

Ruth Bavetta

## *Oranges and Pomegranates*

I'm tired of hearing about weathered barns
and cows and icy Vermont winters.
Sometimes it seems that every poet in America
lives on a farm in New England. Enough

already, give me someone who sings of golden hills
dehydrated under an August sun, of sage
and chaparral, eucalyptus and red-tailed hawks,
and crummy motels hooded with bougainvillea.

Tell me of freeways wide as the Plains of Abraham,
interchanges thicketed like mangrove swamps,
and tides of tile-roofed houses spread out
in mortgaged blots across the land.

Spin songs of palms and pyracantha, of olives
and oranges and pomegranates, of beaches,
tawdry with bottles and cigarette butts,
and the smell of sprinklers on a sun-baked sidewalk.

Let me see Latinos in white straw hats selling oranges
at the freeway off-ramps while ghost coyotes nip
at the tasseled edges of the city. I crave the pure,
magnificent, bloody beauty of a smoggy sunset.

Ruth Bavetta

## Pacific Savings Time

Here on the edge
of the world, we watch fog
float over headlands,
see the sun set in a hemorrhage

of smog. We live on freeways
clogged like butter-filled veins,
all lanes leading nowhere.
Coyotes track house cats

in the hollows of the canyons.
The thirst of lawns is slaked
by water stolen from valleys
no longer green. The saber tooth

is extinct, the tar pits tamed,
the rivers flow concrete.
It's time now
to tell our stories.

T.m. Lawson


## *Brentwood Coyotes*

I've seen him myself, up along
Montana Boulevard, on the sidewalk where
you collect your mail in your sweatpants, where

you jog in place, at night, fingers to your neck
to check your pulse; imagine him
running alongside you, grinning.

But no one will believe me. They think
I've seen a ghost. "No coyotes can come down here."
Is that why you've built your houses on hills?

He trotted like he owned the world, scared
of what it could do, tongue out, mazed
by the cement and the asphalt, the glass hedges

a prismatic trap, a trick to a wolf's eyes:
wolf not yet dog, dog yet not wolf, scavenger
who delights in and wearies of surprise.

But no one will believe me. They think he
doesn't exist. They need to see danger
before their eyes to believe its teeth.

The mountain lives so close to us. Visits us
with eagle and owl, with snake and rabbit;
why not coyote, tonight, in your garden?

Richard Beban

## In Praise of Los Angeles

Here, in a land "without seasons," we don't
wait for weather to tell us what to do.
From the east we absorb hordes of surprised
refugees—topcoats, greatcoats, winter
armor obsolete here. They are not used
to subtlety, trees that refuse to shed.
Spring is a nuance in the air; purple
jacaranda surprise late April
into turning May. Our April is not
preceded by thick, white clouds of breath
& wool. It is simply ascension from March,
a warmer February, cessation
'til October of January rain.
Here, December white is bleached southern sun,
sand along Venice boardwalk, whitewashed
stucco mimicking Mykonos.

Those married to seasons are queasy;
angry at the absence of "real change" they
pine for the mixed colors of maples,
as if Santa Ana-fueled fires
& the occasional earthquakes are not
change enough. They live lives unsettled by
a lack of overt cues, & miss the baby
sparrows, monarchs & cabbage moths, miss
the mixed colors their children are turning.

Cathie Sandstrom

## September Wildfire, Los Angeles Basin

Hot black night. The mountain crowned
with fire. Air so heavy with smoke
dawn sun's a dulled fuchsia disk on gray,
an icon from a Japanese print I could
stare into, imagine its corolla leaping
like the flames I saw from the freeway.

> *Third grade, Ninth Avenue School, Columbus.*
> *We have finished making our Ohio-shaped booklets*
> *of the rivers, burial mounds, pioneers, and now*
> *we are scissoring the mimeo-purple*
> *outlines of maple and oak leaves. Traced*
> *onto construction paper, orange, yellow,*
> *red and brown, we'll cut them again, tape*
> *them to the windows as if they are falling.*

> *Golda Authenreith, spinster,*
> *a pillar in her old-lady's lace-up*
> *Oxfords, her good black dress;*
> *behind her a flurry of leaves.*
> *We sit hushed, hands folded,*
> *while she reads aloud poems*
> *about the color and crispness*
> *of fall, season of harvest,*
> *the brisk air laden with*
> *the fragrance of burning leaves.*

Ash on the kitchen counter: flecks of white
on the dark book I lay down, black on the pale
cutting board, gray on the blue tiles.

The window's opened louvers furred
with a fine dust. The blaze doubled
in size last night. Outside, leaves sag
from the Chinese elm. We breathe
manzanita and sage, fell and feather.
The fire pushes wildlife before it twenty-
five miles east along the San Gabriels.
Thirty years since a burn.

Karen Greenbaum-Maya

## Standing Ovation

Pale orange light carved by tree-leaves
makes sherbet triangles on the sidewalk.
Creamsicle orange, then bright Orange Crush.

More smoke billows up, soft and dirty,
a standing ovation you can see from Vegas.
L.A.: every live act gets a standing ovation.

The air smells of ashtrays, old fireplaces.
Ash sifts down, lays down a rash of fine grit.
You find it on everything's skin, black dander.

The sun is an overripe guava.
The sun is a fake harvest moon.
The moon fakes an eclipse.

Neighbors thought they didn't have to run,
rashly thought they could face off the fire,
somehow it would leave them standing,

thought we'd return with their standing ovation.
Nothing alive still stands. Charred dirt.
The trees, stripped pillars, bleached by the firestorm.

Running shoes melt, dishwasher skeletons,
orange trees become coals piled for barbecue,
hills go to hot orange heaps that smolder by night.

Live coverage from Melrose, Hollywood, Vegas,
ash sifts over everything's skin, black dander.
The sun is an over ripe guava.
Burnt hills are a standing ovation.

Chad Sweeney

## Bloom

The bees are dying toward Beverly Hills
The bees are dying into the sun

At midnight it is day the bees
In Santa Monica our oranges

Fall sideways toward no beginning the
Bees are dying America in the teeth

By waxlight the bees brim up
From no well they have

Left their reflections on the ice
Of eternity the bees are dying in our

Talk of beginning this young country
Their hives follow the names down

On Alvarado by the light of swans
We go crossing our sunglasses into oblivion

The hands of the Indians are buried
Everywhere nothing grows the feet

Of the Tongva are gathering in white shadows we
Forget them the shadows convulse

We announce ourselves upward into teeth
A cowboy hat without its body the bees

On Sepulveda a wheelchair and silence
In our mouths the sea forgets

We wake our way down the processes
Blooming everywhere the actions of our hands


## Cause

A windmill is most
when still

because it might
at any moment
begin to turn,

      just as I sit
my back to what I love most

so a wind may come over

come over the honeysuckle and wire
to fill this one sentence

with motion,

the deer for weeks
bounding over the highway

until there is no highway.

Bronwyn Mauldin

## Alarm Song

On a rooftop across the alley
a spiked gray mockingbird trills
a five-tone car alarm sequence.
Screaming at the top of her lungs,
she aches to be heard over the
construction-freeway-leaf-blower
white noise of the city.
At night I pull the blanket up over my ears,
unable to bear the sound,
the never-ending alarm song
of a mockingbird who cannot sleep
in the eternal amber
of streetlamp sunlight.

Ellaraine Lockie

## *Offerings to the Green Gods*

Not alley stench or gnaw of smog
but scrape of Marshweed's viola/bass tune-up
scour of motors and smell of exhaust
cause the air at the entrance of the Hollywood/Western
Metro station to hold its breath

Then the exhale rush of twenty-some passengers
who sweep across the platform like prairie wind
to settle on a small plot of brown ground
They wear tie-dyed T-shirts, tattoos, brimmed hats
a Batman costume, batik sarong, crocheted cap
One pushes a wheelbarrow holding
bags of soil and two toddlers
A stealth platoon toting succulents, spades
plastic jugs of water and babies on backs

Marshweed music rides the breeze
and ushers the espionage
*Freight train freight train run so fast*
*Freight train freight train run so fast*
*Please don't tell what train I'm on*
*So they won't know what route I've gone*

Mr. Stamen already on hands and knees
issues orders like prayers
A video cameraman follows a woman
who carries a chalkboard with the words
"Guerrilla Gardening" and messages
like "Looking for local person to water"

She asks one of the toddlers
what is his favorite plant
He says "Daddy" through a mouthful of granola
Picks up a feather to stroke his father's cheek
as the father puts a painted lady into the ground
*And the wing is on the bird*
*And the bird is in the nest*
*And the nest is on the branch*

The redhead holding a jade plant introduces
herself as Ginger and her partner as Desert Rose
*The only girl I've ever loved*
*was born with roses in her eyes*
Not even a siren's scream can cloud
the well-oiled hum of this mission
Murmurs as reverent as Sunday morning stop passers-by
who seem to forget train schedules
and the gray hair of frenzy

Thirty minutes later the crusaders pack up
in an undercover of quiet
Leave thermoses of beer for the band
And stir the air once more with their exit
to the train for the next Metro stop
where another brown patch waits to be reborn
and where another band will perform the offertories

*Freight train freight train run so fast*
*Freight train freight train run so fast*
*Please don't tell what train I'm on*
*So they won't know what route I've gone*

Susan Terris

## What It Means to Kill

First—I don't. Even a housefly is shooed past my door.
Every spider is carried out cupped in my hands.
But last week, on a country road I know well, my car was
taking curves at a moderate speed, and there was a quail...

Quails skitter off roads with regal, head-bobbing poise.

Yet this one didn't. I felt her bones crush under
my wheels. *To everything (turn, turn)*...Omen, bad omen.
Why only once have I even held a gun, a rifle, shot at a

clay disk at a ranch near Reagan's old one. Missed, threw
down the weapon, my shoulder purpling from its kick.

But the quail didn't move and I didn't stop. Went on.
Then turned back, worried she'd been decoy
for a covey hidden in dense brush.
The road was smudged yet empty. No chicks, no bird.

Her body quick-claimed, I supposed, by vultures.

Later, I drove there again. This time, at the same place,
more roadkill, a gray/white tomcat with a collar.
I parked and pulled his body to the side of the road.

*To every thing (turn, turn) there is a season*...But wait:
was that a feather and quail-flesh oozing from his belly?

A quail-stuffed cat, ambling home, unaware of
another fast car? But by the next morning, his body, too,

had vanished. How to count up sins?
What is truly good and what is only careless evil?

A week later, at the same curve, a dead skunk.

For days, cars rolled over it, its body even too rank
for the vultures. Flattened, then less and less
until only a swatch of black/white fur on the asphalt.

Quail, cat, then skunk. *A time to be born, a time to...*
bear a skunk off, bit by bit, in the treads of our tires.

Dan Gerber

## *After the Rain*

I spot a young barn owl
standing by the road
peering at his own reflection in a puddle,
or so it seems,
when I pull off on the shoulder to see
if I can help.

Dazed,
probably struck by a car,
though not visibly wounded,
he looks up across the puddle
where I'm standing,
as if to ask about this
wondrous, underground bird he is seeing,
as if to ask if I see it, too.

Karen Greenbaum-Maya

## The Week Before My Friend Breaks Her Ankle...

...the roadrunner crosses the patio, inspecting. He has the zygodactyl foot that steadies the stride, two back toes and two front, parrot's foot, and woodpecker, though the roadrunner has never clutched a branch. He shows no doubt. He applies each foot, dried-twig toes flat against sun-roasted concrete. He advances purposeful as a tightrope-walker. He peers into the dim room through the glass door. We are not quite zoo exhibits, more like friends spotted unexpected in a café. I would mock that thin crest of stringy feathers, a Mohawk greased back, but those deliberate steps silence me. He is an envoy, slowed down so we would stop too, and mark him:

*Watch me watch my step.*
*Now: you watch yours.*

Camille T. Dungy

## *Long Time Gone, Long Time Yet to Come*

where jasmine lemon-sweets wind and salt
slicks the breeze    where sage spices sundrench
there    where the fragrant cloud-nest drives
the pump-beat of my blood    I am home.

long time gone.  long time gone and don't know
when I'm coming back    but see me there.
where the orange tree blossoms and the sky
smells white as line-dried sheets    see me there.

where jasmine lemon-sweets wind and salt
slicks the hair you wear into the breeze.
where cactus fruit is suckling pear
and its sweet-hidden water's everywhere
I am home.  am gone    but I'll be back.
long time gone.  but I'll be coming back.

# Editors' Afterwords

In creating *Fire and Rain: Ecopoetry of California*, I was deeply inspired by two other anthlogies: *The Place That Inhabits Us: Poems of the San Francisco Bay Watershed* (Sixteen Rivers Press, 2010) and *The Ecopoetry Anthology* (Trinity University Press, 2013). The latter anthology inspired me even before it was published, because I heard the coeditors, Ann Fisher-Wirth and Laura-Gray Street, read from and discuss it as an in-progress book at the Poetic Ecologies Conference in Brussels in 2008 and then again at the ASLE (Association for the Study of Literature and Environment) conference in Victoria, British Columbia, in 2009.

*The Ecopoetry Anthology* first inspired me to look at my own poems more rigorously in terms of how they present ecology and what they say about environmental issues. Then, in 2010, as I read the insightful, compelling poems in *The Place That Inhabits Us*, the idea came to me for another anthology of contemporary ecopoetry: one organized by habitat and encompassing all of the major ecosystems of California. Because I was trained in biology and science education before studying English and creative writing, from the start I was concerned with the scientific and environmental aspects of this project as well as with the literary ones. First, I wanted to organize this anthology around habitats, rather than around poets or themes. Second, I wanted to include poems representing all of California's iconic habitats and species: coast and ocean, redwood forests, oak woodlands, Central Valley, mountains, and deserts; sea lions and whales, turkey vultures, condors, giant sequoias, live oaks, Joshua trees, and the extinct but not forgotten California grizzly bear.

Celebrating the extraordinary beauty and diversity of California's ecosystems was only part of my impetus. The other part was showing environmental destruction and change through natural phenomena such as fires, floods, and earthquakes as well as such human impacts as pollution, logging, climate change, and loss of species and habitat.

We are now in the midst of a worldwide environmental crisis. For the past fifty years, global temperatures have been increasing faster than at any other time in human history; dozens of species are going extinct every day. A poetry collection cannot solve these problems, but it can illuminate them and generate discussion, and I hope this anthology will do that.

In addition to encompassing nature poetry and environmental poetry, the terms "ecopoetry" and "ecological poetry" have been applied to experimental poems that, like biological ecosystems, have interacting and interdependent parts. Such poems can offer intriguing experiments with syntax, line breaks, and the appearance of the poem on the page. Embodying systems thinking as discussed by physicist Fritjof Capra in *The Web of Life* (1996), these poems make an important contribution to ecopoetics. Although the subject of such poems is not necessarily ecology, the poems exemplifying this esthetic in *Fire and Rain* (see especially work by Jack Foley, Brenda Hillman, and Chad Sweeney) do indeed reflect on California ecosystems.

I started collecting poems for *Fire and Rain* in 2011. Early on, writer and founder of Berkeley's Heyday publishing company Malcolm Margolin gave me a copy of *No Place for a Puritan: The Literature of California's Deserts* (Heyday, 2009) and suggested that I contact the editor, Ruth Nolan. This was excellent advice because my knowledge of California's deserts was sorely lacking. Having visited the Sonoran Desert in Arizona and Mexico, at least I knew that not all deserts were characterized by camels and barren, shifting sand dunes. But I had not visited California's deserts, although I had lived in California all my life and had visited all of the other habitats represented in this book.

Ruth not only sent me some of her own desert poems but also offered to provide any other assistance I might need on the anthology. I needed a lot! I needed not only a desert expert but also a coeditor, and Ruth valiantly stepped into this role. It has been a pleasure to work with her, and it is not an exaggeration to say that I could not have created this book alone. I could have created something, but it would not have been as good.

Although Ruth and I first discussed this project in 2011, life intervened and we did not get going on it in a big way until 2016, when we issued a formal call for submissions and hundreds of poets sent us well over 1,200 poems. We both read all of them. I admired so many, I was like the proverbial kid in a candy shop: I want that one! And that one! And that one! Fortunately, having Ruth's responses enabled me to see many flaws and virtues in the poems that I might otherwise have overlooked. Often, this led to different decisions than I would have made alone. Many of the choices were difficult, because it would have been impossible to accept all of the wonderful poems we received.

I love the poems in this book so much that I wish I'd written all of them! I know, of course, that I couldn't have done it. I was blessed with Ruth and 147 other collaborators on this project to document the ecology of California in poetry. Many thanks to all!

—Lucille Lang Day

Taste all and hand the knowledge down.
—Gary Snyder, *Turtle Island*

When I was invited to submit my poetry for this anthology by Lucille Lang Day back in 2011, and then asked some years later to be the coeditor of *Fire and Rain: Ecopoetry of California*, I had no idea of the important role this anthology would play in my life.

As a Mojave Desert-based writer, living and working in rural parts of our state, a second-generation Californian, I have often felt marginalized in my geographic-literary presence here, where much emphasis is placed on the cooler and more recognizable geographic-literary interfaces in our vast state. For the first time, perhaps, through my involvement with helping weave together and shape the final book that is *Fire and Rain*, I feel inherently connected to poets in all parts of our Golden State. This book of poems, as a whole, does much to reestablish a continuity and fluidity to our ecologic-poetic landscape that has always lurked just beneath the surface, but for so long has remained widely unrecognized, compartmentalized, and broken.

These poems provide an essential antidote to that and, in fact, build on the old and find the connective pieces to shape a body of ecopoems that rely on both deep land-memories (forgotten, but not unknown) and new discoveries (looking to ecological-historical continuity, past, present, and future). The resulting collection is concurrently powerful, beautiful, heartbreaking, hopeful, transformational, and necessary.

The poems in *Fire and Rain* build their own environments, their own ecologies, a world of poetic language-tongues: a precise and impressionistic canvas of microclimates and hybrid geographies—biological, historical, cultural—like no other in the country, and perhaps the world. The poems provide ecologies that are both freshly imagined and recognizable in their evocation and recognition of the echoes of the native populations who have lived here for millennia.

I have been surprised and gratified by the coming together of this book of poems, coming from the vast range of ecologies of California—from Pacific coastline to the Sierra, inland valley and coastal ranges, and Mojave Desert—including ones that overlap with cities and towns. I have been led, as coeditor, on a magical journey through the astonishing diversity found in the countless microcosms in every fold of its geographies, mile for mile.

What is the ecologic fabric of California, and what are the lessons we learn from exploring our ecologies? How might we use the transformational power of poetry to knit together new understandings?

The metaphor of the fierce struggles in the natural world, and the overlap between these and the struggles for "home" and "relationship"—as derived from the linguistic roots of the word "ecology" ("eco-" comes from the Greek *oikos*, meaning "house" or "dwelling place")—is evoked in these poems in intricate and delightfully visceral poetic explorations that not only shape and define our state's various ecologies but also reveal—with powerful, generous, surprising, and gorgeously written turns of poetic insignia—how we are informed and defined by them, in a dance of ever-reciprocity.

I would like to thank my coeditor, Lucille Lang Day, for her inception of this project and her near-decade-long dedication and hard work in bringing this book to publication. I am deeply honored to have been invited to serve as her coeditor. Being a part of *Fire and Rain*, as a coeditor and a contributor, has changed my life as a poet, professor, and resident of California, and I am, and will remain, humbled and grateful for the experience.

—Ruth Nolan

# Notes on the Poems

"The Hungry Calf" by Elaine Miller Bond (p. 32). Humpbacks were reduced to less than 10 percent of their original population before a hunting moratorium was enacted in 1966. They were on the Endangered Species List in 1973 but have since made a comeback.

"The Gray Whale" by Tricia Knoll (p. 33). Of the three original gray whale populations, only the Eastern North Pacific (a.k.a. Californian) population has recovered from several centuries of extensive whaling. The North Atlantic population is extinct, and the Western North Pacific population has only about 150 individuals remaining.

"Blue Whales" by Gail Rudd Entrekin (p. 34). At up to 98 feet in length and with a maximum recorded weight of 190 tons, the blue whale is the largest animal known to have ever existed. Hunted almost to extinction, blue whales were abundant in nearly all the oceans on Earth until the beginning of the twentieth century.

"Otter" by Ken Haas (p. 37). Hundreds of thousands of sea otters once roamed the North Pacific, but the fur trade brought them close to extinction by 1911, when Russia, Japan, Great Britain, and the United States signed a treaty for the preservation and protection of fur seals. In California, the sea otter population now numbers approximately 2,900.

"Docks, Cliffs, and Tidepools" by Rachel Dacus (p. 58) is Part II of a longer poem called "San Pedro Trilogy."

"*Tu Bishvat* in the Redwoods: A Meditation Suite for the Earth" by Marcia Falk (pp. 65-68). *Tu Bishvat* is a holiday also called "Rosh HaShanah La'Ilanot," which translates from Hebrew as "New Year of the Trees" and is often referred to as Israeli Arbor Day. The poem quotes from these sources:

"And trees—you're allowed to kill trees?' / a small boy blurted…"
  —Zelda, "Ancient Pines" (translated by Marcia Falk)
"You do not belong to you. You belong to the universe."
  —Buckminster Fuller

"The Dudley's Lousewort" by Kirk Lumpkin (pp. 77-78). Dudley's lousewort (*Pedicularis dudleyi*), a flowering plant, is currently known to be found in only two small isolated areas: in and around Portola Redwoods State Park and along the North Fork of the Little Sur River near Big Sur. The Pico Blanco Scout Camp in the Little Sur watershed contains nearly 50 percent of the total population, which was only 2,233 in 2011.

"California Condor" by Erin Redfern (p. 111). With a 9.8-foot wingspan, the California condor is the largest North American bird. It became extinct in the wild in 1987, when all remaining individuals were captured. Since then, it has been bred in captivity and reintroduced in the coastal mountains of Southern and Central California. As of 2018, there were 440 birds total in the wild and captivity. Condors eat carrion and have been poisoned by animals shot with lead bullets and left behind by hunters.

"To Poison Oak" by Kirk Lumpkin (pp. 112-114). In *Secrets of the Oak Woodlands* (2014), author Kate Marianchild writes, "[Poison oak] is "so adaptable…that it may have a wider geographic distribution than any other California native. At least fifty California bird species eat its berries and seeds…In some areas deer eat more poison oak than any other plant."

"Dear Editor" by Mary Makofske (p. 147). Fountain grass is an African species that is planted ornamentally in California. It is tough, vigorous, and drought-resistant; but, having no natural enemies in California, it is invasive, readily out-competing native plants.

"Conductor" by Mary Kay Rummel (pp. 149-150). Wisteria and bougainvillea are not native to California. According to the *Orange County Register*, "Chinese wisteria is the most common species planted in Southern California." Bougainvillea is also planted widely in California, but even the variety called California Gold is native to South America.

"Viriditas" by Jack Foley (pp. 186-188). Theologian and author Matthew Fox writes, "One of the most wonderful concepts that Hildegard [von Bingen] gifts us with is a term that I have never found in any other theologian: the word *viriditas* or greening power" (*Illuminations of Hildegard of Bingen*). The word suggests "veritas," truth, as well as "veridicus," speaking the truth. From the *Wikipedia* entry on the twelfth-century religious philosopher and mystic: "The definition of viriditas or 'greenness' is an earthly expression of the heavenly in an integrity that overcomes dualisms. This greenness or power of life appears frequently in Hildegard's works."

    Foley said *Poetry Flash* editor Joyce Jenkins "challenged me to 'write a nature poem' for her Watershed event. I found my mind returning to Kore/Persephone, especially to her aspect as seed, thrust underground but emerging to flower. I remembered as well W. C. Williams' poem 'Asphodel, That Greeny Flower' and Denise Levertov's book of nature poems, *The Life Around Us*."

"Ocotillo Wells" by W. F. Lantry (p. 195). Lantry writes, "I have no idea why we called the California ebony tarantula (*Aphonopelma eutylenum*) a 'tarantella': I just know that, growing up, we did. Perhaps we were confusing it with the Italian dance, or maybe we were trying to distinguish it from the desert blond tarantula (*Aphonopelma chalcodes*). Both can be found in the Anza-Borrego Desert. It's just one of those quirks of growing up in San Diego county, I guess..."

"Super Bloom" by Helen Wick (pp. 199-201). Increased rainfall from an El Niño year causes the desert to carpet itself in wildflowers. In years of deep, gentle rain, super blooms occur throughout California's deserts, sometimes germinating flowers that are not usually seen in a particular location, indicating that their seeds were dormant for many years. "Fox paw," "wild grape," and "moon glow" are names invented by Wick; the actual names of the plants she's referring to are verbena, gravel ghost, and desert gold, respectively.

"A Grass Song: November," "The Spring at Sinshan," and "A Song Used When Damming a Creek or Diverting Water to a Holding Tank for Irrigation" by Ursula K. Le Guin (pp. 239, 240, and 241). Le Guin wrote to Lucille Lang Day and Ruth Nolan, "These poems are from my novel *Always Coming Home* (1985), which is set in the Napa Valley in an imagined far-future time. The book portrays a human society (from which the poems come) very different from ours; but the descriptions of the flora, fauna, and native ecosystem of the Valley are entirely drawn from our present-day reality."

"The Canyon Wren" by Gary Snyder (pp. 287-288). Snyder says, "This poem is for James and Carol Katz. The Stanislaus River comes out of the Central Sierra. The twists and turns of the river, the layering, swirling stone cliffs of the gorges, are cut in nine-million-year-old latites. We ran the river to see its face once more before it went under the rising water of the New Melones Dam. The song of the canyon wren stayed with us the whole time."

"Dreaming Back the Griz" by Eric Paul Shaffer (pp. 296-297). The California grizzly bear (*Ursus arctos californicus*), a now extinct subspecies of the grizzly bear, was relentlessly hunted and killed following the discovery of gold in 1848. The last reported sighting of a California grizzly bear was in Sequoia National Park in 1924.

"Interlope" by Tobey Hiller (pp. 319-321). In 2017, a female gray wolf, her mate, and their three pups were the second pack of wolves spotted in Northern California since the species went extinct there in 1924. The gray pups were born in Lassen National Forest to the female wolf of unknown origins. Her mate was the son of OR7, a wolf with a tracking device, who was the first of his kind in almost a century to migrate into California from Oregon.

# Appendix

## Rhymes with Reason: Poetry, Science, the Planet, and the Mind

### Lucille Lang Day

When language entered human culture more than fifty thousand years ago, with it came the capacity for humans to use language to deceive as well as to find and share truth. In *Ritual and Religion in the Making of Humanity* (1999), anthropologist Roy A. Rappaport proposed that religion evolved with language as a way to authenticate beliefs and moral prescriptions and to create order within society. Today anthropologists and evolutionary biologists debate whether religion is an evolutionary by-product or an adaptation, but they agree that all human societies exhibit widespread counterfactual and counterintuitive beliefs.

What does this have to do with poetry? Poetry appeared early in human cultures as a vehicle for sharing religious experience and preserving communal history. Indeed, all known human cultures produce poetry, just as all cultures have religion and language. It is no accident that Enheduanna, daughter of Sargon of Akkad (located in present-day Iraq), the first known author to sign her work, was a poet (writing in about 2300 B.C.E., Enheduanna composed poems to the goddess Inanna). Could it be that the linked origins of language, religion, and poetry mean that, at the biological level, hormones and neuron networks evolved to make these cornerstones of culture simultaneously possible?

Music is also found in all cultures. In *The Singing Neanderthals* (2006), archaeology scholar Steven Mithen argues that before grammar-based languages evolved, music and language were one and the same, and that early hominids communicated through musical phrases, much as birds and whales do today. If this is correct, it seems likely that, as pure sounds coalesced into words, the first word-based human communication was intermediate between what we call language and music today; that it was characterized by meter, tone, assonance, alliteration, and onomatopoeia; and that it was, in fact, poetry.

The scientific process as we know it entered human culture much later. Although Babylonians and Egyptians developed bodies of technical knowledge, including practical applications of mathematics and methods for diagnosing and treating illnesses, the earliest forms of what we recognize as modern science were not documented until the fifth century B.C.E. in Greece by Plato and other philosophers. If poetry evolved along with religion and language, but science came later, this could mean that the human brain is hardwired for poetry and religion but not science, and that when we use scientific reasoning, we are exploiting neural structures that evolved for other purposes. This would help explain such findings as the facts that 92 percent of Americans believe in a personal God (Baylor University, 2006), 68 percent believe in angels (Harris Poll, 2005), and 60 percent believe in the devil and hell (Harris Poll, 2005), but just 13 percent believe that humans evolved from lower organisms without God's intervention (Gallup Poll, 2006), which is the most logical conclusion based solely on science.

I am not saying that faith is wrong and logic is right but that faith comes more easily to the human brain, whereas it's desirable to be able to use logic when the occasion calls for it. Such an occasion is now, when the planet Earth is at the brink of disaster. Species are dying out 100 to 1,000 times faster than the natural rate; due to habitat loss and climate change, about one-quarter of the world's mammals, one-third of its amphibians, and one-tenth of birds are currently in danger of extinction. According to the National Oceanic and Atmospheric Administration, the rate of global warming is accelerating and is now about 2 degrees Celsius (3.6 degrees Fahrenheit) per century. If this acceleration continues, an additional 15 to 37 percent of all species will be pushed close to extinction within the next fifty years.

Poetry, I believe, could play an important role in preventing the worst-case scenario for the planet. Because it may represent a more basic mode of thinking, poetry could turn out to be a useful concomitant to scientific discourse for introducing science to children and for communicating scientific ideas, including those of ecology, to the general public. Poetry is a means for processing experience, better understanding ourselves and the world around us, communicating our emotions, discovering new insights, and, significantly, revealing when something has gone awry. By teaching poetry and science simultaneously rather than separately, we may be in a better position to create a scientifically literate public and an ecologically sustainable future.

Ever since poets have been writing, they have been intuitively linking an awareness of the environment to their quest for the divine. The following verses were written by Sappho in the seventh century B.C.E.:

> Come to me from Krete to this holy
> temple, to the apple grove,
> the altars smoking
> with frankincense,
>
> cold water ripples through apple
> branches, the whole place shadowed
> in roses, from the murmuring leaves
> deep sleep descends,
>
> where horses graze, the meadow blooms
> spring flowers, the winds
> breathe softly...
>
> ~
>
> Here, Kypris, after gathering...
> pour into golden cups
> nectar lavishly
> mingled with joys.
> —translated by Diane J. Rayor

Children, too, have an intuitive appreciation of nature. Former US Poet Laureate Robert Hass founded an organization called River of Words to promote children's environmental awareness and literacy through the study and practice of poetry and art. Here is a poem by a child who participated in River of Words:

*My Trip to the Hudson River*

Footprints all around—
Rabbit, deer, dog, coyote, squirrel, wild turkey—
Eyes watching all around.
Fog in distance
Rocks on the shore
Sounds of crows in the background
Smell of snow in the air
Water sits calm and quiet.
Fog disappearing slowly
Buds in the tulip trees
Sound of footsteps in the snow
Shadows of the trees in the water.
  —Devin Felter, age 12

I believe that poetry can be taken a step further in the study of the environment: it can be used not just to communicate appreciation and awareness of nature but also to promote understanding of relevant scientific concepts and issues. I've tried to do this in the following poem:

*History of the Biosphere*

At first no redwoods scraped the sky
with pointed leaves; no globular cones
on ultimate twigs turned slowly
from green to brown as they ripened.

And no calliope hummingbirds
with red-streaked throats and slender beaks
probed the necks of tubular flowers.
There was no oxygen, just a boiling sea

where gases streamed from the Earth's core.
Millennia passed and membranes formed
on rocks until self-replicating sacs
were cells, insensate, sulfur-metabolizing.

The Earth cooled and countless generations
of cells tumbled through the centuries.
Then chloroplasts exhaled oxygen
at last over oceans and land.

The seas filled with sponges, anemones
and corals where crabs could hide
and brightly colored fish could practice
dances to attract mates, long before

the first uncertain creatures crept out
to deposit eggs in crystalline sand.
Now ribosomes and chromosomes repeat
the story, and humans, with neurons

tangled like a rain forest and three billion
nucleotides lined up in their DNA,
gather round the fire to listen,
while the sky darkens with carbon

and the planet—with its orchids, figs,
rubber trees, calliandras and ferns
under canopies dense with hanging lianas—
trembles as it burns and burns.

This poem combines an overview of the evolution of life with a
description, at the end, of a burning rain forest. The questions I
hope to raise are: Is this the outcome we really want? Should this
be the culmination of billions of years of evolution?

Scientific discourse differs from poetry in that it attempts
to eliminate all ambiguity and emotional response. We could not
substitute poetry for scientific discourse and expect science to

progress, and yet there is no reason, except tradition, why poetry should be excluded from the study of science. Why not have students read and interpret poems along with scientific texts? Why not have students record their scientific observations in poetry as well as in "objective" lab notes? Not just for children, but also for adults, poetry might help make scientific ideas and terminology more palatable.

What might such a poem that marries ambiguity and emotion with scientific observation look like? Certainly not like a traditional entry in a scientific lab book. Poet Pattiann Rogers has for many years been writing poems that describe her world carefully and scientifically and at the same time embody both her unique spirituality and the ongoing, timeless human quest for the divine. Her poem "Being Specific," occasioned by her encounter with a spider on a forest path, exemplifies her process:

> *Being Specific*
>
> The beginning subject is narrowed
> first to the yellow toe-claw on the left
> front seven-segmented leg of this one
> specific, totally bright yellow
> spider misplaced, a small spectacle
> moving across the damp, grey
> gravel of the forest path.
>
> Yet the subject, more specifically,
> is the cellular tremble of pulse
> in this particular toe-claw belonging
> to this very spider I see, lost
> from its yellow-orange flowerfield—
> goldenrod, daisy, jessamine.
>
> Still, to be more exact, the sole
> subject here is one colorless shiver
> of molecule inside the one-chambered
> heart of this quite shiny, yellow-
> eyed, golden pea-orb pausing
> on rock at my feet.

But the focus, to designate
further, must be on one atom-
to-atom link inside this arachnid
heart this afternoon, and further,
within this spider-atom, one electron,
and beyond that, one hadron, one quark;
and further beyond that, the last
and finest specification possible,
which is naturally the only
underlying, indivisible universal
that thus possesses like the void
and exhibits like the boundless
and holds distance like the night
and serves like the sun and inhabits
like the stars and therefore exists
as this split-moment's revelation
inside the mind meeting itself
in the recognition of its own
most specific composition.

Like all good scientists, Rogers pays careful attention to details and records them accurately: "yellow toe-claw," "seven-segmented leg," "one-chambered heart," "goldenrod, daisy, jessamine." She is also fluent in the language of science, effortlessly incorporating words like "arachnid," "electron," "hadron," and "quark" into the poem. Finally, she goes beyond observation and scientific facts when she describes "the only / underlying, indivisible universal / that thus possesses like the void / and exhibits like the boundless / and holds distance like the night / and serves like the sun and inhabits / like the stars and therefore exists / as this split-moment's revelation." In these lines she is simultaneously describing an inscrutable life force, consciousness, creativity, and the divine.

~

Getting back to the hypothesis that the human brain is wired more directly for poetry than for science, I believe that more people would be drawn to and enjoy reading Rogers' poem than a scientific treatise on arachnids or subatomic particles. Yet scientific literacy is important. To be informed citizens, people need to know something about science, including arachnids, which are part of ecosystems, and subatomic particles, which are bound to each other with energy that can be released either to destroy the environment or, with further research, to provide a clean energy source that will enable civilization as we know it to continue. Why not tap into our affinity for poetry and use it not only as an end in itself, or even as a vehicle to promote literacy, but also as a tool in the teaching and study of science, along with inquiry, problem solving, and scientific observation and discourse?

Including poetry in the science curriculum could even turn out to be a great boon for science, because poetry is a means for channeling intuition, and intuition is just as important to the scientific enterprise as logical reasoning and careful observation. The history of science is filled with instances where scientists and nonscientists alike have made intuitive leaps, or pre-discoveries, that science later developed the tools and methods to validate. Such pre-discoveries can point scientific research in new directions, and they can be made by poets. In fact, Walt Whitman, Gertrude Stein, and Edgar Allan Poe all made important pre-discoveries that are now accepted as scientific truths. Whitman went against the religious, philosophical, and scientific teachings of his time to argue in his poetry that the mind depends upon the flesh, i.e., that the body and soul are inextricably intertwined. Through her poetic experiments, Stein showed that the brain's neural structures for grammar exist independently of the meanings of words.

Perhaps most impressively of all, in his poem "Eureka," published in 1848, Poe insisted that the universe arose "in one instantaneous flash" from the explosion of a single primordial particle, thus prefiguring the Big Bang theory. He also described black holes, claimed that the universe was expanding, and was the first person to solve Oblers' Paradox, the mystery of why the sky is dark at night. Nineteenth-century astronomers believed that the universe was infinite, but Poe intuited that it is finite in time and space and that night can therefore fall, because the universe is not illuminated by the light of an infinite number of stars. Alexander

Friedmann, who inferred the expanding universe from Einstein's theory of relativity, was a fan of Poe and may have gotten the idea of an expanding universe from him before he set out to demonstrate that it follows from scientific theory.

At this crossroads of human history, we need both scientists who can think humanistically and nonscientists, including politicians, who can think scientifically. We need creative solutions to unprecedented problems in order to halt the destruction of the Earth's ecosystems and prevent catastrophic climate change. Bringing poetry to the science class and vice versa might help prepare citizens to play a role in finding these solutions and scientists to think intuitively as well as logically, so that on our beautiful blue-green planet, life as we know it can continue to thrive.

Note: Lucille Lang Day presented this essay as "Poetry, Ecology, and the Human Brain" at the Poetic Ecologies Conference in Brussels in 2008 and as her keynote speech that year at the 82nd Annual Poets' Dinner in Oakland, California. It appeared online at *PoetryMagazine.com* in 2009, and in print in the *Redwood Coast Review* in fall 2014.

# Poet Index

# About the Contributors

## Editors

LUCILLE LANG DAY has published ten poetry collections and chapbooks, including *Becoming an Ancestor* and *Dreaming of Sunflowers: Museum Poems*. She is a coeditor of *Red Indian Road West: Native American Poetry from California* and the author of two children's books, *Chain Letter* and *The Rainbow Zoo*, as well as a memoir, *Married at Fourteen: A True Story*. Her poems, essays, and short stories have appeared widely in magazines and anthologies, and her many honors include the Joseph Henry Jackson Award in Literature, two PEN Oakland awards, and nine Pushcart nominations. She received her BA in biological sciences, MA in zoology, and PhD in science/mathematics education at the University of California, Berkeley, and her MA in English and MFA in creative writing at San Francisco State University. http://lucillelangday.com

RUTH NOLAN, a former wildland firefighter for the federal Bureau of Land Management's California Desert District, is a widely published writer/scholar whose work focuses on California's deserts. She is a professor of creative writing at College of the Desert, Palm Desert, California. She has received a Bread Loaf Environmental Writers Fellowship and a California Writers Residency Award, and she is the author of the poetry book *Ruby Mountain* as well as the essay collections *California Drive* and *Notes from the Gateway to Death Valley*. In addition, she edited *No Place for a Puritan: The Literature of California's Deserts*. Her short story "Palimpsest," published in *LA Fiction: Southland Stories by Southland Writers*, received a 2016 Editor's Reprint Award from the journal *Sequestrum* and was nominated for a 2016 PEN/Robert J. Dau Short Story Prize for Emerging Writers. She holds her MFA in creative writing from the University of California, Riverside.

## Poets

CYNTHIA ANDERSON lives in the Mojave Desert near Joshua Tree National Park. Her poems frequently appear in journals and anthologies, and she has authored seven collections, most recently *Waking Life* (Cholla Needles, 2017). Cynthia coedited the anthology *A Bird Black As the Sun: California Poets on Crows & Ravens* (Green Poet Press, 2011).

CATHY BARBER lived in San Mateo for nearly twenty years. In 2016 she returned to her native Ohio to be near family. Her work has been published in many journals, including *Kestrel*, *Haight Ashbury Literary Journal*, and *Canary*. She has an MFA in poetry from Vermont College of Fine Arts and an MA in English from CSU East Bay.

ELLEN BASS' most recent book of poetry is *Like a Beggar* (Copper Canyon Press, 2014). Previous books include *The Human Line* and *Mules of Love*. Among her many awards are fellowships from the National Endowment for the Arts and the California Arts Council, two Pushcart Prizes, and a Lambda Literary Award. She teaches in the MFA writing program at Pacific University.

RUTH BAVETTA lives and loves in Southern California. Her poems have been published in *Rhino, Rattle, Nimrod, Tar River Poetry, North American Review, Spillway, Poetry New Zealand*, and many others. She has published three books: *Embers on the Stairs* (Moon Tide Press), *Fugitive Pigments* (FutureCycle Press), and *Flour, Water, Salt* (FutureCycle Press).

RICHARD BEBAN, formerly a Los Angeles-based poet, now lives in Paris, where he works as a photographer. His two poetry books, *What the Heart Weighs* and *Young Girl Eating a Bird*, were published by Los Angeles' Red Hen Press in 2004 and 2006, respectively.

PAUL BELZ is an environmental educator and writer based in Oakland, California. He develops and teaches natural history workshops for preschoolers and school-aged children, their parents, and their teachers. His articles have been published by *Terrain.org, East Bay Monthly, Exchange*, and the blogs Green Global Travel, Green Adventures Travel, and Wild Oakland.

SALLY BLIUMIS-DUNN teaches modern poetry at Manhattanville College. She recieved her MFA in poetry from Sarah Lawrence in 2002, and that same year she was a finalist for *Nimrod*'s Pablo Neruda Prize. Her two books, *Talking Underwater* and *Second Skin*, were published by Wind Publications, and her poems have appeared in many journals.

When ELAINE MILLER BOND was eight years old, her teacher secretly sent her ode to Berkeley's holiday lights to the *Oakland Tribune*. This was Elaine's first poetry publication. She has since worked as a science writer, authored and photographed children's books (*Running Wild* and *Living Wild*), and photographed a science book on prairie dogs.

JOHN BRANTINGHAM is Sequoia and Kings Canyon National Park's first Poet Laureate. His work has been featured in hundreds of magazines, on *Writer's Almanac*, and in *The Best Small Fictions 2016*. He has published seven books of poetry and fiction, including *The Green of Sunset* from Moon Tide Press. He teaches at Mt. San Antonio College in Walnut, California.

NANCY SUE BRINK is a poet, writer, and media-maker whose work is rooted in the people, landscapes, and wildlife of her adopted Northern California home, where she bands migrating raptors and grows tomatoes in her Berkeley backyard. Recent work has appeared in *Veterans of War, Veterans of Peace*, edited by Maxine Hong Kingston.

PATRICIA BRODY lived in the Bay Area in the '70s and commuted daily to the San Francisco peninsula, after Woodstock and before Silicon Valley. She has two MAs and two poetry collections: *American Desire* (New Women's Voices Award, Finishing Line, 2009) and *Dangerous to Know* (Salmon, 2013). She teaches poetry and short-prose workshops for women.

BRI BRUCE is an award-winning author and graphic designer from California's Central Coast and holds a BA in writing from UC Santa Cruz. Her work has appeared in numerous publications and anthologies, and she is the author of *The Weight of Snow, 28 Days of Solitude*, and *The Starling's Song*.

CHRISTOPHER BUCKLEY's *Star Journal: Selected Poems* was published by the University of Pittsburgh Press in 2016. Other recent books are *Spanish Notebook* (Shabda Press, 2017); *The Far Republics*, winner of the 2017 Vern Rutsala Poetry Prize (Cloudbank Books, 2017); and *Chaos Theory* (Plume Editions, 2018). *Cloud Memoir: Selected Longer Poems* is forthcoming in fall 2018.

DANE CERVINE's books include *Kung Fu of the Dark Father, How Therapists Dance*, and *The Jeweled Net of Indra*. Saddle Road Press will publish his new cross-genre work of Zen kōan poems in 2018. His poems have been honored by Adrienne Rich and Tony Hoagland and have won awards from the *Atlanta Review* and *Caesura*. www.DaneCervine.typepad.com

For many years, ABBY CHEW worked at a Quaker boarding school on a farm, where she raised goats and taught humanities. Today, she lives in Echo Park, Los Angeles, with her husband and two dogs. She teaches at Crossroads School for Arts & Sciences.

ROBERT COATS has been writing poetry for 40 years. His work as an environmental scientist takes him outdoors and sometimes provides inspiration and material. His poems have appeared in *Orion, Windfall, Canary, Song of the San Joaquin*, the Pudding House anthology *Fresh Water*, and a full-length book, *The Harsh Green World*, published in 2015 by Sugartown Publishing.

SUSAN COHEN has won a Rita Dove Poetry Award, a Milton Kessler Memorial Prize for Poetry, a Literal Latté award, and other honors, including the 2015 David Martinson-Meadowhawk Prize from Red Dragonfly Press for her second full-length collection, *A Different Wakeful Animal*. She lives in Berkeley and Bodega Bay.

E. K. COOPER writes, "I am a 59-year-old Pomo from the Round Valley Indian Reservation in Northern California. I have been writing for just over four years and I am just now understanding the power of how it nourishes my spirit. Writing has also helped me to remember not only my own rich history but histories of relations who have passed on."

TASHA COTTER is the author of the poetry collections *Some Churches*, *That Bird Your Heart*, and *Girl in the Cave*. Published in the 2015 Delphi Chapbook Series, her work has appeared in journals such as *Contrary Magazine*, *NANO fiction*, and *Booth*. In 2015 she was named runner-up in the Carnegie Center's Next Great Writer contest.

BARBARA CROOKER is the author of six books of poetry: *Radiance*, winner of the 2005 Word Press First Book Award and finalist for the 2006 Paterson Poetry Prize; *Line Dance* (2008), winner of the 2009 Paterson Award for Excellence in Literature; *More* (2010); *Gold* (2013); *Small Rain* (2014); and *Barbara Crooker: Selected Poems* (2015).

RACHEL DACUS is the author of *Gods of Water and Air*, a collection of poetry, prose, and drama, and the poetry collections *Earth Lessons* and *Femme au chapeau*. Her writing has appeared in *Atlanta Review*, *Boulevard*, *Drunken Boat*, and *Prairie Schooner*, as well as in many other journals and anthologies, including *Ravishing DisUnities: Real Ghazals in English*.

CARYN DAVIDSON is a park ranger in the education branch of Joshua Tree National Park. She is also the park liaison for the Artist-in-Residence program, now in its tenth year. Her work has been published in *LA Weekly*, *LAICA Journal*, *The Stone*, *Pacific Crest Trailside Reader*, *GEO*, *Spillway*, *Phantom Seed*, and various Joshua Tree National Park publications.

CAROL V. DAVIS is the author of *Because I Cannot Leave This Body* (Truman State University Press, 2017) and *Between Storms* (TSUP, 2012). She won the T. S. Eliot Prize for *Into the Arms of Pushkin: Poems of St. Petersburg* (TSUP, 2007). She teaches at Santa Monica College and Antioch University Los Angeles.

ALISON HAWTHORNE DEMING's most recent poetry book is *Stairway to Heaven* (Penguin, 2016). She is currently the Agnes Nelms Haury Chair of Environment and Social Justice and teaches in the Creative Writing Program at the University of Arizona.

JIM DODGE is a novelist and poet whose works combine themes of folklore and fantasy, set in a timeless present. He has published three novels—*Fup*, *Not Fade Away*, and *Stone Junction*—and a collection of poetry and prose, *Rain on the River*. He was born in Santa Rosa, California.

CAROL DORF has two chapbooks available, *Some Years Ask* and *Theory Headed Dragon*. Her poetry has appeared in *E-ratio*, *Great Weather For Media*, *About Place*, *Slipstream*, *Mom Egg Review*, *Sin Fronteras*, *The Journal of Humanistic Mathematics*, *Scientific American*, and *Maintenant*. She is the poetry editor of *Talking Writing* and teaches at Berkeley High School.

CAMILLE T. DUNGY is the author of *Guidebook to Relative Strangers: Journeys into Race, Motherhood, and History* and four collections of poetry, most recently *Trophic Cascade*. She has also edited anthologies, including *Black Nature: Four Centuries of African American Nature Poetry*. Her honors include NEA fellowships in poetry and prose, an American Book Award, and two Northern California Book Awards.

IRIS JAMAHL DUNKLE is a former Poet Laureate of Sonoma County, California. *Interrupted Geographies*, published by Trio House Press, is her third collection of poetry. It was featured as the Rumpus Poetry Book Club selection for July 2017. Dunkle teaches at Napa Valley College and is the poetry director of the Napa Valley Writers' Conference.

KEVIN DURKIN's poetry has appeared in *Poetry, New Criterion, Yale Review*, and the anthologies *Poetry Daily, Irresistible Sonnets*, and *Measure for Measure*. In 2013, Finishing Line Press published his collection *Los Angeles in Fog*. A managing editor at the Huntington Library, he lives with his wife and two daughters in Santa Monica.

DONNA EMERSON lives in Petaluma, California. Recently retired from teaching at Santa Rosa Junior College, Donna's award-winning poems have been published in *Denver Quarterly, Calyx*, and the *Paterson Literary Review*. She has published four chapbooks. Her most recent honors include Pushcart nominations, a Best of the Net nomination, and two Allen Ginsberg Poetry Awards.

GAIL RUDD ENTREKIN's most recent books of poems are *The Art of Healing* (coauthored with her husband, Charles Entrekin) and *Rearrangement of the Invisible*. She is editor of the online environmental literary journal *Canary* (canarylitmag.org) and poetry editor of Hip Pocket Press. She has been a finalist for the Pablo Neruda Prize and, in 2016, a winner of the Women's National Book Association Award.

MAUREEN EPPSTEIN's bioregion is the mixed conifer forest, grassy headlands, and rocky shore of the Mendocino Coast of Northern California. She has published three poetry collections—*Earthward, Rogue Wave at Glass Beach*, and *Quickening*—and has taught poetry workshops at the College of the Redwoods Mendocino Coast. www.maureen-eppstein.com

MARCIA FALK is a poet, painter, translator, and Judaic scholar. Her books include *The Book of Blessings: New Jewish Prayers for Daily Life, the Sabbath, and the New Moon Festival; The Days Between: Blessings, Poems, and Directions of the Heart for the Jewish High Holiday Season*; and *The Song of Songs: Love Lyrics from the Bible*.

DEBORAH FASS grew up in Los Angeles and later moved to San Francisco. Her work has won an Academy of American Poets Prize and has appeared in journals including *Terrain.org, Canary*, and *The Fourth River: Tributaries*. Her latest poetry collection is *Where the Current Catches* (Island Verse Editions, 2017).

ANN FISHER-WIRTH's fifth book of poems, *Mississippi*, was published by Wings Press in 2018; it is a poetry/photography collaboration with the acclaimed Delta photographer Maude Schuyler Clay. Ann is the coeditor, with Laura-Gray Street, of *The Ecopoetry Anthology* (Trinity University Press, 2013). She teaches English at the University of Mississippi and also directs the Environmental Studies program.

JACK FOLEY has published 15 books of poetry, five books of criticism, a book of stories, and the two-volume *Visions & Affiliations: A California Literary Time Line, Poets and Poetry, 1940–2005*. His radio show airs every Wednesday on KPFA-FM. In 2010, he received a Lifetime Achievement Award from the Berkeley Poetry Festival, and June 5 was proclaimed "Jack Foley Day" in Berkeley.

CB FOLLETT is the author of 11 books of poems, the most recent of which is *Noah's Boat* (2016), and several chapbooks, including *Boxing the Compass* series. She is the editor/publisher of Arctos Press, was publisher and coeditor (with Susan Terris) of *RUNES, A Review of Poetry*, and was Poet Laureate of Marin County, California (2010-2013).

REBECCA FOUST is the Poet Laureate of Marin County, California, and author of the books *Paradise Drive*; *All That Gorgeous Pitiless Song*; and *God, Seed: Poetry & Art About the Natural World*; as well as the chapbooks *Dark Card* and *Mom's Canoe*.

DIANE FRANK is an award-winning poet and the author of six books of poems, including *Swan Light, Entering the Word Temple*, and *The Winter Life of Shooting Stars*. She teaches at San Francisco State University and the Dominican University of California, leads workshops for young writers as a Poet in the Schools, and directs Blue Light Press.

THEA GAVIN is a native of Orange, California, where she never gets tired of (shoelessly) exploring the nearby coastal sage scrub and chaparral communities. Other sources of inspiration include the Grand Canyon, Oregon's Wallowa County, and all the adventurous wanderers and writers she's met in her journeys. www.theagavin.wordpress.com

TRINA GAYNON is a literacy tutor. Her poems appear in *The Great Gatsby Anthology, The San Diego Poetry Annual, Saint Peter's B-list: Contemporary Poems Inspired by the Saints, Obsession: Sestinas in the Twenty-First Century, A Ritual to Read Together: Poems in Conversation with William Stafford*, and several WriteGirl anthologies.

JOAN GELFAND is the author of three poetry collections and *You Can Be a Winning Writer* (Mango Press). Her *Ferlinghetti School of Poetics*, a poetry film, showed internationally and won a Certificate of Merit from the International Association for the Study of Dreams. Joan lives in San Francisco with Adam Hertz. http://joangelfand.com

DAN GERBER is the author of nine poetry collections, three novels, a book of short stories, and two books of nonfiction. *ForeWord Review*'s Gold Medal Book of the Year Award in Poetry for *Trying to Catch the Horses* is one of his many honors.

DANA GIOIA is an internationally acclaimed and award-winning poet. Former Chairman of the National Endowment for the Arts, Gioia is a native Californian of Italian and Mexican descent. He received a BA and an MBA from Stanford University and an MA in comparative literature from Harvard University. Gioia currently serves as the Poet Laureate of California.

A California resident since 1961, SUSAN GLASS taught English and women's studies at San Jose State University and West Valley College until 2013, when she retired in order to write full-time. Her poetry has appeared in *The Broad River Review*, *Snowy Egret*, and *Magnets and Ladders: Active Voices of Writers with Disabilities*.

TERRI GLASS is a writer of the natural world. She currently teaches in the California Poet in the Schools program in the Bay Area and served as their Program Director from 2008 to 2011. She is the author of a book of nature poetry, *The Song of Yes*, and a chapbook of haiku, *Birds, Bees, Trees, Love, Hee Hee*. https://terriglass.com

HARRIET GLEESON, a transplant from the Southern Hemisphere, lives two miles from the Pacific Ocean on the fringes of a second-growth redwood forest—a rich milieu for creating poetry while walking the dog. She began writing on her retirement when she and her partner moved from the San Francisco Bay Area to California's north coast.

TOM GOFF is an instructional assistant at Folsom Lake College. He has published four poetry chapbooks, including *Twenty Two* (little m press, 2015). His poems on English composer/poet Arnold Bax appear on the Sir Arnold Bax website (arnoldbax.com). Tom is married to poet/artist Nora Laila Staklis; they live in the Lower American River watershed.

LIZ GONZÁLEZ's poetry, fiction, and memoirs have been published widely. Her work appears in *Inlandia: San Bernardino*, the City of Los Angeles 2017 Latino Heritage Month Calendar, *Askew Poetry Journal*, and *Voices from Leimert Park Redux*. She directs Uptown Word & Arts and teaches for the UCLA Extension Writers' Program. lizgonzalez.com

RAFAEL JESÚS GONZÁLEZ, writing bilingually in Spanish and English, has thrice been nominated for a Pushcart Prize. Published in the United States and abroad, he is the City of Berkeley's first Poet Laureate. His book *La musa lunática/The Lunatic Muse*, published in 2009, is in its second printing. rjgonzalez.blogspot.com

GRACE MARIE GRAFTON's most recent poetry book is *Jester*, from Hip Pocket Press. Her previous collections include *Zero, Visiting Sisters, Other Clues, Chrysanthemum Oratorio*, and *Whimsy, Reticence & Laud*. Three of her poems in this anthology are in her next collection, *Lens*, which will be released by Unsolicited Press in 2019.

KAREN GREENBAUM-MAYA, a retired clinical psychologist, German major, two-time Pushcart nominee, and occasional photographer, no longer lives for Art but still thinks about it a lot. She reviewed restaurants for the *Claremont Courier* for five years. Her work appears frequently in journals and anthologies, and her latest poetry collection is *The Book of Knots and Their Untying*.

EMILY GROSHOLZ spent the first two years of her life in California, returned there briefly as a teenager with her family, and years later spent a month as artist-in-residence at the Djerassi Foundation. She teaches philosophy at the Pennsylvania State University and has published eight books of poetry.

SUSAN GUBERNAT's second poetry collection, *The Zoo at Night*, won the Prairie Schooner Book Prize in Poetry and was published in September 2017 by the University of Nebraska Press. Her poems have appeared widely in literary journals. She is a professor in the English Department at California State University, East Bay.

BENJAMIN GUCCIARDI's poems have appeared in *Indiana Review, Orion, Terrain.org, upstreet, Forklift, Ohio* and other journals. He is a winner of the Milton Kessler Memorial Prize from *Harpur Palate*, a Dorothy Rosenberg Prize, and contests from *The Maine Review* and *The Santa Ana River Review*.

KEN HAAS lives in San Francisco, where he works in healthcare and sponsors a poetry writing program at the UCSF Benioff Children's Hospital. His poems have appeared in over 50 journals, including *Freshwater, Helix, Natural Bridge, Nimrod, Poet Lore, Quiddity,* and *Spoon River Poetry Review*. http://kenhaas.org

CC HART was born and raised in California's Central Valley, where forays into the Sierra Nevada deeply informed her childhood. She holds an MFA in writing from the University of San Francisco. Her work has been published in *The Dawntreader, Erstwhile Magazine*, and the neuroscience journal *Multisensory Research*.

ROBERT HASS is a celebrated poet and also a leading critic and translator, notably of the Polish poet Czeslaw Milosz and Japanese haiku masters Bashō, Buson, and Issa. He is the author or editor of more than 20 books of poems, essays, and translations. A professor at the University of Calilfornia, Berkeley, he served as the US Poet Laureate from 1995 to 1997.

Born in the shadow of the world's smallest mountain range, the Sutter Buttes, POLLY HATFIELD resides now amidst rambunctious gardens in Portland, Oregon, where the verdant revolutions hold her heart, alongside her beloved partner and one mammoth striped cat who forever prowls the delicate balance between feral and domestic.

DOLORES HAYDEN's poetry collections are *American Yard* (2004) and *Nymph, Dun, and Spinner* (2010). *Exuberance*, a sequence set in the early years of aviation, is forthcoming in 2019 from Red Hen Press. Her poems have appeared in *Poetry, Raritan, Best American Poetry, Ecotone, The Common*, and *Yale Review*. She has taught at UCLA and Yale.

ELIZABETH C. HERRON is the author of four chapbooks, a book of short fiction, and poems that have been recently published in more than a dozen literary magazines. She is a long-standing member of PEN and a Fellow with the International League of Conservation Writers.

TIFFANY HIGGINS is the author of *The Apparition at Fort Bragg* (2016), selected by Camille T. Dungy; *And Aeneas Stares into Her Helmet* (2009), selected by Evie Shockley; and *Tail of the Whale* (2016), translations from Portuguese of poems by Alice Sant'Anna. Her article "Brazil's Munduruku Mark Out Their Territory When the Government Won't" appears in *Granta*.

NELLIE HILL has published poetry and short stories in a variety of literary journals and magazines as well as in two books and two chapbooks. Journals in which her poems have appeared include *Poetry East, American Poetry Review* (with an introduction by Denise Levertov), *Harvard Magazine, Commonweal*, and *New Millennium*.

TOBEY HILLER writes poetry, flash prose, and fiction. Publications: three books of poetry, a novel, and poetry and prose in a variety of journals and three previous anthologies. Awards: two first prizes for poems (*Milkweed Chronicle, SF Poetry*); stories short-listed for the Reynolds-Price Short Fiction Award and the Los Gatos-Listowel short story contest.

BRENDA HILLMAN is the award-winning author of nine collections of poetry: *White Dress, Fortress, Death Tractates, Bright Existence, Loose Sugar, Cascadia, Pieces of Air in the Epic, Practical Water*, and *Seasonal Works with Letters on Fire*. She is a professor at Saint Mary's College in Moraga, California, and a Chancellor of the Academy of American Poets.

JANE HIRSHFIELD's most recent books are *The Beauty* (poems) and *Ten Windows: How Great Poems Transform the World* (essays), both from Knopf in

2015. A current Chancellor of the Academy of American Poets, her recent work appears in *The New Yorker*, *The New York Times Magazine*, and the Canadian journal *Brick*. She lives in the San Francisco Bay Area.

After high school, DAVE HOLT began setting poems to music. This led to a move from Toronto, Canada, to California, where he followed the muse of storytelling and poetry into SF State University's creative writing program (MA '95). He is Anishinaabe/Ojibway (Chippewa) Indian on his mother's side. His award-winning poetry collection is *Voyages to Ancestral Islands*.

TIMOTHY HOUGHTON's *The Internal Distance: Selected Poems, 1989-2012*, appeared in a bilingual (Italian/English) edition from the Italian publisher Hebenon/Mimesis Edizioni in late 2015. The book was presented in Florence at the Museo Casa di Dante. Recent publications include *Stand*, *Cyphers*, *Oxford Poetry*, and *Agenda*. He conducts bird surveys for Audubon.

PATTY JOSLYN moved back to Mendocino County, California, in 2012 from Vermont, where she worked primarily in end-of-life care. She is fascinated with both death and birth as passages into new realms. As a writer she has published in *El Calendario de Todos Santos*, *Poets Online*, *VOYA (Voice of Youth Advocates)*, and Tupelo Press' 30/30 Project, and her work has been included in several anthologies.

SUSAN KELLY-DEWITT's poetry books are *Spider Season*, *The Fortunate Islands*, *A Camellia for Judy*, *Feather's Hand*, *To a Small Moth*, *Susan Kelly-DeWitt's Greatest Hits*, *The Land*, *The Book of Insects*, and *Cassiopeia Above the Banyan Tree*. Her many awards include a Wallace Stegner Fellowship. She lives in Sacramento, California.

LAURIE KLEIN is the author of *Where the Sky Opens* (Poiema Poetry Series, Wipf and Stock) and *Bodies of Water, Bodies of Flesh*, a prize-winning chapbook. Her poems have appeared in *Terrain.org*, *The Southern Review*, *Natural Bridge*, *Barrow Street*, *Midwest Quarterly*, and other journals and anthologies. She lives in the Pacific Northwest.

LYNNE KNIGHT graduated from Syracuse University, where she was a fellow in poetry and received her MA in creative writing and literature. After teaching for four decades at both the high school and college levels, Lynne now works as a poet and translator. She is the award-winning author of nine poetry collections and chapbooks.

TRICIA KNOLL's poetry collections include her full-length book *Ocean's Laughter* (Aldrich Press) and her chapbook *Urban Wild* (Finishing Line Press). Her poems appear widely in anthologies and journals, including *Written River*, *Calyx*, *Windfall*, and *Mojave River Review*. www.triciaknoll.com

STEVE KOWIT's poetry collections include *The Dumbbell Nebula* and *The First Noble Truth*. He taught at Southwestern College in Chula Vista, California, and lived in the backcountry hills of San Diego County with his wife, Mary. Steve passed away in his sleep in 2015 at the age of 76.

JENNIFER LAGIER has published 14 books, coedits the *Homestead Review*, and helps coordinate Monterey Bay Poetry Consortium readings. Newest books: *Scene of the Crime* (Evening Street Press), *Harbingers* (Blue Light Press), *Camille Abroad* (FutureCycle Press), and *Like a B Movie* (FutureCycle Press). Forthcoming in 2018 is *Camille Mobilizes* (FutureCycle Press). jlagier.net

W. F. LANTRY, native of San Diego, currently in DC, has two full-length collections: *The Structure of Desire*, winner of the 2013 Nautilus Award and *The Terraced Mountain*. Honors include the Hackney Literary Award and poetry prizes from *Potomac Review, Old Red Kimono, Comment, Crucible*, and *CutBank*. He is the editor of *Peacock Journal*.

NOREEN LAWLOR is a poet, artist, and therapist who lives in Joshua Tree. Her fourth book of poetry and paintings, about her last 13 years in Joshua Tree, called *Mostly Mojave*, was published in 2018. She shares that the harsh yet fragile environment of the desert has informed her recent writing.

T.M. LAWSON is a writer and poet living in Los Angeles. She has been published by *Los Angeles Review, Entropy*, and Poets.org, and has forthcoming work in the *Nomadic Journal* and *White Stag*. She is a 2015 Academy of American Poets Prize winner and a 2016 Thompson Prize winner.

URSULA K. LE GUIN, born in Berkeley in 1929, started publishing poetry and fiction in the 1960s. Recent books are *Late in the Day* (poems, 2015) and *Words Are My Matter* (nonfiction, 2016). In 2014 the National Book Foundation awarded her the Medal for Distinguished Contribution to American Letters. She died in January 2018.

CYNTHIA LESLIE-BOLE is a writing coach, editor, and certified Amherst Writers and Artists Method writing group leader who has been published in *Pure Slush, Rootstalk,* and *Moonshine Ink*'s Creative Brew. Cynthia's new collection of poems, *The Luminous In-Between*, invites readers to experience the radiance of one woman's evolution through marriage, motherhood, spiritual individuation, and kinship with nature.

RICHARD MICHAEL LEVINE was a magazine writer and editor for many years. His bestselling nonfiction book is *Bad Blood: A Family Murder in Marin County*. He is also the author of *Catch and Other Poems* and a short story collection, *The Man Who Gave Away His Organs: Tales of Love and Obsession at Midlife.* http://richardmichaellevine.com

ELLARAINE LOCKIE is a widely published and award-winning author of poetry, nonfiction books, and essays. Her eleventh chapbook, *Where the*

*Meadowlark Sings*, won the 2014 Encircle Publications Chapbook Contest. Her newest collection, *Love Me Tender in Midlife*, has been released in the chapbook collection *IDES* from Silver Birch Press.

NAOMI RUTH LOWINSKY is a Jungian analyst and poet. Her chapbook, *The Little House on Stilts Remembers*, won the Blue Light Poetry Prize. Her fourth full-length collection is *The Faust Woman Poems*. Her memoir, *The Sister from Below: When the Muse Gets Her Way*, tells stories about her pushy muse.

After years teaching writers and writing teachers in the San Francisco Bay Area, CATHARINE LUCAS embraces the writer's life, sustained by Zen practice, medieval singing, and a Berkeley garden that mirrors life's impermanence. Her poems have appeared in *Cloudbank 9, Fogged Clarity, Dallas Review, WomenArts Quarterly, Zone 3, The Alembic*, and *Sweet*, among many others. www. catharinelucas.com

KIRK LUMPKIN is a poet, spoken-word and performance artist, lyricist, and environmental activist. He is currently creating all-ages material suitable for outdoor education, including raps in the voices of a Steller's jay and a tanoak tree and pieces in the voices of fire and a creek. www.kirklumpkin.com

MARY MAKOFSKE's latest books are *World Enough and Time* (Kelsay, 2017) and *Traction* (Ashland Poetry Press, 2011), the Richard Snyder Award winner. Her poems have appeared in many literary journals nationwide and internationally and in 18 anthologies. In 2017 she received *Atlanta Review*'s Poetry Prize and a *New Millennium* Writing Award. www.marymakofske.com

EILEEN MALONE lives in the coastal fog at the edge of the San Francisco Bay Area. Her poetry has been published in numerous literary journals and anthologies. Her award-winning collection *Letters with Taloned Claws* was published by Poets Corner Press, and her book *I Should Have Given Them Water* was published by Ragged Sky Press.

JACQUELINE MARCUS' first collection of poems, *Close to the Shore*, was published by Michigan State University Press. Her second collection, *Summer Rains*, was published by Iris Press. Her new chapbook, *Suspended Time*, will be published at Iris Press in fall 2018. She taught philosophy at Cuesta College in San Luis Obispo, California, and is the editor of *ForPoetry.com* and *EnvironmentalPress.com*.

JERRY MARTIEN's occupations have included bookstore clerk, carpenter, and instructor of literature and writing at Humboldt State University. He is also a student of money and culture, publishing such books as *Shell Game: A True Account of Beads and Money in North America*. His poetry collections include *Pieces in Place* and *At the School of Doors*.

BRONWYN MAULDIN is the author of the novel *Love Songs of the Revolution* and the short story collection *The Streetwise Cycle*. She is the creator of *GuerrillaReads*, an online video literary magazine. In September 2016 she was an artist-in-residence at Mesa Verde National Park.

KATHLEEN MCCLUNG's books include *The Typists Play Monopoly* and *Almost the Rowboat*. Winner of the Rita Dove, Shirley McClure, and Maria W. Faust poetry prizes, she is an associate director and sonnet judge for the Soul-Making Keats Literary Competition. She teaches at Skyline College and The Writing Salon and lives in San Francisco. www.kathleenmcclung.com

JUDITH MCCOMBS grew up nomadic, in a geodetic surveyor's family. Her poems appear in *Delmarva, Potomac* and *Saranac Reviews, Innisfree, Nimrod, Poetry, Shenandoah* (Graybeal-Gowen Prize); and in her collection *The Habit of Fire: Poems Selected and New*. She works with The Word Works, George Washington University's "A Splendid Wake" celebration, and Federal Poets, and arranges the Kensington Row Bookshop readings.

JOSHUA MCKINNEY is the author of three collections of poetry: *Saunter*, co-winner of the University of Georgia Press Poetry Series Open Competition; *The Novice Mourner*, winner of the Dorothy Brunsman Poetry Prize; and *Mad Cursive*. He teaches at California State University, Sacramento. An amateur lichenologist, he is a member of the California Lichen Society.

STEPHEN MEADOWS is a Californian of pioneer and Ohlone descent whose poems have appeared in anthologies and journals nationwide. He is a 20-year veteran of public radio, where he has interviewed scores of musicians and visionaries. The author of *Releasing the Days* (Heyday), he resides with his family in the foothills of the Sierra Nevada.

A. D. MILLER has served the arts community of the San Francisco Bay Area for more than four decades as a teacher, writer, editor, publisher, and radio and television programmer and producer. His memoirs are *Ticket to Exile* and *Fall Rising*. His latest poetry collection is *The Sky is a Page: New and Selected Poems*.

FLORENCE MILLER, author of *Upriver: New and Selected Poems*, taught creative writing and advised the literary magazine at McClymonds High School in Oakland, California. The Emmy Award-winning documentary *Can You Hear Me*, by Allen Willis, was based on her students' poems. She is a Pushcart nominee and a founding member of the Shakespeare's Sisters collective.

JACOB MINASIAN received his MFA from Saint Mary's College of California. His work has appeared in or is forthcoming from Poets.org, *Gyroscope Review, Causeway Lit, Linden Avenue Literary Journal, These Fragile Lilacs, Museum of Americana*, and *RipRap Literary Journal*, among others. Originally from California, he currently lives in Cincinnati, Ohio.

MARY B. MOORE has three recent books: *Amanda and the Man Soul* (Emrys Writing Prize, 2017, chapbook); *Flicker* (Dogfish Head Poetry Prize, 2016, full-length); and *Eating the Light* (Sable Books Award, 2016, chapbook). Poems appear in *Nimrod, Georgia Review, Nasty Women Poets, The Orison Anthology, Birmingham Poetry Review, Drunken Boat, Cider Press Review,* and elsewhere.

KAY MORGAN's poetry has been published in several anthologies, appeared online in *The Avocet* and *The Moon Magazine*, and is forthcoming in *Reed Magazine*. She lives, gardens, and writes on the seacoast of New Hampshire, though her roots are in the beaches of Southern California.

BONNIE MOSSE lives in San Diego, where she is retired from teaching world literature. She enjoys singing, hiking, playing Scottish fiddle, reading, gardening, and knitting. She writes for nonprofits working to fight climate change, the most critical issue of our time, but solvable by people of good will.

STEPHANIE NOBLE's poems have been published in *Atlanta Review, IthacaLit, Pilgrimage Magazine, Buddhist Poetry Review, DoveTales, Mindful Word, Light of Consciousness, Unsilenced: The Spirit of Women,* and others. A 2014 Pushcart Prize nominee, she is the website administrator for the Marin Group of the Sierra Club and teaches insight meditation. stephanienoble.com

JUDITH OFFER has had two daughters, five books of poetry, and dozens of plays. (Eighteen of the latter, including six musicals, have been produced.) She has read her poetry at scores of poetry venues but is particularly delighted to have been included in the Library of Congress series and on NPR's *All Things Considered*. www.JudithOffer.com

J. C. OLANDER, bio-educator with California Poets in the Schools since 1984, blends performance with spoken word, creating musical image phrasings dramatizing relative experiences—poetry arising from oral traditions—a sound poet exploring meanings of words, phrasings, ideas arranged in sound rhythm patterns. *River Light* is his first book of poetry.

CANDACE PEARSON grew up in the "other" California—that vast stretch known as the Central Valley—and the landscape still informs her poetry. Her full-length collection, *Hour of Unfolding*, received the Liam Rector First Book Prize for Poetry from Longwood University, and her poems have appeared in fine journals and anthologies nationwide.

A native of New Jersey, VINCENT PELOSO has been a California resident since 1979. A finalist for the 1990 Discovery/The Nation Prize, in 1999 he was a California Poets and Writers poet-in-residence at the Ink People Center for the Arts. From 1994 to 2008, he hosted a poetry program on KHSU radio, in Arcata, California.

EVELYN POSAMENTIER is the author of *Poland at the Door* (Knives Forks and Spoons, 2011). Her work has appeared in the *Yale Journal for Humanities in Medicine, Tule Review, New York Quarterly, Drunken Boat, 3:AM Magazine, Free Verse,* and *American Poetry Review*, among others. Her latest book is *Royal Blue Car* (RAW ArT PRESS, 2016).

Novelist and poet BARBARA QUICK lives with her husband, violist Wayne Roden, on a little farm and vineyard outside of Cotati, in the wine country of Northern California.

ZARA RAAB grew up in Mendocino County, where her family has lived—ranching, lumbering, farming, and building—for five generations. Her books are *Fracas & Asylum* and *Swimming the Eel* (David Robert Books, 2010, 2013). Her book reviews and poems have appeared in *Verse Daily, River Styx, West Branch, Arts & Letters, Crab Orchard Review*, and other journals.

ERIN REDFERN is a writing mentor in San Jose. Her work has appeared recently in the *Naugatuck River Review,* the *New Ohio Review*, and the delicious anthology *Ice Cream Poems* (World Enough Writers). Her first chapbook is *Spellbreaking and Other Life Skills* (Blue Lyra Press Delphi Series, 2016). www.erinredfern.net

KIM ROBERTS is the author of *A Literary Guide to Washington, DC: Walking in the Footsteps of American Writers from Francis Scott Key to Zora Neale Hurston* (University of Virginia Press, 2018) and five books of poems, most recently *The Scientific Method* (WordTech Editions, 2017). She coedits the journal *Beltway Poetry Quarterly*. www.kimroberts.org

SYLVIA ROSS is the author of five books, including *East of the Great Valley*, a novel about an Indian child who survives genocide. In 2010, Ross' children's book, *Blue Jay Girl*, won a publication award from the Tule River Indian Reservation. Although she is of Chukchansi descent, Sylvia was born and raised in Los Angeles.

MARY KAY RUMMEL was Poet Laureate of Ventura County, California, from 2014 to 2016. Her eighth book of poetry, *Cypher Garden*, was published by Blue Light Press in 2017, and *The Lifeline Trembles* won the 2014 Blue Light Prize. She performs her poems in many venues and teaches at California State University Channel Islands.

CATHIE SANDSTROM's poems have appeared in *Ploughshares, RUNES, Lyric, Ekphrasis, Comstock Review, Cider Press Review*, and *New Plains Review*, among others. Her work appears in anthologies including *Wide Awake: Poets of Los Angeles and Beyond, All We Can Hold*, and *Beyond the Lyric Moment*. Her manuscript *All the Land Around Us* was a finalist for a Perugia Press Prize.

NANCY SCHIMMEL grew up in California, first in Berkeley, with summers in Santa Cruz, and then from fifth grade on in Long Beach, with summers in the San Gabriel Mountains and family trips to the high desert. She returned to Berkeley to go to UC Berkeley, and settled in the Bay Area, working as a librarian and then as a storyteller and singer/songwriter.

EVA M. SCHLESINGER is the author of four poetry chapbooks, including *Ninnies Who Whinny* (2018). She's received the Literal Latté Food Verse Award and contributed to *Cooking with the Muse, Changing Harm to Harmony: Bullies & Bystanders Project*, and *Cricket*. She enjoys photographing nature and drawing wildly colorful, whimsical animals.

JOYCE SCHMID's recent poetry has appeared in or is forthcoming from *Missouri Review, Poetry Daily, New Ohio Review*, and other journals and anthologies. She has a BA from Harvard and has studied Russian literature at Columbia, where she met a San Francisco man who said that living in the East felt like being in exile. So they moved to Palo Alto, California.

STEPHANIE SCHULTZ's poems have appeared in *Fracture: Essays, Poems, and Stories on Fracking in America* and *South Dakota Magazine*. She received her MFA in creative writing from Hamline University and lives in St. Paul, Minnesota. In 2016, her poem "Golden Hour in Sage Creek" won First Prize in the National Park Service's Centennial Project Contest.

KURT SCHWEIGMAN is coeditor of *Red Indian Road West: Native American Poetry from California*, and his poetry appears in *Shedding Skins: Four Sioux Poets* (Michigan State University Press). The first spoken-word poet to receive an individual artist fellowship in literature from the Archibald Bush Foundation, he is an enrolled member of the Oglala Sioux Tribe, Pine Ridge Reservation.

ERIC PAUL SHAFFER's seventh book of poetry, *Even Further West*, was published by Unsolicited Press in April 2018. Other books include *A Million-Dollar Bill*; *Lāhaina Noon*; *Portable Planet*; and *Living at the Monastery, Working in the Kitchen*. Shaffer teaches composition, literature, and creative writing at Honolulu Community College.

HEIDI M. SHERIDAN was born and educated in California and currently lives in New Jersey. Her poems have appeared in many literary journals. She is Assistant Professor of English at Ocean County College. She received her MA in English at Cal Poly, San Luis Obispo, and her MFA in poetry at Drew University in New Jersey.

GINNY SHORT is currently a student at the Regis University Mile High MFA program in Denver, Colorado, studying poetry and creative nonfiction. Her day job as an ecologist in the field of conservation and plant and animal ecology takes her into the extreme conditions of the deserts of Southern California, where she finds ample inspiration for her writing.

KAREN SKOLFIELD's book *Frost in the Low Areas* (Zone 3 Press) won the 2014 PEN New England Award in poetry, and she is the winner of the 2016 Jeffrey E. Smith Editors' Prize in poetry from *The Missouri Review*. Skolfield teaches writing to engineers at the University of Massachusetts Amherst.

GARY SNYDER is the author of many books of poems and essays, including *This Present Moment* (2015) and *The Great Clod: Notes and Memoirs on Nature and History in East Asia* (2016). He is also an environmental activist and has been called the Poet Laureate of Deep Ecology. His awards include a Pulitzer Prize and an American Book Award for poetry.

JAN STECKEL was a pediatrician who took care of Spanish-speaking children until chronic pain persuaded her to change professions to writer, poet, and medical editor. Her poetry book *The Horizontal Poet* (Zeitgeist Press, 2011) won a 2012 Lambda Literary Award. She is also the author of two award-winning chapbooks.

DAVID ST. JOHN is the author of 11 collections of poetry, including *The Last Troubadour* (2017), as well as a volume of essays, interviews, and reviews entitled *Where the Angels Come Toward Us*. A Chancellor of the Academy of American Poets, he is University Professor and Chair of English at the University of Southern California, and lives in Venice Beach.

ELIZABETH STOESSL is a retired librarian who lives in Portland, Oregon. The Monterey Peninsula was once home to her, and she returns there often. Her poetry has been published in numerous journals and anthologies, including *Measure*, the *Naugatuck River Review*, the *Sow's Ear Poetry Review*, *VoiceCatcher*, and *The Poeming Pigeon: Love Poems*.

VINCE STORTI (1944-2017) graduated from UC Berkeley. He was the founder and editor of *North Coast Literary Review*. In addtion to poetry, his creative pursuits included music, painting, auditory investigations, film, and pen-and-ink visualizations. He said he worked to "create visual and literary pieces which investigate conscious and unconscious realms."

CHAD SWEENEY is the author of five books of poetry, including *White Martini of the Apocalypse* (Marick Press), *Parable of Hide and Seek* (Alice James), *Arranging the Blaze* (Anhinga Press), and *Wolf's Milk: The Lost Notebooks of Juan Sweeney* (Forklift Books). Chad teaches in the MFA program at California State University, San Bernardino, where he edits *Ghost Town* (ghosttownlitmag.com).

JENNIFER K. SWEENEY is the author of *Little Spells* (New Issues Press, 2015); *How to Live on Bread and Music* (Perugia Press, 2009), winner of the 2009 James

Laughlin Award and the 2009 Perugia Press Prize; and *Salt Memory* (Main Street Rag, 2006), winner of the 2006 Main Street Rag Poetry Award. She lives in California.

SONJA SWIFT writes toward a place of understanding, both of herself and of our world. Writing is her creative medium for grappling with the complexity of our times. She was born and raised on a subtropical fruit farm and longhorn cattle ranch in Los Osos, California, and currently lives in San Francisco.

SUSAN TERRIS' most recent book is *Take Two: Film Studies* (Omnidawn). She is the author of seven books of poetry, 15 chapbooks, and three artist's books. Journal publications include *The Southern Review, Denver Quarterly*, and *Ploughshares*. A poem of hers from *Field* appeared in the anthology *Pushcart Prize XXXI*. She served as editor of *Spillway*. www.susanterris.com

JUDITH TERZI's poetry has appeared in journals such as *Atlanta Review* (International Publication Prize, 2015), *Caesura, Raintown Review, Spillway*, and *Unsplendid*, and in anthologies such as *Times They Were A-Changing: Women Remember the '60s & '70s* and *Wide Awake: The Poets of Los Angeles and Beyond. If You Spot Your Brother Floating By* is her latest chapbook.

LYNNE THOMPSON is the recipient of an Individual Artist Fellowship from the City of Los Angeles and the author of two full-length poetry collections, *Beg No Pardon*, winner of the Perugia Press Prize and the Great Lakes Colleges Association's New Writers Award, and *Start with a Small Guitar* (What Books Press). One of her poems received the Stephen Dunn Poetry Prize.

J. C. TODD, a Pew Fellow and recipient of the Rita Dove Poetry Award, is the author of *On Foot/By Hand* and *FUBAR*, two collaborative artist's books (Lucia Press, 2018, 2016), and of *What Space This Body* (Wind Publications, 2008). Poems have appeared in *The Paris Review, American Poetry Review,* and *Beloit Poetry Journal*. http://www.pcah.us/people/j_c_todd

JAMES TOUPIN, a descendant of a gold rush immigrant, was born and raised in San Francisco and graduated from Stanford and UC Berkeley. Circumstance sent him to Washington, DC, however, for his professional career, and he eventually retired as general counsel of the US Patent and Trademark Office. His poems have appeared in dozens of journals, garnering a couple of Pushcart nominations.

PATTI TRIMBLE is a poet, essayist, and visual artist living in California and Sicily. Her poems are widely published and she performs in the United States and Europe. Current projects include *Nomad Poems*, written in Sicily and California; a memoir of her work with abstract expressionist painters; and co-translations of Arabic poetry. Patti was a co-founder of the Tuolumne Poetry Festival in Yosemite. https://pattitrimble.com

ARIN VASQUEZ is a senior at the Ruth Asawa San Francisco School of the Arts. Arin, whose discipline is creative writing, says, "I am 17 years old and agender (I use they/them pronouns) and I've loved writing since I was a very little kid. I am Salvadorian and speak both Spanish and English, and have lived in San Francisco my whole life."

JEANNE WAGNER is the winner of several national awards, most recently an *Arts & Letters* Award, a *Sow's Ear* Chapbook Prize, and a *Sow's Ear* Prize for an individual poem. Her first book, *The Zen Piano Mover*, won the Stevens Poetry Manuscript Prize. Her most recent book, *In the Body of Our Lives*, was released by Sixteen Rivers Press in 2011.

LENORE WEISS received an MFA in creative writing from San Francisco State University. Her poetry and stories have been widely published online and in print journals. Books include *Cutting Down the Last Tree on Easter Island* (West End Press, 2012), *Two Places* (Kelsay Books, 2014), and *The Golem* (Hadassa Word Press, 2017). www.lenoreweiss.com

SARAH BROWN WEITZMAN, a past National Endowment for the Arts Fellow in Poetry and Pushcart Prize nominee, has had work in *New Ohio Review, Poet & Critic, North American Review, Bellingham Review, Rattle, Mid-American Review, The MacGuffin, Poet Lore, Spillway, Miramar*, and elsewhere. Pudding House published her chapbook, *The Forbidden*.

JUDY WELLS' latest poetry collection, *The Glass Ship* (Sugartown, 2014), completes her trilogy of Irish-themed works, including *Everything Irish* and *Call Home* (both from Scarlet Tanager Books). *Dear Phebe*, a poetry and prose collection about her Dickinson ancestors, will be published by Sugartown in 2018. And yes, she is related to Emily Dickinson!

KARI WERGELAND, who originally hails from Davis, California, is a librarian and writer. Her poetry has appeared in *Jabberwock Review: A Journal of Literature and Art, New Millennium Writings, Pembroke Magazine*, and many other journals. Her chapbook, *Breast Cancer: A Poem in Five Acts*, is available from Finishing Line Press.

LISBETH WHITE is a poet, editor, and Expressive Arts Therapist. A 2016 Pushcart Prize nominee, Lisbeth is also an alumna of the VONA/Voices of Our Nations Arts Foundation and the Callaloo creative writing workshops. Her poems have been published by or are forthcoming in *Visitant Winter Tangerine, Obsidian: Literature & Arts in the African Diaspora*, and *Kweli*.

ANNE WHITEHOUSE was born and raised in Birmingham, Alabama. She graduated from Harvard College and Columbia University and now lives in New York City. She is the author of five poetry collections—*The Surveyor's Hand*,

*Blessings and Curses, Bear in Mind, One Sunday Morning*, and *The Refrain*—as well as a novel, *Fall Love*.

HELEN WICK is a poet and artist from Petaluma, California. While completing her BA in creative writing at Colorado College, she began to observe the changing climate of California more astutely. The topic culminated in a collection of poems she wrote after spending the spring of 2016 in Death Valley.

BRENDA YATES is the Pushcart-nominated author of *Bodily Knowledge* (Tebot Bach) and the recipient of a Patricia Bibby Memorial Prize and an award from the Beyond Baroque Literary Arts Center. She has poems in *Mississippi Review, City of the Big Shoulders: An Anthology of Chicago Poetry* (University of Iowa Press), and *The Southern Poetry Anthology, Volume VI: Tennessee* (Texas Review Press).

ANDRENA ZAWINSKI's latest book is *Landings* from Kelsay Books. She has two previous award-winning poetry collections: *Traveling in Reflected Light* and *Something About*. She is editor of *Turning a Train of Thought Upside Down: An Anthology of Women's Poetry* (Scarlet Tanager Books), runs the San Francisco Bay Area Women's Poetry Salon, and is the features editor at *PoetryMagazine.com*.

# Acknowledgments and Credits

*M*any people contributed insights, suggestions, and encouragement that helped make this anthology a reality. I would especially like to thank Malcolm Margolin for cheering me on when this book was just an idea and for recommending that I get in touch with several of the poets whose work appears here, including my coeditor, Ruth Nolan; Marcia Falk for bringing her keen eye and aesthetic judgment to bear on my questions about the design; and my husband, writer Richard Michael Levine, for his unwavering support during the seven years I worked on this project, including 2017, when the submissions were in stacks—sorted and resorted, read and reread—on our dining room table for most of the year. —L. L. D.

Thanks to all of the California poets whose works miraculously grace, celebrate, and sustain our state's many storied places in these pages and beyond. I'd also like to thank my family and friends for their encouragement of my literary endeavors, in particular my work coediting *Fire and Rain: Ecopoetry of California* with the indefatigable Lucille Lang Day. —R. N.

Cynthia Anderson, "Joshua Tree Weeping," printed with permission of the author.

Cathy Barber, "Scrub Jay," printed with permission of the author. "The Waiting Season" from *Roux Magazine* (2004) and "Return" from *Slippery Elm* (2014), reprinted with permission of the author.

Ellen Bass, "Taking My Old Dog Out to Pee Before Bed" from *The Sun* (2015), reprinted with permission of the author. "Their Naked Petals" from *Like a Beggar*, © 2014 by Ellen Bass, reprinted with the permission of The Permissions Company, Inc., on behalf of Copper Canyon Press, www.coppercanyonpress.org.

Ruth Bavetta, "Oranges and Pomegranates," "Pacific Savings Time," and "Kramer Junction," printed with permission of the author.

Richard Beban, "In Praise of Los Angeles" from *What the Heart Weighs* (Red Hen Press), © 2004 by Richard Beban, reprinted with permission of the author.

Paul Belz, "Elephant Seal on the Beach," printed with permission of the author.

Sally Bliumis-Dunn, "Sea Lions," printed with permission of the author.

Elaine Miller Bond, "The Hungry Calf," printed with permission of the author.

John Brantingham, "Your Story of Water," "Up on Whitney," and "Alta Peak," printed with permission of the author.

Nancy Sue Brink, "On the Day He Left for War" and "Have I Told You About the First Time I Saw White Pelicans Over Manzanar?," printed with permission of the author.

Patricia Brody, "Demeter Shops Local," printed with permission of the author.

Bri Bruce, "Feel" and "Storm," printed with permission of the author.

Christopher Buckley, "No Other Life" from *Crosswinds Poetry Journal* (2016) and "Drought" from *Spillway* (2015), reprinted with permission of the author.

Dane Cervine, "The Only Truth I Know" from *How Therapists Dance* (Plainview Press), © 2013 by Dane Cervine, reprinted with permission of the author.

Abby Chew, "Ohlone Tiger Beetle" and "Island Barberry," printed with permission of the author.

Robert Coats, "Logging Old Growth, 1964" from *The Harsh Green World*, © 2015 by Robert Coats, reprinted with permission of Sugartown Publishing.

Susan Cohen, "Golden Hills of California" from *Redactions: Poetry & Poetics* (2015), "Ode to the Brown Pelican" from the *Atlanta Review* (2012), and "Credo" from *California Quarterly* (2015), reprinted with permission of the author.

E. K. Cooper, "Salmon Time" and "Where Have They Gone?," printed with permission of the author.

Tasha Cotter, "Solar" from *Superstition Review* (2017), reprinted with permission of the author.

Barbara Crooker, "Leaving the White In" from *Barbara Crooker: Selected Poems* (FutureCycle Press), © 2015 by Barbara Crooker, reprinted with permission of the author.

Rachel Dacus, "Docks, Cliffs, and Tidepools" ("San Pedro Elegy," part 2), printed with permission of the author. "Bowing to the Gods of Upheaval" from *IthacaLit.com* (2012), reprinted with permission of the author.

Caryn Davidson, "Among the Tortoises," printed with permission of the author.

Carol V. Davis, "On a Stretch of Coastline," printed with permission of the author.

Lucille Lang Day, "Tracking," "Muir Woods at Night," "Lake Leonard," "Eye of the Beholder," "Mount St. Helena," and "History of the Biosphere" from *Infinities* (Cedar Hill Publications), © 2002 by Lucille Lang Day. "Naturalists" from *Becoming an Ancestor* (Červená Barva Press), © 2015 by Lucille Lang Day.

*on the Nature of Things* (Milkweed Editions, 2008), edited by Pamela Michael, introduction by Robert Hass, reprinted with permission of River of Words.

Ann Fisher-Wirth, "Light. Olympic Valley, California" from *Blue Window* (Archer Books), © 2003 by Ann Fisher-Wirth. "At McClure's Beach, Point Reyes National Seashore, California" from *Five Terraces* (Wind Publications), © 2005 by Ann Fisher-Wirth. "No Vow" from *Dream Cabinet* (Wings Press), © 2012 by Ann Fisher-Wirth. All reprinted with permission of the author.

Jack Foley, "Viriditas" from *Grief Songs* (Sagging Shorts, Sagging Meniscus Press), © 2017 by Jack Foley, reprinted with permission of the author.

CB Follett, "Once Here" from *Noah's Boat* (Many Voices Press), © 2016 by CB Follett, reprinted with permission of the author.

Rebecca Foust, "Seeds of the Giant Sequoia" from the *Atlanta Review* (2008) and "Sonoma Oak" from *Bayou* (2008), reprinted with permission of the author.

Diane Frank, "Mendocino Late Night" and "In the Mendocino Woodlands" from *Swan Light* (Blue Light Press), © 2013 by Diane Frank, reprinted with permission of the author.

Thea Gavin, "Fire Cycle," "Spinning SoCal," "Nothing Rhymes with Orange," and "Born in the Land," printed with permission of the author. "Definitely Home" from the Newsletter of the California Native Plant Society, Orange County Chapter (2011), reprinted with permission of the author.

Trina Gaynon, "Landscapes: San Fernando Valley," printed with permission of the author.

Joan Gelfand, "Russian River Watershed" and "California Cobra," printed with permission of the author.

Dan Gerber, "After the Rain" from *Particles: New and Selected Poems*, © 2007 by Dan Gerber, reprinted with the permission of The Permissions Company, Inc., on behalf of Copper Canyon Press, www.coppercanyonpress.org.

Dana Gioia, "California Hills in August" and "Rough Country" from *99 Poems: New and Selected* (Graywolf Press), © 2016 by Dana Gioia, reprinted with permission of the author.

Susan Glass, "Fainting in the Mojave" and "Chance," printed with permission of the author.

Terri Glass, "Wind Turbines of Altamont Pass" from *About Place Journal* (2015), reprinted with permission of the author.

Harriet Gleeson, "Charmed Circuit," printed with permission of the author.

Tom Goff, "You, Robinson Jeffers" and "The Work of the Monitor," printed with permission of the author.

liz gonzález, "Fall in the Chaparral," printed with permission of the author.

Rafael Jesús González, "Bajo Monte Shasta/Below Mt. Shasta" from *Raven Chronicles* (2016), reprinted with permission of the author.

Grace Marie Grafton, "Earthquake Country," "Canyon, Santa Barbara," "Succession (2)," and "Tangle," printed with permission of the author.

Karen Greenbaum-Maya, "Long Lake Blues" and "The Week Before My Friend Breaks Her Ankle…," printed with permission of the author. "Standing Ovation" from *New Verse News* (2009), reprinted with permission of the author.

Emily Grosholz, "The Gold Earrings" from *The Stars of Earth: New and Selected Poems*, © 2017 by Emily Grosholz, reprinted with the permission of Able Muse Press.

Susan Gubernat, "Yosemite," "To Return as Owl," and "In the Desert," printed with permission of the author.

Benjamin Gucciardi, "Scavengers," printed with permission of the author.

Ken Haas, "Otter," printed with permission of the author. "Birthday Poem" from the *Marin Poetry Center Anthology* (2013), reprinted with permission of the author.

CC Hart, "Halfway to Keeler, California," printed with permission of the author.

Robert Hass, "To Be Accompanied by Flute and Zither," printed with permission of the author. "Abbotts Lagoon: October" from *Bay Nature* (2011), reprinted with permission of the author.

Polly Hatfield, "Del Monte" and "Paraffin Moon," printed with permission of the author.

Dolores Hayden, "For Rent" from *American Yard* (David Robert Books), © 2004 by Dolores Hayden, reprinted with permission of the author.

Elizabeth C. Herron, "Who Remembers," printed with permission of the author. "Fawn on Bodega Highway" from the *Lindenwood Review* (2016), reprinted with permission of the author.

Tiffany Higgins, "There Is One Lone Hawk Who Seems," printed with permission of the author.

Nellie Hill, "After the News," printed with permission of the author. "Sunol Song Master" from *Snowy Egret* (2005), reprinted with permission of the author.

Tobey Hiller, "#2: Status Report" and "#5: Red" excerpted from "Interlope" and printed with permission of the author.

Brenda Hillman, excerpt from "Hydrology of California" from *Practical Water*, © 2009 by Brenda Hillman, reprinted with the permission of Wesleyan University Press.

Jane Hirshfield, "Today, Another Universe" from *Terrain.org* (2016), reprinted with permission of the author.

Dave Holt, "Waiting on Spring" and "Volunteer Work Day on the Mountain," printed with permission of the author.

Timothy Houghton, "Redwoods: Northern California" from *The Height in Between* (Orchises), © 2012 by Timothy Houghton, reprinted with permission of the author.

Patty Joslyn, "Elk Prairie" and "I Live Here," printed with permission of the author.

Susan Kelly-DeWitt, "Flood Plain" from *Mockingbird* (1995) and "Valentine" from the *Suisun Valley Review* (2004). "Salmon" from *To a Small Moth* (Poet's Corner Press), © 2001 by Susan Kelly-DeWitt. "Egrets Along the Yolo Causeway" from *The Fortunate Islands* (Marick Press), © 2007 by Susan Kelly-DeWitt. "Bliss" from *Spider Season* (Cold River Press), © 2016 by Susan Kelly-DeWitt. All reprinted with permission of the author.

Laurie Klein, "In Conflagrante," "Return Engagement," and "No One Wrings the Air Dry," printed with permission of the author.

Lynne Knight, "Small Deer, Small Lilac," printed with permission of the author.

Tricia Knoll, "The Gray Whale" from *Ocean's Laughter* (Aldrich Press), © 2015 by Tricia Knoll, reprinted with permission of the author.

Steve Kowit, "*Perognathus Fallax*" from *The Dumbbell Nebula* (Roundhouse Press, Heyday Books), © 2000 by Steve Kowit. "The Bridge" and "Raven" from *The First Noble Truth* (University of Tampa Press), © 2007 by Steve Kowit. All reprinted with permission of Mary L. Kowit.

Jennifer Lagier, "Last Stand," from *Dead Snakes* (2015), reprinted with permission of the author.

W. F. Lantry, "Giant Forest," "Sailing Stones," "Ocotillo Wells," "Anza Borrego," and "Tehachapi," printed with permission of the author.

Noreen Lawlor, "Creosote" from *Cholla Needles* (2017), reprinted with permission of the author.

T.m. Lawson, "droughtfall" and "Brentwood Coyotes," printed with permission of the author.

Ursula K. Le Guin, "A Grass Song: November," "The Spring at Sinshan," and "A Song Used When Damming a Creek or Diverting Water to a Holding Tank for Irrigation" from *Out Here: Poems and Images from Steens Mountain Country* (Raven Studios), © 2010 by Ursula K. Le Guin, reprinted with the permission of Curtis Brown, LTD.

Cynthia Leslie-Bole, "Redwood" from *The Luminous In-Between* (Azalea Arts Press), © 2016 by Cynthia Leslie-Bole, reprinted with permission of the author.

Richard Michael Levine, "Turning Seventy at a B&B on Clear Lake" from *Catch and Other Poems* (Scarlet Tanager Books), © 2015 by Richard Michael Levine, reprinted with permission of the author.

Ellaraine Lockie, "Offerings to the Green Gods" from the *Broad River Review* (2011). Reprinted with permission of the author.

Naomi Ruth Lowinsky, "Where Coyote Brush Roams" and "Because the Mountain Is My Companion" from *The Book of Now: Poetry for the Rising Tide* (il piccolo editions, 2012), reprinted with permission of the author.

Catharine Lucas, "After New Rain" from *Zone 3* (2015), reprinted with permission of the author.

Kirk Lumpkin, "The Dudley's Lousewort" and "To Poison Oak," reprinted with permission of the author,

Mary Makofske, "Dear Editor," printed with permission of the author.

Eileen Malone, "*Velella Velella*," reprinted with permission of the author.

Jacqueline Marcus, "Waiting for Winter Rains," printed with permission of the author.

Jerry Martien, "Losing the Lines" from *Wild Earth* (2002). "Afternoon River Ragtime" from *Pieces in Place* (Blackberry Books), © 1999 by Jerry Martien. "In the Pines" from *Earth Tickets* (Bug Press), © 2017 by Jerry Martien. All reprinted with permission of the author.

Bronwyn Mauldin, "Alarm Song" and "Dead Snake on the Trail," printed with permission of the author.

Kathleen McClung, "Whistle Keepers, 1883" from *Heron Tree* (2016) and "Gualala Winter" from the Maria W. Faust Sonnet Contest (sonnetcontest. org/2016-winners), reprinted with permission of the author.

Judith McCombs, "Refugio Beach, California, 1950," printed with permission of the author. "Pictures Not in Our Albums" from *The Habit of Fire: Poems Selected and New* (The Word Works), © 2005 by Judith McCombs. Reprinted with permission of the author.

Joshua McKinney, "In Earnest" and "Point of Reference," printed with permission of the author.

Stephen Meadows, "Drought" and "Waterhole" from *Releasing the Days* (Heyday), © 2011 by Stephen Meadows, reprinted with permission of the author.

A. D. Miller, "Apocalypse Is My Garden" from *Apocalypse Is My Garden* (Eshu House Publishing), © 1997 by Adam David Miller, reprinted with permission of the author.

Florence Miller, "Upriver" and "Delta Afternoon" from *Upriver: New and Selected Poems* (dvs publishing), © 2012 by Florence Miller, reprinted with permission of the author.

Jacob Minasian, "Half Moon Bay," printed with permission of the author. "Wine Country" from Poets.org (2016), reprinted with permission of the author.

Mary B. Moore, "Economy," "Abundance," "Ecology of the Siskiyou Watershed," and "Rock Is the Premise" from *Flicker* (Broadkill River Press), © 2016 by Mary B. Moore, reprinted with permission of the author.

Kay Morgan, "Before the Oil Spill," printed with permission of the author.

Bonnie Mosse, "Desert Sunflowers" and "San Elijo Lagoon," printed with permission of the author.

Nguyen Phan Que Mai, "From the Deep Earth" from *The Secret of Hoa Sen*, translated by Bruce Weigl, © 2014 by Nguyen Phan Que Mai. Translation © 2014 by Nguyen Phan Que Mai and Bruce Weigl. Reprinted with the permission of The Permissions Company, Inc., on behalf of BOA Editions Ltd., www.boaeditions.org.

Stephanie Noble, "In this Land of Wind and Tinder," printed with permission of the author.

Ruth Nolan, "Mopping Up," "Ouroboros—Amargosa River," "Ghost Flower: *Mohavea Confertiflora*," "King Clone," and "Old Woman Springs," printed with permission of the author. "Black-Chinned Hummingbird" from *Ruby Mountain*

(Finishing Line Press), © 2016 by Ruth Nolan, reprinted with permission of the author. "Mopping Up" received the 2018 Los Angeles Poetry Society Award.

Judith Offer, "Strawberry Patch" from *The First Apples*, © 1977 by Judith Offer, reprinted with permission of the author.

J. C. Olander, "Sierra Foothill Birding" from *December Birds*, © 2004 by J. C. Olander, reprinted with permission of the author.

Candace Pearson, "Alfalfa Light" from *Hour of Unfolding* (Briery Creek Press), © 2018 by Candace Pearson, reprinted with permission of the author.

Vincent Peloso, "Wounded," "Clear Cuts," and "This Burl," printed with permission of the author.

Evelyn Posamentier, "Peanut Shells," printed with permission of the author.

Barbara Quick, "Cotati," printed with permission of the author.

Zara Raab, "The Sawmill Smokes Above the Village," printed with permission of the author.

Diane J. Rayor, translation of Sappho, Fragment 2 from *Sappho's Lyre: Archaic Lyric and Women Poets of Ancient Greece* (University of California Press), © 1991 by Diane J. Rayor, reprinted with permission of Diane J. Rayor.

Erin Redfern, "Some Knots," printed with permission of the author. "California Condor" from *Soundings* (2016), reprinted with permission of the author.

Kim Roberts, "The Invasive Weed Syndicate," printed with permission of the author.

Pattiann Rogers, "Being Specific" from *Song of the World Becoming: New and Collected Poems 1981–2001* (Milkweed Editions), © 2001 by Pattiann Rogers, reprinted with permission of the author.

Sylvia Ross, "Cultural Capitulation" from *Acorns and Abalone* (Bentley Avenue Books), © 2017 by Sylvia Ross, reprinted with permission of the author.

Mary Kay Rummel, "Conductor," printed with permission of the author.

Cathie Sandstrom, "Good Bones Endure" and "September Wildfire, Los Angeles Basin," printed with permission of the author.

Nancy Schimmel, "The High Desert" from We'Moon Calendar (2015), reprinted with permission of the author.

# Also from Scarlet Tanager Books

*Bone Strings* by Anne Coray
poetry, 80 pages, $15.00

*The Rainbow Zoo* by Lucille Lang Day
illustrated by Gina Aoay Orosco
children's book, 26 pages, $18.00

*Wild One* by Lucille Lang Day
poetry, 100 pages, $12.95

*The "Fallen Western Star" Wars: A Debate About Literary California*
edited by Jack Foley
essays, 88 pages, $14.00

*Catching the Bullet & Other Stories* by Daniel Hawkes
fiction, 64 pages, $12.95

*Luck* by Marc Elihu Hofstadter
poetry, 104 pages, $16.00

*Visions: Paintings Seen Through the Optic of Poetry*
by Marc Elihu Hofstadter
poetry, 72 pages, $16.00

*Embrace* by Risa Kaparo
poetry, 70 pages, $14.00

*Catch and Other Poems* by Richard Michael Levine
poetry, 82 pages, $18.00

*crimes of the dreamer* by Naomi Ruth Lowinsky
poetry, 82 pages, $16.00

*red clay is talking* by Naomi Ruth Lowinsky
poetry, 142 pages, $14.95

*The Number Before Infinity* by Zack Rogow
poetry, 72 pages, $16.00

*Red Indian Road West: Native American Poetry from California*
edited by Kurt Schweigman and Lucille Lang Day
poetry, 110 pages, $18.00

*Call Home* by Judy Wells
poetry, 92 pages, $15.00

*Everything Irish* by Judy Wells
poetry, 112 pages, $12.95

*Turning a Train of Thought Upside Down: An Anthology of Women's Poetry*
edited by Andrena Zawinski
poetry, 100 pages, $18.00